EVER THE LEADER

EVER THE LEADER

SELECTED WRITINGS, 1995–2016

William G. Bowen

Edited and with an introduction by Kevin M. Guthrie

With an afterword by Hanna Holborn Gray

PRINCETON UNIVERSITY PRESS

PRINCETON AND OXFORD

Copyright © 2018 by Princeton University Press and ITHAKA

Requests for permission to reproduce material from this work should be sent to
Permissions, Princeton University Press

Published by Princeton University Press,
41 William Street, Princeton, New Jersey 08540

In the United Kingdom: Princeton University Press,
6 Oxford Street, Woodstock, Oxfordshire OX20 1TR

press.princeton.edu

Jacket photograph by Brian Wilson, courtesy of Mary Ellen Bowen.

Page 33, excerpt from "Ithaka" in C. P. Cavafy: *Collected Poems Revised Edition*
translated by Edmund Keeley and Philip Sherrard, edited by George Savidis. Translation
copyright © 1975, 1992 by Edmund Keeley and Philip Sherrard. Reprinted by permission
of Princeton University Press.

Page 100, Lyrics from "This Is My Song" by Lloyd Stone and Georgia Harkness, stanzas
1–2 © 1934 (Stanzas 1 and 2), © 1964 (Stanza 3) Lorenz Publishing Company (admin. by
Music Services). All Rights Reserved. Used by Permission.

All Rights Reserved

ISBN 978-0-691-17787-8

British Library Cataloging-in-Publication Data is available

This book has been composed in Sabon LT Std and Trajan Pro

Printed on acid-free paper. ∞

Printed in the United States of America

10 9 8 7 6 5 4 3 2 1

CONTENTS

~

ACKNOWLEDGMENTS

This book would not exist were it not for the effort of two long-time friends and colleagues. I first met Sarah Turner, now a professor of economics and education at the University of Virginia, in the early 1990s, when we were both working at the Mellon Foundation. Sarah collaborated with Bill on a number of books and articles over the years and is therefore very familiar with his work. Sarah played a key role in developing this book by selecting the initial set of articles that make up this compilation. She also strategized with me on the organization for the book and provided valuable comments on the introduction. Johanna Brownell was Bill's research assistant for twelve years and is a member of the "family." She organized and took care of everything professional for Bill 24/7, 365 days a year. She was forever on call and knows literally where everything pertaining to Bill's professional activity lives. Her dedication to Bill and all he stood for survives his death. The idea for this book was originally Johanna's, and she has provided invaluable support in this effort, helping to locate articles, edit entries, and make sure that everything is represented accurately. I am indebted and grateful to Sarah and Johanna for their inspiration, guidance, and support even as I take full responsibility for any errors or omissions in this compilation.

INTRODUCTION

~

In 1987, Princeton University Press published *Ever the Teacher*, a collection of William G. Bowen's writings while he served as president of Princeton University (1972–88). It is a reference work that documents not only the major issues facing higher education during that period but also provides guidance on one uniquely talented man's efforts to address those issues. A notable attribute of that collection is how relevant it remains today, thirty years later. Some of the issues addressed include the university's role in society; the purposes of a liberal education; diversity, opportunity, and financial aid; and reflections on the importance of preserving everyone's right to speak on campus. In his work Bill was both fearless and prodigious. The collection of writings and speeches from his sixteen-year tenure as Princeton's president not only address a set of issues so challenging that they remain on the front pages today, but they also represent a nearly comprehensive overview of the broad issues facing a university president, and indeed higher education in general. That encyclopedic compendium totals six hundred pages!

Ever the Teacher is long not because its editor, Bob Durkee, refused to make choices. It is long because of Bill's unparalleled productivity and the incredible originality and depth of intellectual rigor in his work. There was so much to choose from. And so it was as I dove into the task of reviewing Bill's work after Princeton, during which time he served as president emeritus of the Andrew W. Mellon Foundation and as the founding chairman of ITHAKA. After the publication of *Ever the Teacher*, Bill published sixteen books and a long list of booklets, book chapters, and articles, a selected list of which is included in the appendix. If you have opened this book and are interested in learning about higher education and leadership, that reading list combined with *Ever the Teacher* is a compelling core curriculum.

If the issues in *Ever the Teacher* have stood the test of time, and if Bill documented so carefully and thoroughly his ideas through his research and publications after that, why publish *Ever the Leader*? One answer is implied by the title, that the emphasis in the selection of the works should be on leadership; but truthfully, there is much leadership to be found in *Ever the Teacher*. A second answer is an obvious one: that the issues addressed get more contemporary treatment. Most important in this regard is the advent of new information and network technologies, an issue of great interest to Bill, which was only just beginning to have an impact in 1988 and has accelerated relentlessly since that time. But the third answer, and the most important one from my perspective in terms of leadership, is that Bill accomplished all that he did in a very special way, and this book offers an opportunity to share his approach more widely. Those of us who knew Bill had the good fortune to see the joy and passion he brought to every task he took on, the unquenchable motivation he had to make a lasting difference, and the deeply and consistently held principles that governed all of his work. These humanistic qualities and his commitment to others were key parts of what made his leadership so special and impactful, qualities that are hard to infer or discern from the formal arguments made in a published book or scholarly article. They are also qualities that depend less on Bill's rare gifts and talents, and more on choices he made—and that anyone can make—about what kind of person and leader one wants to be. This brief introduction, and the selection of works included in this book, are my attempt to convey those special qualities to present and future leaders who never had the chance to know Bill Bowen.

In pursuing that task, I must confess to the fact that I do so without objectivity. Our relationship began in June 1984, just following my graduation from Princeton, when I was surprised to receive a congratulatory handwritten note from "President Bowen." I didn't know him at the time other than to have said hello while walking across campus or after a football game, and did not understand why he would write to me. But that note opened a door that gave me the courage just a few months later to reach out to him, a contact that led to a thirty-two-year relationship that not only determined the course of my professional life but also had a profound impact on me personally as well. He was a father figure, mentor, partner, and friend.

This pattern of reaching out to near strangers and drawing them into his orbit of influence was not unusual for Bill—far from it. Over the years I witnessed him initiating, developing, and nurturing such relationships with people of all walks and stations. He wrote to the accomplished and the neophyte, to the privileged and the disadvantaged. But, as with me, these notes were just the entry points to much deeper relationships that were characterized by Bill's desire to use his talents and standing to help others, and most often to help others less fortunate than he. I cannot begin to count how many people regarded Bill as a close personal friend or had a relationship with him that they considered life altering.

Bill's personal attributes start with an intellect that was unmatched. He was supremely brilliant and was as fast as he was smart. He completed his PhD in labor economics at Princeton in three years, was a full professor by the age of 32, and became provost of the university at age 34. He became Princeton's president when he was just 38. As Taylor Reveley said at Bill's memorial service:

> I've never known anyone whose work ethic, sheer energy, and delight in the chase was as robust as Bill's. Work for him was not work as most mortals experience it. This was, in part, I believe, because he was so good at what he did, drawing on his powerful intellect (really, a giant throbbing brain), on stamina akin to that of a bull elephant, and on sheer quickness, his capacity to produce telling results far more swiftly than is the norm.

Working with him later in his career, I marveled at this rare combination of intellectual firepower, speed, and determination. He combined those qualities with a remarkable ability to communicate in all forms with one voice. All of his writing—his speeches; his papers, articles, and books; his emails—and his conversation sprang from his mind fully formed, brilliant yet accessible. If you were a competitive type, you learned quickly that you would never be able to outthink him or outwork him. You just counted yourself fortunate for the opportunity to work with him. As Mike McPherson once said, writing a book with Bill was like being strapped to the outside of the space shuttle as it was taking off.

Despite his enormous intellect and his ability to think around and beyond others, he never, ever was lazy in his thinking. Bill chose difficult and important problems to tackle and pursued them with rigor and discipline. What is remarkable as you read these writings and speeches is the consistency of his approach. Time after time he breaks down and defines a problem carefully, marshals evidence to support his argument, and then defends that argument forcefully and with courage, regardless of criticism or controversy.

In the time since Bill left Princeton, he gave over two hundred speeches—or at least that is how many we found in the files! In selecting the writings and speeches for this volume, I have attempted to include works that supplement the previously published books and articles and that demonstrate the principles and values that defined Bill's particular form of leadership. These writings and talks are organized into the following six chapters:

Chapter 1: University Values
Chapter 2: Extending Opportunity
Chapter 3: Athletics, Admissions, and Campus Culture
Chapter 4: Technology and Scholarly Communications
Chapter 5: Technology, Education, and Opportunity
Chapter 6: Profiles in Leadership

The book opens with several talks and commentaries in which Bill reflects on important challenges facing universities. In each of these he addresses the particular topic at hand, whether it be the impact of new technologies, the growing bifurcation of wealth, or controversial speakers on campus, in the context of what he regarded as enduring values that are essential to universities. Bill's intellect was tethered to principle.

The first of the talks is the Romanes Lecture delivered at Oxford University in 2000, which outlines Bill's expectations for what technology and the associated "markets" were likely to impose on higher education. In it he demonstrates his singular capacity to reduce an important and complex topic to its essential core. He defines what he argues are universities' "most essential purposes." He says:

> [Universities' most essential purposes] include educating students broadly so that they may lead productive lives in a civilized society; serving as engines of opportunity and social mobility; creating new knowledge of every kind including work that either has no immediate market value or may even threaten some commercial end; encouraging and protecting the thoughtful critic and the dissenting voice; and defending cultural, moral and intellectual values.

Bill's view was that the shift of communications mechanisms from the physicality of ink on paper to bits on a network would draw universities into commercial marketplaces and activity. For universities to understand and embrace their essential purposes was so important—is so important—because there is both challenge and opportunity in the use of electronic technologies. He reminds us: "The disinterested pursuit of learning, commitments to tolerance and social justice, the belief that learning is enhanced by studying with those who have different perspectives and come from different walks of life—these and other core elements of university life defy the logic of the marketplace."

For most of the challenging problems he chose to address, there are no easy answers; Bill used to say that the answer to any interesting question is "It depends." He demonstrated in such matters the need to define clearly what is important, to collect evidence on the effects associated with various choices and outcomes, and to rigorously defend one's decisions. He often argued that what was most important was to do the right things for the right reasons. Taylor Reveley tells the story of a moment shortly after he became president of William and Mary, when he asked Bill what was the one thing he should watch out for at all costs. Bill instantly replied: "Don't let other people set your agenda." Do the right things for the right reasons.

Although he was reluctant to talk about himself or explain what motivated him, upon reflection it seems that the core of Bill's motivation came from a drive to preserve opportunity, particularly for those who have historically been denied it. He himself had been from a lower-middle-class family and was the first in his family to attend college. As Jerome Davis, a former student and friend for nearly fifty years, said at Bill's memorial service:

> From the beginning I saw that his approach to delicate and complicated educational, social, and racial issues started with a deep respect for others as his peers.... Bill made it his business to advocate for those not historically recognized to be "worthy of Princeton"— initially women, blacks, and browns; and later, among others, students from low-income families lacking a tradition of higher education.

This particular moral compass sets the direction for the papers and talks that have been selected for chapter 2. One aspect of Bill's approach that emerges from these talks is a willingness to state his position clearly and strongly and to defend it. In "Life on the River," Bill states:

> Educational institutions, in my view, are obligated *by principle* to do two things: (a) create as rich a learning environment as possible for everyone on their campuses; and (b) contribute to meeting the needs for larger numbers of exceptionally well-prepared students of color of a society that is far too stratified by race. If someone disagrees with those objectives, so be it. But let us not be reluctant to state them and argue for them.

He later goes on to express his frustration with people's unwillingness to speak their minds in support of race-sensitive admissions. Despite the fact that 80 percent of white graduates surveyed as part of the *Shape of the River* research agreed with these admissions policies, many people express an unwillingness to say so on the record. Bill responds: "Why not? What is there to be afraid of? Are we going to allow ourselves to be intimidated by controversy?"

Bill extends these arguments further in the other entries in this chapter to justify providing an admissions advantage for students from low socio-economic backgrounds who have to overcome long odds to compete for spots in selective colleges. In "Extending Opportunity: 'What Is to Be Done?'" (2005), Bill highlights the gap between the rhetoric of college admissions offices that claimed to give special attention to applicants from economically or culturally deprived backgrounds and what the data actually show: no admissions advantage. He models the statistical increases in numbers of students that would be admitted from these backgrounds if they received the same benefit as children of alumni. He states: "All that we are suggesting is that high-achieving students from modest backgrounds deserve at least some break when being considered for admissions—it would be splendid if rhetoric and reality were brought into closer balance."

Bill's attention to admissions and its impact on college communities was not limited to those students who he felt should get favorable treatment; he also studied the impact on campus communities of admissions preferences offered those he did not feel should be so favored; namely, recruited athletes. Although this topic was covered extensively in *The Game of Life* (2001) and *Reclaiming the Game* (2003), chapter 3 includes two talks on the subject: (1) the Edge Lecture at Princeton, in which Bill presented research from *Reclaiming the Game*, and (2) "Why You Came," which Bill delivered at a dedication for a new student center at Centre College, where he assessed the impact of athletics on life at a small Division III college.

I included these talks for three reasons. First, the Edge Lecture demonstrates Bill's meticulous commitment to careful research and gathering of evidence. Second, this topic was important to him, not because he did not care for sports—quite the contrary, he was both a college athlete and a sports fan—but because he felt that the degree of commitment to sports had reached a point that was in conflict with the values of the university. Third, and finally, his commitment to address this issue all the way back in the late 1990s demonstrates one of Bill's other leadership talents, his ability to envision a problem or opportunity ahead of its time. Nearly twenty years after this research was conducted, people may continue to argue with the conclusions about the impact of having larger numbers of recruited student athletes on campus, but there are very few people—coaches, parents, or athletes—who believe that the time and effort invested in the recruiting of student athletes is in proper balance with the role of athletics and education for high school and younger athletes. It was the impact of the recruiting on the campus community and on the athletes themselves that troubled him most, and he saw before others what might be the longer-term impact of those policies. As Bill says in the Centre College talk: "Looking beyond the campus, we should not underestimate the 'signaling effects' of current practices (especially giving substantial admissions advantages to recruited athletes) on secondary schools, prospective students, and their families." The idea that an 8-year-old child would be pressured to specialize in a single sport (or even in a single role in a sport—say that of a relief pitcher or face-off specialist) to improve his chances for admission to college would seem absurd if it were not true. Bill was so right about that, but it has gone far beyond even what he imagined.

Chapter 4 includes talks and papers that further illustrate Bill's inclination and ability to see around the proverbial corner, in this case related to the impact of technology on scholarly communications. The chapter starts with a speech Bill delivered to librarians about JSTOR in the fall of 1995. It is an entertaining talk, in part because Bill's entrepreneurial instincts and persuasive skills were on full display. He was selling! Even so, he didn't abandon his commitment to rigorous research, as even the justifications for JSTOR's fee structure are backed with scholarly citations. The talk is also a reflection of Bill's willingness to make big bets and to stake his reputation on big ideas. He believed that institutions should focus on a small number of grand initiatives—what he used to like to call "a few tall trees"—and he was not afraid to back them. Although JSTOR is now a highly successful enterprise and an important part of college research and teaching infrastructure, it was not pre-ordained to be the case, and Bill used his considerable powers of persuasion and leverage not only to get it started, but also to maintain it. Without his leadership, there would be no JSTOR.

Bill's ability to anticipate the future was brought into even sharper focus by a speech he delivered as part of a celebration of the New York Public Library's Centennial in the spring of 1996. In this talk he reflects on the impact of new technologies on libraries, first highlighting the need to embrace opportunities to harness increasing productivity to do more with less. In anticipating the economic impacts of technological change, he foresaw economic and operating principles that have become a hallmark of successful Silicon Valley tech firms. The first is a basic product development tenet; he states that one of the lessons he learned through his "intimate and at times grueling involvement with the JSTOR adventure, is that in the field of technology, perhaps especially, we learn principally by doing, and then correcting our errors." The second was a fundamental business principle; he anticipates what has come to be called the freemium business model when he expresses one of JSTOR's challenges as the need to "find a sane balance between the need to make the 'basics' equally available to all, and the desirability of assigning some costs, and especially the costs of 'extras,' to those who can and should help to cover them." It is a balance that JSTOR still works to strike.

His willingness to focus so much of his time and energy on the business and pricing model for JSTOR and similar initiatives was less a reflection of his background as an economist and more a practical realization that new initiatives needed to be sustainable. Bill often spoke about the fact that foundations and governments were disinclined to provide perpetual subsidies and that new enterprises needed to develop their own recurring revenue streams. He reiterates this point in his celebration of the successes of MIT's OpenCourseWare (OCW) project in 2004. He says:

> In today's environment, when there is much heated debate as to whether it is ideologically acceptable to seek to recover any part of the costs of a digital project by imposing user fees of one kind or another, it is well to recall that the decision about the pricing of OCW (make it free to the world) was not ideologically driven. Rather, it grew out of a careful analysis of the pros and cons of different approaches. Let me suggest to my economist friends at MIT and elsewhere that there is a real need for good analytical thinking about the circumstances in which one distribution/pricing approach or another makes the most sense. In brief, I think that the right pricing structure depends on, among other things, the applicability

of the "exclusion principle," the shape of costs curves, the ability to segment markets, and the availability of alternative ways of achieving "fair access" without sacrificing sustainability.

Bill was a self-proclaimed "convert" to the idea that information technologies would make productivity gains available in teaching and learning that would be both "better and cheaper." Having been the co-author with Will Baumol of the principle that the cost of teaching and education increases inexorably because its dependence on "manual" labor limits gains in productivity (Baumol's cost disease), his support for technology's likely impact surprised some. But he had seen that outcome realized in scholarly communications, and more specifically with JSTOR, and he saw similarities in the potential for shared activity and collaboration in teaching and learning, especially in fields and for courses that "have a right answer." These notions are brought together in a number of talks and papers that make up chapter 5, in which Bill speculates on the potential that the increasing need to reduce costs in higher education might be addressed by intelligent uses of technology.

Despite his advocacy for the potential of technology, he was never a full-blown technology enthusiast. He lamented what he regarded as a paucity of quality research and called incessantly for more research about what works to improve learning outcomes both in the classroom and online. As always, he thought there was no single right answer to the question and that thoughtful, nuanced approaches would be necessary. In the Stafford Little Lecture at Princeton in 2014 he expressed his view that the notion of a demise of face-to-face instruction because of online technologies was "unthinkable." He framed his response by articulating what he explained as the nuanced skills of great teaching that enable students to

> [learn] how to frame questions in value-laden subjects, how to distinguish evidence from opinion, how to take account of different points of view, how to formulate one's own position on complex questions, how to express oneself verbally and in writing, how to engage with others as a member of an intellectual community, and even how to approach an understanding of "life lessons."

He did not believe that an online experience could replace the benefits that came from interacting face-to-face with a teacher and other students, and he was convinced that there would always be demand—and by that he meant people willing to pay—for that opportunity.

Nevertheless, the potential for productivity gains in teaching certain subjects appealed to Bill precisely because he thought they might help to extend the opportunity for education to more people. He saw ways that technology could be used to extend access to education to more students by, among other things, helping address the increasing length in time-to-degree and by reducing the costs of teaching. He was disturbed, therefore, by what he regarded as a lack of willingness among faculty to find ways to control costs associated with teaching. He states:

> Unappealing as it may be to focus on costs (which of course can mean unwelcome changes in faculty staffing and in faculty roles), and satisfying as it may be to focus instead on the glories of teaching in both old and new modes, it borders on the irresponsible to ignore the pressures to control costs—and the concomitant need to make the most intelligent educationally sensitive trade-offs that can be identified.

Through the aperture of technology and its impact on teaching and learning, a whole range of challenges came into focus for Bill, including those related to ownership of intellectual property, proper development of teaching methodologies and content, the tensions between teaching faculty and tenured research faculty, equity of access to quality education, and, finally, shared governance. These areas of interest are covered in this chapter as well as in his two most recent books, *Higher Education in the Digital Age* and *Locus of Authority*.

Unlike what is true of the other topics covered in this volume, we don't have the benefit of hindsight and the passage of time to evaluate whether Bill's views in these areas accurately predicted the outcomes. We are living through this transformation as we speak, and so the story is yet to be written of how digital and network technologies are going to impact education. The talks and papers in this chapter therefore provide historical, current, and near-future assessment of the changes going on around us; they provide valuable food for thought and reflection in their own right, in addition to having value as case studies in leadership.

Chapter 6 offers a series of tributes Bill delivered about people whom he admired. They are marvelous in a number of dimensions. First, they describe wonderful accomplishments of inspiring people, all of whom we would do well to emulate. Second, they convey succinctly some of the essential qualities of superb leadership, but also Bill's particular form of leadership. In delivering these talks, he illuminated the very qualities that he most valued. Third and finally, they are beautifully rendered reflections on special people whom he knew and loved.

His remarks at such events as retirements and funerals were not always formal, but they were always thoughtful. At the retirement celebration for Margaret Massiah, the beloved housekeeper of many years at the Mellon Foundation, Bill summed up the love everyone felt for her and reflected it back when he said something I will never forget: "You get the relationships you deserve." And he meant it.

Bill was obviously a man of many talents, but even more he was a man of many relationships. He invested in them without expectation of return. This was true of his relationships with his colleagues, former colleagues, staff, associates, friends, and sometimes even strangers! I saw him offer advice and invaluable counsel nearly every single day. Make a call to open the door for an important job. Find the right doctor for a sick friend. Make his apartment in New York City available as a refuge for someone from out of town. Extend countless kindnesses. He was, fundamentally, a generous man. He was generous with his time. He was generous with his intellect. He was generous with his relationships.

As Jerome Davis said so eloquently: "Bill Bowen was the kind of man who helps us measure ourselves. It is not so much a question of how people feel or felt about him, but of wanting to be worthy of the love, time, attention, guidance, care, and support he gave to so many, and to some of the most vital causes of our time. He seemed energized by ... a love for people and an enthusiasm for helping them."

I am obviously profoundly grateful to have had the opportunity to work so closely with this special man for nearly thirty years. It was a labor of love to work with someone who had such a love of labor. His form of leadership was like being on a dogsled team with him in the role of lead dog. You are running along and after a while you start taking it a little easy and you realize, "Wait a minute, this sled is still flying along and I don't think I'm doing much," and right about that moment the lead dog turns back and barks, "Excellent work! A+!" And you resume your running even harder. Bill led from the front, and while doing so had an amazing ability to bring out the very best in others. And so it is with this book. Bill has done the work yet again, and I am along for the ride.

I cannot close this introduction without paying tribute to Mary Ellen Bowen, Bill's wife of sixty years. Together since the fourth grade, they were not just husband and wife; they were true intellectual partners, as I experienced many times over the years working with Bill. "That's a good idea," he would say, "but last night I was speaking with Mary Ellen, and she thinks ..." So one cannot reflect on the impact of this man without recognizing Mary Ellen. I want to thank her here for welcoming me as a member of the extended family and for giving us permission to publish this book, allowing me to intrude on her life for work yet again. Probing through files and personal papers gave me an opportunity to have a special conversation with Bill, and enabled me to partner with him this one last time.

Kevin M. Guthrie

EVER THE LEADER

CHAPTER 1

UNIVERSITY VALUES

AT A SLIGHT ANGLE TO THE UNIVERSE

THE UNIVERSITY IN A DIGITIZED, COMMERCIALIZED AGE

~

William G. Bowen
October 17, 2000

THE ROMANES LECTURE, OXFORD UNIVERSITY

It would be a great privilege for anyone, and it is an especially great privilege for a sometime academic from across the sea, to give the Romanes Lecture. To be joined, in even a small way, to such a distinguished list of predecessors, going back to Gladstone and including many scholars whose writings I have long admired, is a most humbling experience. Adlai Stevenson once remarked that "flattery is all right—if you don't inhale" (a phrase since made memorable by another American with Oxford connections).

DEFINITIONS AND THEMES

The title I have chosen for this lecture, "At a Slight Angle to the Universe," is taken from E. M. Forster's description of the Greek poet Cavafy. I will return to the title at the end of the talk, when it

Editor's note: The Romanes Lecture is the annual public lecture of Oxford University delivered at the Sheldonian Theatre. A distinguished public figure is invited by special invitation of the Vice-Chancellor. The lecture was established in 1891.

Author's note: I am grateful to David H. Bayley, John D'Arms, Ira Fuchs, Sarah Levin, Pat McPherson, Thomas Nygren, Roger Schonfeld, James Shulman, Dennis Sullivan, Michele Warman, and Harriet Zuckerman for helpful comments and suggestions.

will be clearer, I think, why I have chosen it. My purpose today is to consider the implications for the university of two powerful intersecting forces: the revolution in information technology that is so pervasive (on which I will concentrate) and the associated, but separate, increase in the reliance on the market to solve problems of all kinds.

Let me begin by proposing working definitions of our key concepts that may help to clarify why "digitization" and "commercialization" are inevitably linked and why, together, they propel the university into a new world. It is useful to remember that despite all of the hyperbole, *things*, even in this new age, will continue to be *things*. As Professor Negroponte of MIT has put it, "If you make cashmere sweaters or Chinese food, it will be a long time before we can convert them to bits."[1] But universities are not known for their steamed dumplings. Rather, they have long been concerned with intangibles: ideas, concepts, and knowledge. Their "products" draw upon information and are packaged as information—which, unlike dumplings, can be broken down into the digital equivalent of atoms. When this is done, the life of the university changes in profound ways: students and faculty are now surrounded by e-mail, websites, electronic archives, search engines, voice and image transmission, and the wonders of Internet2. So, for the purposes of this talk, I use "digitization" to mean the electronic assembling, disassembling, and transmitting of the basic elements of intellectual capital. These include words, sounds, pictures, and data. The ability to take these sources apart, send them easily over distances, and reconstruct them renders the walls around universities far more porous.

Once those walls are pierced in this way—that is to say, once both the basic materials and the fruits of the work of academic institutions are easily gathered and sent—the very currency of the university becomes dramatically more accessible and these institutions find themselves drawn increasingly into the realm of commerce. New economic possibilities abound—especially in an age when the market is king and everything (or nearly everything) seems

[1] Nicholas Negroponte, *Being Digital* (New York: Alfred A. Knopf, 1995), p. 12.

to have a price and to be for sale. As Thomas Friedman writes in his recent book on globalization: "Ideologically speaking, there is no more mint chocolate chip. There is no more strawberry swirl, and there is no more lemon-lime. Today there is only free-market vanilla.... In the end, if you want higher standards of living in a world without walls, the free market is the only alternative left."[2]

Innumerable manifestations of the broadening reach of market mechanisms are seen on many campuses, certainly in the United States. The universities themselves have become highly sophisticated in collecting large streams of revenue from the licensing of patent rights; faculty increasingly expect to be paid extra not only for developing patentable inventions but also for helping to create e-commerce "products"; many graduate students want to be regarded as paid employees and to affiliate with old-style industrial unions like the United Auto Workers; and students seem to require the promise of compensation in such exotic forms as chances to win mountain bikes to cooperate with survey research.[3] I suspect that it would be easy to add UK examples.

By "commercialization," thought about in this context, I mean the changing way in which the wares of the academy are transferred from one person (or one entity) to another—not solely through interactions in cloistered realms devoted to the free exchange of ideas, but also in settings where ideas and information are bought and sold like wooly goats and port wine. "Commercialization," in this setting, has at least a mild connotation of impurity. The selling of autos is not regarded as "commercialization"—that transaction is, and always has been, "commercial." Places or products that are "commercialized" are those—at least to my ear—that have not always been subject to the dictates of the market and, some would

---

[2] Thomas Friedman, *The Lexus and the Olive Tree* (London: Harper Collins, 1999), p. 86.

[3] See Karen W. Arenson, "Columbia Sets Pace in Profiting Off Research," *New York Times*, August 2, 2000, p. B1, and Dan Carnevale and Jeffrey R. Young, "Who Owns On-Line Courses? Colleges and Professors Start to Sort It Out," *Chronicle of Higher Education*, December 17, 1999, p. A 45. See Catherine R. Stimson's insightful article on the NYU graduate student situation ("A Dean's Skepticism about a Graduate-Student Union," *Chronicle of Higher Education*, May 5, 2000, www.chronicle.com/article/a-deans-skepticism-about-a/4588). Information on rewards necessary to elicit cooperation with survey research is taken from personal correspondence with Professor Michael Nettles of the University of Michigan. One alumni survey listed a trip to Paris as a prize.

argue, ought not to be. Let us remember that there is a deep ambivalence in the relationship between the university and the market—there always has been and always will be. *Scientia gratia Scientiae* may be the mantra for certain individuals and for certain fields at certain times, but institutions that depend on external support have never been that pure. What digitization does is accelerate the possibilities and the pace of commercial trafficking. When both new techniques and digitized content can pass so easily through walls as beautiful as those around us, the possibilities for transforming *intellectual* capital into *capital* capital provoke a most challenging set of questions.

A principal theme of this lecture is that universities are not businesses (though they have many business-like aspects). They are highly unusual institutions with missions and attributes unlike those of any other entity in either the for-profit or the not-for-profit world. Society depends on them to do much more than produce "products" at a fair price. In keeping with most other economists, I love the market (it is, as it were, "our baby"). But I also know the limits of markets as definers of values and allocators of resources, and one of my greatest concerns is that, either inadvertently or by design, universities will be so bemused by market opportunities that they will lose sight of, or downplay, their most essential purposes. These include educating students broadly so that they may lead productive lives in a civilized society; serving as engines of opportunity and social mobility; creating new knowledge of every kind, including work that either has no immediate market value or may even threaten some commercial end; encouraging and protecting the thoughtful critic and the dissenting voice; and defending cultural, moral, and intellectual values that no one can "price" very well.

If these venerable institutions become too market-driven, and come to be regarded in too instrumental a way (by themselves as well as by others), they could lose the distinctive "angle to the universe" that they need to retain if they are to function at their best. This does not mean, however, that they can or should turn away from their new opportunities. The key, as I will argue throughout this lecture, is to define and defend the right "middle ground," even as we recognize that, as Isaiah Berlin said in an earlier Romanes Lecture, it is "a notoriously exposed, dangerous, and ungrateful position."[4]

THE GROWING IMPORTANCE OF THE UNIVERSITY— AND ATTENDANT PRESSURES ON IT TO "PERFORM"

Before discussing both the opportunities and the dangers before us, let me pause and remind us, ever so briefly, of why we are playing for such high stakes in debating the role of the university in a digitized and commercialized age. I can be very brief because the basic points are so well understood. In essence, the revolution in information technology and the unforgiving nature of today's international competition combine to enhance the value of well-functioning educational systems. Statesmen and politicians everywhere understand that individuals and countries that fall off the "learning curve" (or that operate below its higher reaches) will pay a big price.

I need do no more than reference the substantial body of literature that documents the purely economic returns to investments in higher education.[5] It is easy to understand intuitively that human

[4] Isaiah Berlin, "Fathers and Children: Turgenev and the Liberal Predicament," Romanes Lecture, reprinted in three parts in the *New York Review of Books*, October 18, November 1, and November 15, 1973. The quote appears in part III, November 15, 1973, p. 9.

[5] Such returns are reflected, albeit imperfectly, in pay differentials associated with different levels of educational attainment, calculations of private and societal returns, and estimates of the spillover benefits of investments in both education and research. Some of the major works in this field include Gary S. Becker, *Human Capital: A Theoretical and Empirical Analysis, with Special Reference to Education*, 3rd edition (Chicago: University of Chicago Press, 1993); Richard Brundell, Lorraine Dearden, Alissa Goodman, and Howard Reed, "Higher Education, Employment and Earnings in Britain," Institute for Fiscal Studies, London, 1997; Edward F. Denison, *Accounting for United States Economic Growth, 1929–1969* (Washington, DC: Brookings Institution Press, 1974); Richard B. Freeman and Lawrence F. Katz, "Introduction and Summary," in *Differences and Changes in Wage Structure*, ed. Richard B. Freeman and Lawrence F. Katz (Chicago: University of Chicago Press, 1995); Claudia Goldin and Lawrence F. Katz, "The Returns to Skill in the United States across the Twentieth Century," Working Paper 7126, National Bureau of Economic Research, Cambridge, MA, 1999; Susan Harkness and Stephen Machin, "Graduate Earnings in Britain, 1974–95," Research Brief 95, Department for Education and Employment, London, 1999; John Schmitt, "The Changing Structure of Male Earnings in Britain, 1974–1988," in *Differences and Changes in Wage Structure*, ed. Richard B. Freeman and Lawrence F. Katz (Chicago:

capital will be more highly valued in an information-intensive world than in a world dependent in greater degree on manual labor and inherited capital. Seen in this light, universities are perceived—correctly—as societal assets of immense value. They will be heavily responsible, for better or worse, for how well societies make material provision for their citizens.

But this is not the only reason that they matter so much. In last year's Romanes Lecture, Mr. Blair gave equal attention to the *social* case for investments in education. He emphasized what he called "the price of missed opportunities"—for individuals as well as for society.[6] Even those of us sheltered in New York are aware of subsequent discussions in this country about admissions policies at a certain well-regarded British university—a topic I will avoid altogether except to note how sad it is when discussions of serious subjects appear to depend so heavily on argument by anecdote and incomplete information. In any event, large numbers of us will surely agree that in a digitized and commercialized age it is even more important than it was before that access to the most prized educational opportunities be made available to individuals of ability and ambition from every background. How best to pursue equal opportunity in ways that strengthen, not weaken, colleges and universities is a huge subject all its own that I cannot pursue today, except to note that whenever anything increases in value we naturally care more about who gets it.

NEW OPPORTUNITIES FOR SCHOLARSHIP AND TEACHING IN A DIGITAL AGE

Universities must pay careful attention to digitization for the simple reason that it will provide innumerable new opportunities to improve and extend teaching and research, and it is these opportunities, some of which I will now outline, that have to be balanced

University of Chicago Press, 1995), pp. 177–204; James Steel and Colin Sausman, "Report 7: The Contribution of Graduates to the Economy: Rates of Return," Report to the National Committee of Inquiry into Higher Education Headed by Sir Ron Dearing, 1997, www.leeds.ac.uk/educol/ncihe/report7/htm.

[6] "The Learning Habit," Romanes Lecture delivered by the prime Minister, Rt. Hon. Tony Blair, December 2, 1999, especially pp. 3 and 7.

against the associated temptations and risks, many of which have a commercial dimension. Websites and e-mail addresses have become the stuff of daily life, both inside and outside the academy. A cartoon that I have in my office depicts a woman explaining to another woman why she has a patch on each arm: "The patch on the right is for cigarettes; the one on the left is for e-mail."[7] Many walls created by distance, time zones, and the need to work directly with physical objects have been breached, and there is much more to come as new technologies emerge and costs of hardware, software, and connectivity continue to fall. A colleague speaks of the impending arrival of "omni-connectivity," by which he means the ability to access information *at any time, from anywhere*.[8]

But what kinds of scholarly resources will there be for scholars to access? Hanna Gray, president emeritus of the University of Chicago, has observed that in many respects the electronic content produced by digitization projects often closely resembles the real objects (the "hard copies") from which it was created—much as the first printed books were intended to look as much as possible like the hand-written manuscripts produced in monasteries.[9] But this is, as Professor Gray noted, surely too limited a vision, and I want next to describe just one example of the many new kinds of specialized scholarly resources that can be built with digital technologies (apart from "courseware" and distance learning projects, which I will discuss later). My example is the JSTOR collection of scholarly journals, an electronic archive whose history I know well because the Mellon Foundation initiated its development and I continue to serve as chairman of the not-for-profit entity that is responsible for it. Focusing on the lessons learned from this one project has the advantage of making concrete a number of points that have broad applicability, and I will return to the JSTOR example several times in this lecture.

[7] *New York Magazine*, July 19, 1999, p. 32.

[8] Comment by Ira Fuchs, vice president for research in information technology at the Mellon Foundation, New York, unpublished paper prepared for the trustees of the foundation.

[9] Professor Gray is the Harry Pratt Judson Distinguished Service Professor of History and president emeritus of the University of Chicago, as well as chairman of the board of trustees of the Mellon Foundation; she made this comment at a dinner for university presidents sponsored by the Hewlett and Mellon foundations.

The JSTOR Collection of Scholarly Journals

"JSTOR" may be familiar to a number of you. It is a highly searchable electronic archive of journal literature that contains the full contents, back to inception, of over 120 leading scholarly journals in core fields of the arts and sciences—excluding only current issues.[10] The JSTOR archive contains high resolution images (exact replicas) of more than 6 million pages of journal literature; additional content is being added every day, and when the earliest issues of the *Transactions of the Royal Society* are digitized later this year, it will be possible to call up on your computer screen some of Newton's first published papers. While the JSTOR system displays images, it also contains ASCII text files that are used to facilitate searching. Users can submit searches by author, title, subject, or even by a descriptive phrase; locate relevant articles; and then print them out.[11] Thus JSTOR offers atypically convenient access to the content of a "library" that never reports that something is "out" (since any number of users can read the same article simultaneously), that delivers articles directly to a person's desk (with no defaced pages), and that never closes.

These features explain why JSTOR has been received so enthusiastically by libraries and the wider scholarly community. Over 850 libraries in forty countries (including Oxford and fifty-three others in the United Kingdom) have paid the site license fees required to obtain access to JSTOR. Usage continues to grow at a phenomenal rate—having more than tripled in the United Kingdom over the last twelve months. It is expected that more than 2.5 million articles will be printed from the database in the current calendar year. Usage has been heaviest, not surprisingly, at research-intensive universities such as Oxford (which now ranks among the top ten uni-

[10] To protect the revenue that publishers derive from selling subscriptions to current issues, JSTOR does not provide access to the most recently published content. JSTOR employs a "moving wall" to separate current issues from the back files, with the "duration" of the moving wall dependent on the wishes of the publisher.

[11] Recently the *Economist* reported that Fred Shapiro, a scholar at Yale Law School, had used JSTOR to identify a first usage of the term "software" that predated any previously known citation. "How Software Got Its Name," *Economist*, June 3, 2000.

versities worldwide in terms of its usage of JSTOR). But in many ways the enthusiastic reception of the archive at less well-known places has been even more gratifying. JSTOR provides a small Appalachian college in the United States with the same access to journals such as *Science* and the *Renaissance Quarterly* as is enjoyed by graduate students at Manchester or Stanford. It closes in some degree the "digital divide" by allowing universities in countries such as Mexico, South Africa, Russia, and Greece to acquire a rich repository of journal literature without building space or hiring staff.

The implications for scholarship and teaching are profound. They range from simply making it easier for students to work with important articles to changing fundamentally the literature that faculty and students consult. One side-benefit of JSTOR is that it allows us to track the usage made of the journal literature in its database— something that could never be done in a paper-only world. Of the 391,000 full-length journal articles in JSTOR in 1999, over two-thirds (69 percent) were viewed and nearly half (46 percent) were printed at least once in that year. Experience to date has demonstrated, convincingly, that older articles are valuable. The average age of the ten most frequently consulted articles in economics is more than fifteen years; the average age of the most frequently consulted articles in mathematics is more than thirty years. These findings are a useful rebuttal to the line of thought that equates anything electronic with a suspicion, if not a rejection, of old verities. The most basic scholarly contribution of JSTOR may be its ability to "unlock" access to older journal literature.

Enhancing Course Content and Providing Distance Learning

While information technology has had, and will have, manifold effects on how scholars do research (and I have not even mentioned applications in the field of science, such as the key role played by computer scientists and sophisticated software in the mapping of DNA, the imaging of art, or the greater ease with which scholars all over the world can collaborate), it will also have major effects on the *teaching functions* of colleges and universities. It is much too early to pass judgment on the wide variety of ways electronic technologies are being used to supplement as well as supplant the work done traditionally by the lecturer, but it is evident already that the importance of different technologies varies dramatically from discipline to discipline: animated graphs are particularly useful in fields such as economics and applied mathematics; virtual environments are especially helpful in studying organic systems in biology and medicine; and feedback applications are particularly effective in language teaching and in instruction in proof technique in logic courses.

One interesting research question, directly relevant to the earlier discussion of the implications of information technology for broadened access to educational opportunities, is whether being able to answer questions or participate in discussions via computer, in a more anonymous and less "social" way, is especially helpful to students who may be uncomfortable in traditional settings. I am reminded of another of my favorite cartoons with which you may be familiar, one showing a large dog at a computer keyboard, looking down at a smaller dog at his feet; the large dog says, "On the Internet, nobody knows you're a dog."[12] A related question is whether the self-paced nature of much instruction of this kind is particularly valuable for disadvantaged students with weaker preparation.

Online enhancements of existing courses grade off naturally into what are sometimes called "cybercourses"—courses in which, according to one definition, "little or no instruction takes place in the traditional physical classroom."[13] As the popular press tells us every day, numerous colleges and universities, including "virtual

[12] Peter Steiner, *New Yorker*, July 5, 1993, p. 61. Anonymity apparently encourages increased participation not only by students from disadvantaged backgrounds but also by women. Marion Walton and Stella Clark observed that in an online writing course they taught at the University of Cape Town, women were more likely to contribute to discussions that took place online than in the classroom. In fact, in the online discussions, over 60 percent of the comments were made by women. Marion Walton and Stella Clark, "Extending Interactivity: Academic Literacy in an Online Writing Environment" (Cape Town: University of Cape Town, 1998).

[13] See Peter Navarro, "Economics in the Cyberclassroom," *Journal of Economic Perspectives*, Spring 2000, pp. 119–32. This article contains an extensive survey of experience with one hundred cybereconomics courses at nearly fifty institutions and also contains a helpful list of references to other studies.

universities," have established a wide variety of distance learning initiatives. Today 20 percent of students at the United Kingdom's Open University [OU] are said to be studying interactively.[14] Other universities, acting alone or in concert with others, are establishing for-profit subsidiaries to deliver educational content of many kinds, including courses, to essentially all comers. One of the best known is Fathom.com, which was founded by Columbia University in collaboration with the London School of Economics and Political Science, Cambridge University Press, the British Library, the New York Public Library, and the Smithsonian.[15] A Stanford–Princeton–Yale–Oxford alliance is focusing on delivering specially created course content to alumni and others.[16] Just last week the Higher Education Funding Council announced the formation of an "eU" in Britain.[17]

This range of initiatives (and others too numerous to mention) is both promising and risky. But I am not one of those who believes that the residential university is an endangered species. Not at all. For as far ahead as any of us can see, there will be a demand—by which I mean not only a desire, but a desire backed up by the willingness to pay—for an education at both undergraduate and graduate levels that continues to emphasize the informal as well as

[14] See www.open.ac.uk/about and www.open.ac.uk/factsheets.NewTech.pdf as well as Thomas K. Grose, "Distance Education the UK Way," *Prism-Online*, November 1999, and Grenville Rumble, *The Costs and Economics of Open and Distance Learning* (London: Kogan Page, 1997), for information on the costs and quality of the OU.

[15] More recent additions to the group of collaborators are the University of Chicago, the RAND Corporation, the American Film Institute, and the Woods Hole Oceanographic Institution.

[16] See Sarah Carr, "Princeton, Stanford and Yale Plan Alliance to Offer Online Courses to Alumni," *Chronicle of Higher Education*, March 17, 2000, p. A 47, and Sarah Carr, "U of Oxford to Join Princeton, Stanford and Yale in a Distance-Education Venture," *Chronicle of Higher Education*, September 25, 2000, www.chronicle.com/article/U-of-Oxford-Joins -Princeton/105513. Most recently, the consortium has announced the selection of Herbert Allison as the CEO of the enterprise, which is now called the University Alliance for Life-Long Learning. The four participating universities have announced that they will invest $12 million in the alliance, which expects to offer short (noncredit) courses by the end of next year. If the experiment works, the alliance will offer courses to a broader public, perhaps in a for-profit mode. See Charles Forelle and Michael Horn, "Universities Commit $12M to E-Learning," *Yale Daily News*, September 29, 2000, https://web.archive.org/web/20020719 093849/http:/www.yaledailynews.com:80/article.asp?AID=12805.

[17] Jim Kelly, "UK Universities Plan Online Global College," *Financial Times*, October 10, 2000, p. 11.

formal modes of learning that are possible in a collegiate setting. Properly conceived, information technology will enhance, but not replace, traditional modes of teaching and learning. It will also permit the delivery of educational content to a wider variety of others interested in subjects that lend themselves to distance learning—at home and at odd hours.

COMMERCIAL OPPORTUNITIES: THE CASE FOR MARKET INVOLVEMENT BY UNIVERSITIES

Incorporating the motivations of for-profit entities into the institutional fabric of not-for-profit educational institutions is inevitably controversial, and most academics may be more inclined to see the negative side of the argument than the positive side. But whatever one's intuitive feelings, it is useful to recognize four advantages of a commercial approach.

The first and most obvious point is implicit in much of what has already been said. Both for-profit offshoots and alliances with for-profit entities such as Pearson and UNext.com may address real financial needs by generating flexible funds that can be used at the discretion of the institution to support its core educational and research purposes. To quote Alan Gilbert, chairman of Universitas 21 and vice chancellor of the University of Melbourne in Australia: "What we want to do is to preserve our universities as the best campus-based institutions in the world where we can continue to offer philosophy and classics and things like that which are hard to pay for in commercial terms, but which you can do if you are well-resourced."[18]

It is hard, however, to assess the potential. John Chambers, CEO and chairman of Cisco Systems, has put forth this claim: "Education over the Internet is going to be so big it is going to make e-mail usage look like a rounding error."[19] Chambers's optimism may or may not prove to be well founded. All of these ventures are in such

[18] Quoted in Zell Miller, "10 Crucial Things the Next President Should Do for Colleges," *Chronicle of Higher Education*, July 14, 2000, p. B4.

[19] Thomas L. Friedman, "Next, It's Education," *New York Times*, November 17, 1999, p. A25.

early stages of development that one cannot know with confidence how much revenue they can generate. An experienced business executive, Elton White, regularly asks: "But will the dog eat the dog food?" We just don't know, and any number of "high hopes" could be disappointed.

There is, however, a great deal to be said for seeking to diversify the revenue sources of universities if this can be done in a responsible way. Being overly dependent on government funding or on any single source is problematic from every standpoint: experience in the United States suggests that it is easier to generate large revenue streams from many tributaries—including student fees, industry support, endowments, and current donations—than it is from any single source. (This is one of the main points I tried to make nearly forty years ago when I was a visitor at the London School of Economics and wrote several papers for the Robbins Commission.[20]) Moreover, diverse sources of funding can protect institutional autonomy by giving institutions greater freedom to decide for themselves what fees they should charge and what salaries they should pay, as well as which students they should admit, what research they should pursue, and what curricula they should offer. In the British context, Alan Ryan, warden of New College, has put the matter this way: "It is essential to bring the marketplace further into the academy. This means allowing colleges and universities to pay faculty what they can afford, and to charge students what they will pay."[21]

A second advantage of commercialization, and one that is often overlooked, has to do with the location and management of risk. A for-profit mode of organization provides a mechanism for raising the capital that is essential to launch projects that require considerable start-up funding—and to do so without putting so many of

[20] See William G. Bowen, "Financing Higher Education," in *Economic Aspects of Education: Three Essays* (Princeton, NJ: Department of Economics, Princeton University, 1964). Similar arguments have been made frequently in the United Kingdom. See, for example, "Funding Higher Education" in *Higher Education for the 21ˢᵗ Century*, DfEE, available at http://webarchive.nationalarchives.gov.uk/20030731060248/http://www.lifelonglearning.dfes.gov.uk:80/dearing/drten00.htm, and "Who Should Pay for Higher Education?," chapter 18 in Report of the National Committee of Inquiry into Higher Education Headed by Sir Ron Dearing, 1997.

[21] Alan Ryan, "The American Way," *Prospect*, August–September 1999, www.prospect magazine.co.uk/magazine/theamericanway.

the core resources of the university at risk. Fathom.com received an initial infusion of funds from its principal academic sponsor, Columbia University, but it is committed to raising the bulk of its working capital from outside investors. If the enterprise fails, Columbia will lose much less money that it would have lost had it made the entire initial investment itself. Similarly, for-profit investors can save a project that might otherwise die of financial starvation. The co-founders of Africana.com, Harvard University professors Henry Louis Gates Jr. and Anthony Appiah, have just sold their website to Time Warner Inc. because of their need for long-term financing. In Gates's phraseology, "The revenue model was slow to develop."[22]

Third, market incentives can encourage faculty and others inside the academy, sometimes regarded as too hidebound, insular, and aloof, to be more responsive to the needs of the larger society. Similarly, there is an advantage in being able to look at market comparisons in assessing whether a given service is being provided efficiently. Market tests offer a useful objectivity.

Fourth, well-developed Internet market mechanisms may enable faculty members to reach far wider audiences than would have been possible otherwise. This was a principal reason given by Columbia for the creation of Fathom.com. As its president, George Rupp, put it: "We want to make sure that our core intellectual capital is not picked off by outside for-profit vendors. But for that, we have to be able to say to our faculty that we will devise ways they can communicate with a wider audience, which many of them would like."[23]

LESSONS LEARNED AND WARNING FLAGS

I come now to the proverbial other side of the coin: lessons learned to date and "warning flags" that can be ignored only at one's peril. First on my list is the need to cope with *the rapid pace of techno-*

---

[22] Quoted in David D. Kirkpatrick, "Co-Founders of Africana.com Sell Venture to Time Warner," *New York Times*, September 7, 2000, p. C2.

[23] Quoted in Karen W. Arenson, "Columbia to Put Learning Online for Profit," *New York Times*, April 3, 2000, p. B3.

logical change. I am told that computer power continues to follow Moore's Law and to double every eighteen months. Video, voice, text, and multimedia are converging in data transmission. Extremely high-speed networks, like the Abilene backbone of Internet2, are enabling new applications. Searching techniques are becoming ever more sophisticated. Progress will continue to be made in designing multi-lingual interfaces. New tools will be developed for linking citations and online documents, for authenticating both electronic documents and users, and for managing intellectual property rights. No technology platform, no technical "fix," stays in place for long.

Nonetheless, in spite of much experience with the recurring transformations of electronic technologies, even knowledgeable people sometimes "forget" the implications. It can be all too tempting to launch a new electronic resource without considering how it is to be maintained. That is a serious mistake. Any project that seeks sustainability must have continuing access to the technical capacity and budgetary resources needed to migrate from one platform to another. In this arena—and in this era—one-time investments are almost certain to be ephemeral. It is well to remember Fuchs's Law, "The time to acquisition is longer than the time to obsolescence," or its corollary, "When you get what you ordered, you don't want it."[24]

A second, related, lesson is *the need to be realistic in thinking about costs* and to avoid the ever-present danger of believing that great things can be accomplished "on the cheap." All aspects of the process of creating and delivering electronic content are expensive—which is the main reason that issues of technology interact so directly with issues of cost. The faster the pace of change, the more expensive it is likely to be to keep up. It is not difficult to spend several hundred thousand dollars developing a multimedia course of high quality. Nor can the initial up-front costs be regarded as once-and-for-all expenditures, given constantly changing technology and the recurring need to update materials and modes of presentation.

---

[24] Attributed to Ira Fuchs, vice president for research in information technology at the Andrew W. Mellon Foundation.

What is more surprising, and even more important to keep in mind, is the high *variable* cost currently associated with the use of cyber teaching units. One careful observer offers this comparison: "A cyberprofessor trades the 'chains' of lecturing in a classroom for a predictable number of hours at a specific time and place for the more unpredictable 'freedom' of being accessible by e-mail and other technologies.... Many cybercourse instructors find themselves being drawn into an endless time drain."[25] Similarly, a faculty report at the University of Illinois suggests that "sound online instruction is likely to cost more than traditional instruction" and that "the scenario of hundreds or thousands of students enrolling in a well developed, essentially instructor-free online course does not appear realistic."[26] The demise of the California Virtual University is, as the *Chronicle of Higher Education* observed, "a sobering reminder of how hard it is to run a successful 'portal' for online education."[27]

For these and other reasons, all the talk of using technology to "save money by increasing productivity" has a hollow ring in the ears of the budget officer who has to pay for the salaries of a cadre of support staff, more and more equipment, and new software licenses—and who sees few offsetting savings. The experience to date of essentially every college or university official has been that technologically induced gains in "productivity" (defined as output divided by units of input) have almost always been taken in the form of better research, improved access to information, and so on (more output), rather than in the form of savings in inputs.

But this could change. Even though I am the co-creator of what has come to be known in the literature as "Baumol's disease" or "Bowen's curse" (the notion that costs in service-intensive fields

[25] Navarro, "Economics in the Cyberclassroom," p. 129. On a single campus, at any rate, the economies of scale appear to be far smaller than is generally assumed; several studies have reported that "the marginal cost of servicing each additional student does not fall at anywhere near the same rate as with a traditional course." Navarro, "Economics in the Cyberclassroom," p. 128.

[26] "Teaching at an Internet Distance," Report of a 1998–1999 University of Illinois Faculty Seminar, December 7, 1999, http://web.archive.org/web/20011217152332/www.vpaa .uillinois.edu/tid/report/toc.html.

[27] Jeffrey R. Young, "Veteran of California Virtual U. Blames a Flawed Business Plan for Its Demise," *Chronicle of Higher Education*, May 12, 2000, www.chronicle.com/article /Veteran-of-California-Virtual/105644.

such as education and the performing arts inevitably rise faster than they do in the economy at large),[28] I am now persuaded that electronic technologies can lead to lower costs. There may be at least one "slumbering giant" who could awaken and change the situation quite dramatically—namely, the textbook publishing oligopoly, which has an incentive to invest in further technological development of courseware that should allow artificial intelligence, for example, to take over some of the more repetitive tasks that now require the time of staff and keep variable costs high.[29]

JSTOR is another, quite different, case in point. While the jury may be out (and out for a long time) on the cost-effectiveness of many types of courseware, some of the electronic resources designed to facilitate scholarship and research can, in principle, lead to substantial system-wide savings. Needless to say, there were significant up-front costs involved in creating JSTOR. There are also recurring costs associated with maintaining the database, adding content each year, keeping current with technological advances, and providing the needed infrastructure (including user services). Fortunately, however, JSTOR not only improves dramatically the ability of scholars to find and use journal literature; it also offers the prospect of savings for library systems, even after taking account of the user fees that libraries pay.[30]

[28] See William J. Baumol and William G. Bowen, *Performing Arts–The Economic Dilemma: A Study of Problems Common to Theater, Opera, Music and Dance* (New York: Twentieth Century Fund, 1966). The phrases "Baumol's disease" and "Bowen's curse" are used in the literature to refer to the phenomenon described earlier. See, for example, L. Deboer, "Is Rock'n' Roll a Symptom of Baumol's Disease?," *Journal of Cultural Economics* 9, pp. 48–59, and Charles T. Clotfelter, *Buying the Best: Cost Escalation in Elite Higher Education* (Princeton, NJ: Princeton University Press, 1996), p. 35.

[29] See Navarro, "Economics in the Cyberclassroom," pp. 125–26. The major publishers are investing heavily in the development of cybernet course content, as well as in the infrastructure that would be needed to deliver the content. As a result, it should become possible, before too long, for institutions to deliver electronic content that is well conceived and free of copyright problems. It is the large publishers that can achieve real economies of scale. More generally, a number of the factors that keep costs high today could turn out to be transitional. As styles of teaching and available technologies become better aligned and as faculty are less inclined to mimic techniques carried over from an earlier day, costs are likely to fall. Many forms of teaching could become better and cheaper.

[30] Libraries pay a one-time archive capital fee, which is intended to defray part of the capital cost of creating the roughly five million pages of digitized content that reside in the archive. Participating libraries also pay an annual access fee that helps cover the running costs. For detailed pricing information, see https://about.jstor.org/.

One important long-term benefit is the opportunity JSTOR offers libraries to economize on stack space. Those that already possess the hard copies of JSTOR journals have the option of moving them out of "prime real estate," which can then be used for other purposes. Going forward, the existence of JSTOR reduces the need to build new shelf space. Libraries that do not have the hard copies are able to gain access to this substantial corpus of literature for a tiny fraction of the costs that would have been involved in building space to house it, never mind acquiring it in the first place and paying staff to catalogue it. On a system-wide basis, these potential savings in capital costs are huge—roughly $140 million at present, according to one estimate, and growing steadily.[31] This kind of resource also offers potentially large savings in operating costs by eliminating the need to handle the paper copies of journals that can now be accessed electronically.[32] In the future, when JSTOR is linked to the electronic versions of current issues (as will surely

[31] The capital costs associated with housing the backfiles of the journals in JSTOR (assuming that a library has the full runs) are estimated to amount to roughly $175,000 in a typical case, and these costs will only increase over time as more content is added. There are at present over eight hundred participating libraries, which suggests a current system-wide saving of roughly $140 million. This figure was derived as follows. JSTOR estimates that there are seven thousand volumes in the current database. Jay Lucker, the former university librarian at MIT and a consultant on academic library construction projects, estimates that academic libraries cost on average $250 per square foot to build and that such libraries store ten bound periodicals per square foot. Personal communication with Sarah Levin. Dividing $250 per square foot by ten volumes per square foot yields a cost per volume of $25, and multiplying by seven thousand volumes yields an overall cost of $175,000 to store the JSTOR collection in print. These numbers and this methodology are in keeping with those used in the literature in this field. See Malcolm Getz, "Storing Information in Academic Libraries," 1994, mimeo, and Michael D. Cooper, "A Cost Comparison of Alternative Book Storage Strategies," *Library Quarterly* 59, no. 3 (July 1989): 239–60. It is important to note that in major university libraries it is not unusual to have two or three print copies of the JSTOR journals, as they are the core journals in their fields, so the savings in these libraries could be double or triple the number stated above.

[32] According to one estimate, a major library should expect to save roughly $20,000 per year and a small library something like $5,000 per year. The New York Public Library, which is a non-circulating closed-stack library, has estimated that it spends $1.94 to retrieve and reshelf a typical journal volume. Even if we cut this estimate in half in recognition of the unusually complex nature of the New York Public Library, and use a figure of $1.00 per retrieval, the savings are substantial. The estimates in the text use the $1.00 per retrieval figure and are based on crude counts of the number of times hard-copy JSTOR journals were taken from the shelves at the University of Michigan and at "test-site" college libraries *in the pre-JSTOR days*. This is the relevant reference point, not the much higher usage now being experienced through access to JSTOR.

happen), there will be further savings in cataloguing and process-ing costs. Also, JSTOR reduces the wear and tear on journals and the attendant costs of preservation and conservation.

These savings—which can exceed the fees charged to libraries by factors ranging from two to ten, depending on the type of library—result directly from using information technology to cen-tralize the storage function while simultaneously enhancing access to content. The economies of scale are extraordinary, since the core database needs to be created only once, and it is possible to grant access to additional sets of library patrons at modest incremental costs. It will of course take time for the habits of librarians and li-brary users to change, but we are already seeing examples of how libraries can collaborate to store the hard copies of journals in in-expensive regional centers; some smaller libraries feel that they can discard the hard copies altogether, relying on larger research uni-versities and entities like JSTOR to take responsibility for the ar-chiving function.[33]

There is a broader point that deserves emphasis. In deciding whether a resource such as JSTOR is worth what it costs in their particular setting, institutions need to take account of *all* elements of the financial equation, including the long-term implications for building plans, capital costs, and maintenance. Not all librarians are inclined to think in such terms (sometimes making comments like "We have enough space now" or "Somebody else is responsi-ble for providing space and paying for maintenance and operating costs"); it is easy to think of JSTOR as merely another competitor for inclusion in a strained acquisitions budget. Fortunately, the

[33] A survey done in 1999 by JSTOR found that 20 percent of the respondents had al-ready moved journals to remote storage and that an additional 24 percent have plans to do. These numbers will continue to increase as libraries gain confidence in the archiving reli-ability of JSTOR. To cite one example of what libraries are doing, the librarian at Maryville College in Appalachia reports that she is completely withdrawing JSTOR backruns up to 1980. She is moving them into the basement and will then try to sell them for a year or so. In her words: "What we cannot sell by next year will go out the door. It will be hard to see these nicely bound volumes go (after first offering them to the faculty with the caveat that they can *not* donate them to the library on their retirement), but we do need the shelf space and I would not even want to ask for more space. Also, students do not touch the paper once the info is online; this is just a fact of life these days." Chris Nugent of Maryville Col-lege, e-mail to Kristen Garlock of JSTOR.

"access-only" benefits of JSTOR are so dramatic that many librar-ies have signed up on this basis alone—ignoring the long-term sav-ings in capital and operating costs. But this is not the way decisions of this kind should be made. In a digital world, a broader institu-tional perspective needs to be applied to resource allocation deci-sions. This is a major organizational lesson taught by experience with JSTOR, and it will have even greater applicability when con-sidering other applications of technology that are more diffuse and harder to tie to specific cost elements.

There is a third set of issues that permeates the electronic world and that can be every bit as vexing as failing to provide for rapid changes in technology or failing to analyze costs correctly. I am referring to *the handling of intellectual property rights*. Seemingly endless controversy can be associated with the ownership of and licensing of rights to everything from electronic course content, to images of works of art, to software such as compression algorithms. A week does not go by without a report of some new lawsuit, and it is perilous indeed to assume that anyone can predict confidently what the courts will conclude in an arena that is fairly described as "unsettled" (to say the least).

Under particularly severe scrutiny at the moment are vendors of electronic databases containing material that appeared originally as hard copy.[34] In the world of art, it is tempting for museums and research libraries to seek a "safe harbor" by restricting electronic representations of their images to "thumbnails" that are of limited

---

[34] In one noteworthy case, *Tasini v. New York Times, Inc.*, 206 F. 3d 161 (2nd Cir. 2000), six freelance writers sued the *New York Times*, Time Incorporated Magazine Company, *Newsday*, the *Atlantic Monthly*, Mead Data Central Corporation, and University Microfilm International for taking articles previously published in periodicals and arranging for them to be reproduced and distributed in databases of digitized individual articles without per-mission and without the provision of additional compensation to the right holders. The writers won, and, due to the *Tasini* ruling, such suits are becoming more common. (As one colleague put it, we now live in a world of "search and sue!") As an outgrowth of the *Tasini* case, the National Writers' Union, whose president is Jonathan Tasini, the lead plaintiff in the *Tasini* case, has established a Publication Rights Clearinghouse to facilitate and enforce the payment of royalties to freelance writers. See Felicity Barringer, "Online Agreement Near for Writers' Group," *New York Times*, August 3, 2000, p. C6. In recognition of such legal challenges, *U.S. News and World Report* is reported to be pulling content from some microform editions, with disturbing consequences for libraries that thought they could rely on the availability of the content.

use to scholars. The most contentious suits of all have affected the copying and distribution of movies and popular music—which is, not surprisingly, where the economic stakes are highest.[35]

This is not a battle between good and evil. It is important, in my view, that an appropriate balance be found between the entirely legitimate interests of the owners of content and the need to find definitions of "fair use," and to craft licensing agreements, that will not negate the educational benefits of electronic technologies. Experience in negotiating agreements with both journal publishers and entities such as the Dunhuang Research Institute in China convinces me that when there is a shared set of objectives, trust, and mutual respect, it is possible to reconcile the multiple interests of participants. One lesson is the importance of confronting such questions directly and openly in the early stages of framing projects of this kind. Another lesson, of equal importance, is that terms such as "balancing" and "reconciling" are essential: ideological insistence on the pre-eminence of the rights of either the content owner or the user will lead nowhere.

Fourth and last on my list is the need to be concerned about the effects of market opportunities on *faculty incentives*.[36] If faculty can earn significant amounts of extra money by working on online projects of one kind or another, it is natural to wonder what the effects will be on the priorities they set for themselves. There is a risk that faculty, and many of the most outstanding faculty, will be distracted from their core functions of scholarship and classroom teaching. Such distractions may result from the responses of individual faculty members to the pull of the marketplace, but faculty

[35] For example, the Recording Industry Association of America sued Napster over the distribution of copyrighted music. On July 26, 2000, Judge Marilyn Hall Patel of the US District Court for the Northern District of California issued a preliminary injunction against Napster and ordered the online music provider to stop the trade of copyrighted music. *A&M Records, Inc. v. Napster, Inc.,* nos. C 99–5183 MHP and C 00–0074 MHP (N.D. Cal. July 26, 2000). Citing "substantial questions of first impression," on July 28, 2000, a panel of appellate judges granted an emergency stay of the district court's injunction, thereby permitting Napster to continue operating pending a decision in the appeal of the preliminary injunction. Oral argument on the appeal was held on October 2, 2000, and an opinion is expected to be issued soon.

[36] Concern over the effects of outside funding of all kinds on university priorities is longstanding. See Eyal Press and Jennifer Washburn, "The Kept University," *Atlantic Monthly* 285, no. 3 (March 2000): 39–54.

may also be drawn away from their core pursuits with the tacit if not overt encouragement of their own universities. Issues of governance and potential conflicts of interest also arise when faculty members have personal stakes in activities affected by policies that they, along with their colleagues, are responsible for shaping. On the other hand, too pristine a posture by the university (attempting to deny faculty any opportunity to be involved in what some will see as "cutting-edge" opportunities to do new things *and* to make money) can lead faculty to seek such opportunities outside the university structure altogether.[37]

These issues may become even more vexing if electronic technologies lead to greater specialization and change the division of labor in universities. At present, the functions of discovering knowledge, putting it into teachable form, distributing it to students, and then certifying their grasp of the material are usually tied together. Generally speaking, there is one "price" for the bundle, with the price paid either by the student who pays tuition or by whatever private or public funders finance the university that is the home of this set of activities. But applications of electronic technologies may lead to an "unbundling" of these functions. Technically sophisticated intermediaries may take over responsibility for translating content created by traditional academics into electronic "courseware," which may then be distributed by still other intermediaries to a wide array of learners. Under this scenario, will separate charges be imposed at each step along the "knowledge chain"? How will faculty incentives be affected, and who will pay for the scholarship that started the process?

HOW "BUSINESS-LIKE" SHOULD UNIVERSITIES BE?

A recurring theme of this talk is the need to seek a sensible "middle ground," an injunction that applies not only to specific issues such as how to balance competing ownership interests and how to

---

[37] Faculty may be tempted to protect their "ownership rights" by separating such work as completely as they can from their normal lives as professors. For a lengthy discussion of these issues, see Scott Carlson, "When Professors Create Software, Do They Own It, or Do Their Colleges?," *Chronicle of Higher Education*, July 21, 2000, www.chronicle.com/article /When-Professors-Create/29189.

structure faculty incentives but also more broadly when we ask the larger question, "How 'business-like' should universities be?" Underlying the concerns expressed by many (including the use of marketplace language such as "brands," which has worrying symbolic overtones for some faculty[38]) is the fundamental risk of "mission drift." As economist Burton Weisbrod puts it: "When nonprofits' pursuit of revenue drives them to act like private firms, ... there are dangers of goal displacement, as the social mission slips from sight.... Aggressive marketing and merchandising produce almost inevitable conflict, sometimes forcing organizations to choose between 'capitalist appetites' and ... integrity."[39] While the not-for-profit entity must certainly pay attention to its own "bottom line" and operate efficiently, it has to keep its own mission firmly in mind. One highly experienced leader of both for-profit and not-for-profit entities, John C. Whitehead, offers this useful distinction: "A for-profit board has an obligation to *get out* of a bad business while a nonprofit board may have an obligation to *stay in*, if it is to be true to its mission."[40]

A for-profit orientation can take a university in directions quite different from those that it would follow otherwise. A good example is the handling of student aid. A for-profit or "proprietary" educational institution will presumably offer financial aid (or "discounts" from its stated fees) if and only if such discounts end up improving the financial health of the organization by increasing marginal revenues more than marginal costs. A not-for-profit university, on the other hand, may see its mission as including an obligation to spend money on financial aid to attract the best students,

[38] In the debate over the creation of a for-profit subsidiary at Cornell, Risa L. Lieberwitz, an associate professor in the School of Labor and Industrial Relations, was quoted as saying: "If we are starting to talk about Cornell as a brand name, then we are in trouble. I don't see what I do as a professor as promoting a brand name. We are talking about brands without the slightest bit of self-consciousness, and that is just jarring to me." See Sarah Carr, "Faculty Members Are Wary of Distance-Education Ventures," *Chronicle of Higher Education*, June 9, 2000, p. A41. Similarly, in announcing the sale of Africana.com, Professor Gates was quoted as saying: "We didn't want a lot of cheap ads that would dilute *the brand*." *New York Times*, September 7, 2000, my emphasis.

[39] Burton Weisbrod, ed., *To Profit or Not to Profit: Commercialization in the Non-Profit Sector* (Cambridge, UK: Cambridge University Press, 1998), p. 304.

[40] Quoted in William G. Bowen, *Inside the Boardroom* (Hoboken, NJ: Wiley, 1994), p. 23.

whatever their means, or to increase diversity, even though such spending will be a drain on its resources.[41]

JSTOR offers a useful case history of the importance of adhering to a not-for-profit mindset. When JSTOR was first established, it was evident that there was more money to be made in providing electronic access to the current issues of journals than to the backfiles. JSTOR targeted the digitization of the backfiles nonetheless because of the perceived importance to scholars, and to the library community, of both enhancing access to this "less commercial" part of journal literature and saving shelf space. Since it was contrarian (from a commercial perspective), this emphasis on the backfiles surprised many people. Early on, the head of one widely known commercial entity told me: "Mr. Bowen, no sane man would do what you propose." He may even have been right—from his perspective. Which is precisely the point.

Subsequent decisions have also been different from those that would have been taken had JSTOR "gone public" and followed the for-profit path advocated by some. Let me cite two examples. In deciding which fields of knowledge to include in the database, JSTOR has attempted to determine where the needs of scholars are the greatest, not where there is the best chance of selling a product. Thus the JSTOR database includes fields like history, philosophy, and literature, whereas it does not yet include business. Then, in setting fees, a determined effort was made to encourage the participation of smaller and less wealthy institutions all over the world. The assistance of foundations has been instrumental in giving effect to these decisions, which have been motivated by objectives and values analogous to those that lead institutions to provide need-based financial aid.

[41] In the for-profit educational world, discounting can be seen as a form of price discrimination, whereas student aid is an "investment" for educational institutions that could have recruited well-qualified students without such outlays. See David J. Breneman and William G. Bowen, "Student Aid: Price Discount or Educational Investment?," *Brookings Review* 11, no. 1 (Winter 1993): pp. 28–31, and William G. Bowen, "The Student Aid/Tuition Nexus," in *Ever the Teacher* (Princeton, NJ: Princeton University Press, 1988), pp. 538–43. The second reference shows how failure to distinguish for-profit from not-for-profit motivations can lead to entirely wrong conclusions about public policy—in this case the effect of changes in federal financial aid programs on tuition.

To be clear, I am certainly not arguing that for-profit providers of one service or another are "bad"; JSTOR itself employs for-profit providers (such as vendors of scanning services) when they can provide the best value for money *in helping JSTOR achieve its purposes*. What *is* crucial is the objective being served and the mission of the enterprise setting the objective. This is no trivial point. In working with the providers of other forms of digitized content (in, for example, the art world), we have had to explain that it is important to retain the freedom to work with whatever agent, be it a for-profit or not-for-profit entity, can best distribute the archive in ways that are consistent with educational and cultural values.

It is also true that not-for-profit entities can sometimes act like their for-profit cousins. For example, we have encountered scholarly journals and occasionally learned societies that were interested primarily in shaping digitization projects to yield the maximum revenue for their organizations. This is understandable, since such entities are often hard pressed to cover their own running costs and are always in search of new sources of funds. In this regard, they have something in common with universities! But there are larger interests to be served, and in shaping the digitized/commercialized world that is evolving, it is important to encourage not-for-profit entities, including universities and university presses, to take as all-encompassing a perspective as possible. A major role for foundations, in my view, is to promote broader orientations. Appropriately targeted subsidies can do a great deal to align interests. More generally, the revolution in information technology creates many new opportunities for productive collaborations, some of which will be missed if there is an excess of competitive zeal that is market-driven.

THE SEARCH FOR BALANCE: THE NEED TO REMAIN "AT A SLIGHT ANGLE TO THE UNIVERSE"

There are no pat answers to the many questions I have raised in this lecture. The longer-term implications for universities of the paired forces of digitization and commercialization are poorly understood.

This should not surprise us. Many of these developments are genuinely new; there is a dizzying array of "moving parts" (and fast-moving parts at that); and, finally, the intellectual framework and the empirical reference points needed to analyze many of the issues are underdeveloped, if they exist at all. In such circumstances, there is a natural temptation to "wing it"—to "do something" so as not to appear slow of foot—even though the likely consequences of the "something" are far from clear. But there are risks associated with just plunging ahead, especially since what we often like to call "experiments" are inordinately hard to reverse in academic settings. Having learned some lessons the hard way, I am a strong advocate of carrying out the same kind of systematic research in this area that we embrace so naturally in more traditional fields.

There is also a temporal perspective that must be honored. Universities are among our oldest institutions, and it would be most unfortunate if the time horizons common to so much of commercial society came to dominate academic planning. Stock prices fluctuate wildly if companies miss quarterly earnings estimates by pennies. New ideas, on the other hand, germinate over long periods and almost always take longer to correct than they did to create.

Above all, I hope we will remember that universities exist to serve purposes that transcend many of the concerns of the work-a-day world. The disinterested pursuit of learning, commitments to tolerance and social justice, the belief that learning is enhanced by studying with those who have different perspectives and come from different walks of life—these and other core elements of university life defy the logic of the marketplace and the auction block. To some people, universities now seem more "for sale" than they have ever been. I hope this is not the case, since I am convinced that their value (including their value to those who would "buy" them) derives in large measure from the fact that they are *not* for sale.

While universities can lose their way by yielding to some combination of complacency and temptation, they can also be pressured by external forces into adopting priorities that are too narrow or overly restrictive. There is a real danger that funders in both the United States and the United Kingdom (especially governmental entities) will expect universities to be so responsive to the market that larger and longer-term objectives will be sacrificed. The society at large needs to give universities the time, the "space," and the resources that they need to work through new and complex issues in thoughtful and principled ways.

I return now, as I conclude, to Forster's famous description of Cavafy:

> They turn and see a Greek gentleman in a straw hat, standing absolutely motionless at a slight angle to the universe.... He may be prevailed upon to begin a sentence—an immense complicated yet shapely sentence, full of parentheses that never get mixed and of reservations that really do reserve; a sentence that moves with logic to its foreseen end, yet to an end that is always more vivid and thrilling than one foresaw.... It deals with the tricky behavior of Emperor Alexius Comnenus in 1096, or with olives, their possibilities and price ... or the dialects of the interior of Asia Minor.... And despite its intellectual richness and human outlook, despite the matured charity of its judgments, one feels that it too stands at a slight angle to the universe; it is the sentence of a poet.[42]

Faced with both new opportunities and new temptations, universities will need an effective combination of internal clarity concerning what matters most and the right kind of external support if they are to retain the perspective of the poet—if they are to continue to stand, with Cavafy, "at a slight angle to the universe."

[42] Here is a fuller excerpt from E. M. Forster's description of Cavafy: "They turn and see a Greek gentleman in a straw hat, standing absolutely motionless at a slight angle to the universe.... Yes, it is Mr. Cavafy, and he is going either from his flat to his office, or from his office to the flat. If the former, he vanishes when seen, with a slight gesture of despair. If the latter, he may be prevailed upon to begin a sentence—an immense complicated yet shapely sentence, full of parentheses that never get mixed and of reservations that really do reserve; a sentence that moves with logic to its foreseen end, yet to an end that is always more vivid and thrilling than one foresaw. Sometimes the sentence is finished in the street, sometimes the traffic murders it, sometimes it lasts into the flat. It deals with the tricky behavior of Emperor Alexius Comnenus in 1096, or with olives, their possibilities and price ... or the dialects of the interior of Asia Minor. It is delivered with equal ease in Greek, English, or French. And despite its intellectual richness and human outlook, despite the matured charity of its judgments, one feels that it too stands at a slight angle to the universe; it is the sentence of a poet." E. M. Forster, "The Poetry of C. P. Cavafy," in *Pharos and Pharillon* (New York: Alfred A. Knopf, 1961), pp. 91–92. I am indebted to my colleague and friend Edmund M. Keeley for this reference.

THE TWO FACES OF WEALTH

~

William G. Bowen
October 21, 2000

REMARKS AT THE INDUCTION OF
MORTON O. SCHAPIRO AS 16TH PRESIDENT
OF WILLIAMS COLLEGE

In my remarks today, I want to consider what I think of as "the two faces of wealth": the temptations and the opportunities. I asked various friends if they could suggest a scriptural or religious text, and a former colleague at the [Mellon] Foundation found the following quotation from the Midrash Tanhuma: "The rich should ever bear in mind that his wealth may merely have been deposited with him to *be a steward over it*, or *to test what use he will make of his possessions*" (my emphasis).

THE TEMPTATIONS OF WEALTH

I begin with the not-so-nice face of wealth: the temptations that go along with it—temptations that can afflict both individuals at a college such as Williams and the college per se. One risk is that wealth will be seen as an end in itself rather than as a means to much worthier ends. Being surrounded by affluent classmates as well as manifestations of institutional affluence can lead to problems of many kinds. Students from modest backgrounds may feel intensely

Author's note: I would like to thank Susan Anderson, Idana Goldberg, Pat McPherson, Cara Nakamura, Roger Schonfeld, James Shulman, Dennis Sullivan, and Harriet Zuckerman for help in preparing these remarks.

uncomfortable and out of place. There are also across-the-board attitudinal risks, which include the notion that the main reason for going to college is to make lots of money—to gain for oneself the affluence that is so much in evidence here. Attending an excellent college or university does enhance an individual's economic prospects, and that's fine; but it is a bit alarming, at least to me, that more and more entering students seem to be focused primarily on the financial benefits that they associate with attending a prestigious institution. In 1971, just under half (49.9 percent) of all entering freshmen said that a very important reason for attending college was "to be able to make more money." In 1996, the comparable percentage was 72.4 percent.[1] As Mike McPherson has pointed out, presidents of colleges and universities do not help the situation when they stress the purely financial value of the "investment" that they are asking students and their parents to make in the institution.

Needless to say, the values and motivations that students reveal in college are developed in large part long before they arrive on campus, and colleges are sometimes blamed for behavior that has deep roots. I remember well an exchange of letters in the *Princeton Alumni Weekly*. The first letter was from the mother of a freshman who had just visited her son. She had been dismayed by the condition of his room and complained bitterly that the university was allowing him to "live like a pig." In the next issue, another parent responded: "How can you blame the University for having failed, in three months, to correct a problem that you obviously failed to correct in 18 years?" Still, a college such as Williams does bear responsibility for (a) selecting the students who enroll and (b) then affecting, in some measure, how they come to see themselves and their world.

Having just finished working with James Shulman on a study of intercollegiate athletics (titled *The Game of Life: College Sports*

---

[1] Similarly, in 1966, 43.8 percent of entering freshmen said that being "very well off financially" was an "essential" or "very important" objective in life; in 1996, the comparable percentage was 74.1 percent. These data are from Alexander W. Astin et al., *The American Freshman: Thirty Year Trends, 1966–1996* (Los Angeles, CA: Higher Education Research Institute, Graduate School of Education and Information Studies, University of California–Los Angeles, 1997).

and Educational Values [Princeton, NJ: Princeton University Press, 2001]), I am keenly aware that colleges are deciding all the time which kinds of students, with the embedded motivations and value systems that they bring with them, will be given the opportunity of studying at privileged institutions. In our view, some admissions deans and other decision-makers have moved too far away from a day when it was thought appropriate to look for candidates who were good at more than one particular thing (who were not the wrong kinds of "trufflehounds," in the memorable phrase of my great teacher Jacob Viner). In our book we argue for admitting students who will come to college for "the right reasons," which to our way of thinking include wanting to take full advantage of the broad learning opportunities offered by liberal arts colleges such as Williams and then putting what they have learned to work for the benefit of the larger society. "In the long run," Thoreau wrote, "[people] hit only what they aim at. Therefore, though they should fail immediately, they had better aim at something high."[2]

Once students have been selected, and arrive on campus, they are then subject to the messages that the college community sends them. One of these messages should be that it is fine to be idealistic, that everyone and everything need *not* be for sale, and that all the scorecards that matter in life are *not* denominated in dollars. This message is especially important in a society such as ours, in which there is so much emphasis on what the distinguished University of Chicago economist Frank Knight once called "the business game." Writing in the mid-1930s, Knight observed:

> However favorable an opinion one may hold of the business game, he must be very illiberal not to concede that others have a right to a different view and that large numbers of admirable people do not like the game at all. It is then justifiable at least to regard as unfortunate the dominance of the business game over life, the virtual identification of social living with it, to the extent that has come to pass in the modern world.[3]

[2] See Carl Bode, ed., *The Portable Thoreau* (New York: Penguin, 1982), p. 282.
[3] Frank H. Knight, *The Ethics of Competition and Other Essays*, 2nd edition (New York: Harper and Bros., 1936), p. 58.

Another message that I believe deserves strong emphasis in a results-oriented society is the importance not only of the destination one chooses, but of the journey itself: it matters so much how we get where we're going and what we learn along the way. This theme has been expressed beautifully by one of my favorite poets, Constantine Cavafy, who lived in Alexandria in the early 1900s. His poem "Ithaka," which refers to the island home to which Odysseus returned after the Trojan War, contains these stanzas:

> As you set out for Ithaka
> hope your road is a long one,
> full of adventure, full of discovery.
> ....
> May there be many summer mornings when
> with what pleasure, what joy,
> you enter harbours you're seeing for the first time;
> ....
> and may you visit many Egyptian cities
> to learn and go on learning from scholars.
>
> Keep Ithaka always in your mind.
> Arriving there is what you're destined for.
> But don't hurry the trip at all.
> Better if it lasts for years,
> so you're old by the time you reach the island,
> wealthy with all you've gained on the way,
> not expecting Ithaka to make you rich.
>
> Ithaka gave you the marvelous journey.
> Without her you wouldn't have set out.
> She has nothing left to give you now.
>
> And if you find her poor, Ithaka won't have fooled you.
> Wise as you will have become, so full of experience,
> you'll have understood by then what these Ithakas mean.

Attitudes toward wealth can not only affect one's destination in life and lead to impatience with long journeys and side-trips (to visit Egyptian cities and learn from their scholars); they can also affect self-perceptions. One of the most insidious aspects of being part of a wealthy, prestigious institution is that the association can lead to a most unfortunate blend of pomposity, smugness, and complacency. The *assumption* of superiority is what gives elitism a bad name. Being here does not entitle anyone to anything—except the opportunity to learn. Mary Kay Ash, the founder of Mary Kay cosmetics, was right when she said: "Nothing wilts faster than a laurel rested upon." This is a great college, but it must not allow its past achievements, and certainly not its accumulated wealth, to blind it to the need to be better. The important tests are always those that lie ahead.

Last on my list of the dangers associated with wealth is a quite practical one: wealth can make it too easy to stand pat, to avoid trying new things. It is no coincidence, I think, that one of the most innovative efforts to use library space more effectively is being made at a small Appalachian college (Maryville College). Wealth can make it much harder to realize that the answer to the question of "which" should not be "both."

It is of course possible to be so attuned to the dangers of wealth that one romanticizes the life of the impoverished artist who is shivering in her garret. In teaching the history of economic thought, Jacob Viner used to like to quote the following pronouncement from a seventeenth-century English sermon: "The poor man in the sun is happier than the rich man in his castle." Viner, always the skeptic, would then add: "I believe it when the poor man tells me." Viner respected the ways in which market incentives can improve economic performance, but he was always careful to separate wealth creation from the much more daunting question of how wealth should be used. As the passage quoted earlier from the Midrash Tanhuma reminds us, the challenge for a college such as Williams is to be a good steward of the riches it has acquired. And so I turn now to the second face of wealth: the opportunities that it conveys to do good in the world.

THE OPPORTUNITIES WEALTH OFFERS

A key test of stewardship is how resources are allocated. It is not my place to tell the trustees, the president, the provost, and others at Williams how to deploy their funds, but I would like to make a modest plea for spending money in ways that will augment the scholarly and educational values for which Williams stands rather than on what might be called amenities. I confess that I have limited sympathy for spending ever larger sums of money on overly elaborate dorms and student centers, state-of-the-art athletic facilities, and more and more student services that really do smack of "consumerism." It is unfortunate, in my view, that competition for able students from middle- and higher-income families seems so often to focus on such amenities. While I understand that Williams cannot be oblivious to such trends, I hope it will not use its wealth to accelerate these arms races.

There are, as all of you know, many other uses for scarce funds (and funds are always scarce at a good place, where ability and imagination are joined to high ambition). Teaching able students how to frame questions, to analyze, to argue, and to write clearly and compellingly remains a very labor-intensive process, especially if done in a personalized way that respects the individuality of the learner. In my experience, there is no substitute for "hands-on" teaching of this kind, expensive as it is. For example, learning to do good empirical social science requires not just the mastery of techniques but also extensive guidance (practice) in using them, and also the cultivation of a skeptical mind.

The answer to most interesting questions is "It all depends," and one of the real contributions of a college like Williams is to help students learn the importance of examining both sides of every horse (every purple cow?), to appreciate nuance, and to live with ambiguity. To be sure, the results of inculcating this kind of thinking can be unsettling. It is much easier, much more comfortable for some, and certainly much cheaper, to teach materials that yield clear-cut answers. But such an approach fails to capture the richness—and the moral complexity—of the human condition. In his Romanes

Lecture titled "Fathers and Sons," Isaiah Berlin provided examples of the moral dilemmas faced by nineteenth-century Russian writers as many of them sought to balance a yearning for absolutes with the complex visions that they simply could not push from their minds—and to do so in a terribly troubled time and place. Berlin spoke with special empathy about Alexander Hertzen and others, "who see, and cannot help seeing, many sides of a case, as well as those who perceive that a humane cause promoted by means that are too ruthless is in danger of turning into its opposite.... The middle ground," he said, "is a notoriously exposed, dangerous, and ungrateful position."

A generous endowment of resources can be used not only to stake out that ungrateful middle ground but also to resist "trendiness." In these days when more and more educational activities are both digitized and commercialized, I hope Williams will consider carefully whether particular initiatives do or do not serve the fundamental educational mission of the place. The same principles apply to selecting traditional course content. An upsurge of interest nationally in business subjects need not pressure a Williams into downplaying the classics—if it chooses to use its resources in that way. In deciding how much to spend on any activity, it is of course necessary to weigh costs and benefits. But this should always be done with the educational mission of the college as the touchstone. There are programs that are intrinsically costly but that need to be supported nonetheless because of what they contribute to the life of the college, its sense of itself, and its ability to fulfill its mission.

One "money-losing" activity that seems to me of paramount importance, and an especially good test of whether resources are being used appropriately, is need-based financial aid. Williams is obviously in a position to attract more "full-pay" students if it were to choose to do so—or to use carefully calibrated infusions of "merit aid" to recruit outstanding students who can pay at least something. Many colleges and universities are moving increasingly in such directions, and often they have no real alternative. (This is true, for instance, of Denison, where I was an undergraduate and, until recently, a trustee.) But if a college or university has a choice, it seems to me extremely important that it contribute what it can, through its student aid policies, to the further strengthening of opportunity in America. Our country has done better than many recognize in continuing to make high-quality higher education available to those who can benefit most from it, whatever their circumstances. Nevertheless, at given levels of pre-collegiate preparedness, large disparities remain in the probability of going to an excellent college or university simply as a consequence of family circumstances. For example, Caroline Hoxby of Harvard calculates that the probability of attending one of the "highest-tuition" colleges was 57 percent for '92 high school graduates with "high" college preparation who also came from families who earned $95,000 or more; the corresponding probability for students with comparable preparation from families in the $20,000 to $35,000 income range was 29 percent.[4]

At the risk of entering an even more sensitive terrain, let me also say just a word about tuition policy. People of good will have different points on view on this subject, as on essentially all others. My own position is that students from affluent families can and should pay a significant fraction of the costs of their own education, especially since they end up benefiting so handsomely from having gone to a Williams and since the true costs of a Williams education are so much higher than the tuition that is charged. I am one of those old-fashioned folks who continues to favor emphasizing high student aid rather than low tuition. Since I also believe that *all* students benefit from diversity—measured along both socioeconomic and racial dimensions—I see nothing whatsoever wrong with using tuition revenues, as well as other sources of funds, to support well-conceived student aid programs.

---

[4] "High" college preparation is defined for these purposes as having had SAT verbal and math scores that together average above 600 and having ranked in the top 25 percent of one's high school class. See Caroline M. Hoxby, *The Rising Cost of College Tuition and the Effectiveness of Government Financial Aid* (Washington, DC: US Government Printing Office, 2000), especially the table on p. 126. This was testimony prepared for the US Senate Committee on Governmental Affairs Hearing on The Rising Cost of College Tuition and the Effectiveness of Government Financial Aid. For another excellent discussion of how access to higher education depends on family resources, see Thomas J. Kane, *The Price of Admission: Rethinking How Americans Pay for College* (Washington, DC: Brookings Institution Press, 1999), especially chapter 4.

There is a system-wide aspect to all of this. A very difficult question for a place like Williams, that is privileged in so many ways, is whether, or in what degree, it has an obligation to think about the effects on other, less favorably situated, colleges when it makes decisions in areas ranging from tuition policy to athletics. As a fierce competitor in all days, I am certainly in favor of doing what is necessary to recruit top faculty talent and to make the quality of the educational program the envy of all other places. To seek excellence along these dimensions (to seek to be "elitist," if you will, in these respects) seems to me entirely appropriate. But I also believe that consideration needs to be given to ways of collaborating as well as competing and that it is appropriate to ask whether a particular mode of competition will have decidedly harmful effects on other good colleges that are less well endowed. I am proposing what may sound like an impossible balancing act (balancing narrow institutional self-interest against broader sector interests), but I believe that good stewards have no choice but to confront such questions, especially at a time when disparities in wealth between excellent colleges are increasing. And, where there is a will, a sensible "middle way" can be found.

For me, wise decisions to spend money on the arts and sciences, and to devote resources to costly subjects and costly methods of teaching as well as to generous student aid programs, do more than justify present endowments. They also justify the constant need to raise more money. I hope no one who cares about Williams misinterprets my warnings about the possible abuses of wealth as license to close one's wallet when President Schapiro enters the room. Unless I badly misjudge him, he will find exciting new opportunities to make a difference, and he will need your help to give life to them. When I was more actively engaged in fundraising myself, I liked to remind the alumni of Princeton (hardly a poor institution) that "progress begets needs" (and that I thought Princeton could make better use of their money than they could!). As one of my friends on the faculty who was being wooed by another university after having won a Nobel Prize in physics said to me: "Excellence can't be bought, but it has to be paid for."

Most basic of all, having a strong resource base and generous supporters allows a well-led college or university to hold onto its own values and to turn away, if need be, offers of funds that would take it in inappropriate directions. I remember well explaining to a potential foreign donor whose country wanted, in effect, to "buy" a program of special interest to it, that Princeton was not for sale—and that that was precisely why it was a place of quality that deserved support.

Having read earlier a brief passage from Cavafy's poem "Ithaka," I want now to conclude by suggesting that Cavafy—and the somewhat detached perspective of poetry itself—have particular relevance for all of us in higher education these days. At a time when there are more and more pressures to be market-oriented and to serve the perceived needs of the market, it is worth remembering that colleges and universities have always had an otherworldly side. They are meant to be places of the imagination, of thoughtful contemplation of questions that have no answers. In the long run, I believe, these venerable institutions will serve the society best if they are able to resist becoming mere captives of it, if they are able to keep some distance from society's more mundane claims on us. Our colleges and universities need to retain their independence, their ability to march to the beat of their own drummers, their ability to stand, as E. M. Forster once said of Cavafy, "at a slight angle to the universe."

ENDURING VALUES

OPENNESS AND MUTUAL RESPECT

~

William G. Bowen
May 18, 2014

REMARKS AT HAVERFORD COMMENCEMENT, "SECOND BITE"

Here I am again—taking advantage of the privilege of being given at this commencement a "second bite at the apple," in the wake of the troubling, sad situation created by the conflict between Haverford protestors and Chancellor Birgeneau. I was presumptuous enough to volunteer to speak on this subject, as an outsider, and President Weiss was kind enough—brave enough, not knowing what I would say!—to allow me to offer a personal homily on the enduring values of openness and mutual respect.

Let me be clear at the outset that I am not judging the controversy over Bob Birgeneau's handling of unrest at Berkeley. I have neither the facts nor the inclination to do so. I would suggest only that people interested in the cross-pressures on a chancellor at Berkeley seeking to respond to extraordinarily difficult, testy demands should consult the brilliant memoir of a Quaker-inspired person, Clark Kerr, which recounts the choices he made (with mixed results, as he was the first to insist) in the mid-1960s.

Editor's note: Bowen had agreed to speak at the 2014 Haverford Commencement when the original keynote speaker, Robert Birgeneau, bowed out due to mounting student protests concerning his handling of a 2011 incident at the University of California, Berkeley, where he was chancellor. The commencement speech was delivered in two parts. The first part, not included here, was his commencement remarks as originally drafted. The second part, included here and referred to here as the "second bite," was written after President Dan Weiss gave Bowen permission to speak longer on the delicate issue of Birgeneau.

Second, I want to suggest, with all due respect for the venerable right to protest—which I would defend to the end—that it is a serious mistake for a leader of the protest against Birgeneau's proposed honorary degree to claim that Birgeneau's decision not to come represents a "small victory." It represents nothing of the kind. In keeping with the views of many others in higher education, I regard this outcome as a *defeat*, pure and simple, for Haverford— no victory for anyone who believes, as I think most of us do, in both openness to many points of view and mutual respect.

I am reminded of the experience of Richard Lyman, another graduate of a Quaker-inspired college located somewhere in this vicinity, who was president of Stanford at a time when he felt obligated to call in the police. Conservative alumni, who had been sharp critics of Lyman's liberal tendencies, applauded his action. But Lyman was having none of it. He replied that any time police had to be involved, as he resolutely believed was necessary in the situation he confronted, it was a defeat for the university, not a victory for anyone. There are no winners in such situations—or in overly contentious replays of them.

In this instance, I am disappointed that those who wanted to criticize Birgeneau's handling of events at Berkeley chose to send him such an intemperate list of "demands." In my view, they should have encouraged him to come and engage in a genuine discussion, not to come, tail between his legs, to respond to an indictment that a self-chosen jury had reached without hearing counter-arguments. I think that Birgeneau, in turn, failed to make proper allowance for the immature, and, yes, arrogant inclinations of some protestors. Aggravated as he had every right to be, I think he should be with us today.

The better course of action is illustrated, I think, by two other situations regarding honorary degrees, one of which I participated in as president of Princeton in the 1970s and one of which took place more recently at Notre Dame.

As president of Princeton, I presided over a commencement at which George Shultz, then a member of Nixon's cabinet in the Vietnam days of the 1970s, was awarded an honorary degree for a lifetime of service as the quintessential public servant—and for having demonstrated, over and over again, impeccable integrity, as for instance when he told a congressional committee investigating the Iran–Contra affair that the day he had to take a lie detector test to convince people that he was speaking the truth as he understood it was the day he would leave government. The congressmen backed down, and Shultz then proceeded to answer all questions asked of him, personally and with no lawyer by his side to protect him; he didn't feel he needed any such "protection." Still, and not surprisingly, many people, and many students especially, objected to the awarding of an honorary degree to Shultz—even as the university took pains to explain that conferring an honorary degree did not imply agreement by the university, or any component of it, with all of the views and actions of the recipient. That standard would effectively preclude, de facto, recognizing any person active in public life. But the protestors were respectful (mostly), and chose to express their displeasure by simply standing and turning their backs when the secretary was recognized. Secretary Shultz, in turn, understood that the protestors had every right to express their opinion in a non-disruptive fashion, and he displayed the courage to come and accept his degree, knowing that many of the faculty and staff (a strong majority, I would guess, this person included) thought that the Nixon conduct of the Vietnam War was a tragic mistake. Princeton emerged from this mini-controversy more committed than ever to honoring both the right to protest in proper ways and the accomplishments of someone with whose views on some issues many disagreed.

My second example is the handling by Notre Dame of the invitation to President Barack Obama to come to campus, speak, and receive an honorary degree. Not surprisingly, many loyal Notre Dame adherents objected vigorously, on the simple ground that Obama's views on issues such as abortion were at odds with the teachings of the Catholic Church. The hero of this dispute was Father Ted Hesburgh, the legendary president of Notre Dame who had long since retired. Speaking in defense of the invitation to President Obama, Father Hesburgh said that Notre Dame was both a "lighthouse" where the beliefs of the Church could be promulgated without qualification, and a "crossroads" where people of every faith and every belief could come to discuss controversial issues and learn from each other. Obama came and spoke at a university with very different traditions than this one but that also deservedly takes pride in being a "crossroads" as well as a "lighthouse."

My thanks for allowing me to express these personal thoughts. I am, as you may have deduced, neither as graceful nor as forgiving as President Weiss, who recognizes so well that students, along with all the rest of us, make mistakes and need to learn from them. There are indeed days when we all need to eat humble pie. This is but one reason, among others, why we should be grateful that Dan Weiss is president of Haverford today. It is my hope that this regrettable set of events will prove, under President Weiss's leadership, to be a true "learning moment," and that Haverford will go forward, as I am confident that it will, as a great liberal arts college committed, as always, both to the principle of non-violent protest and to the enduring values of openness and respect for diverse views. Thank you, once again.

DEMANDING UNIVERSITIES TO DIVEST IS OFTEN BAD POLICY

~

William G. Bowen
March 27, 2015

WASHINGTON POST OP-ED

Campaigns urging colleges and universities to divest stock holdings are again on the rise, focused today more often than not on holdings in *fossil fuel companies*. Many of the arguments against divestment as a general tactic are by now well known. They include practical ones, such as the difficulty of divesting fully when portfolios contain index funds, hedge funds, and other complex instruments; concerns about adverse effects on the ability of endowments to support education and research as fully as they could if they were unconstrained; and doubts about the effectiveness of divestment in bringing about changes (which are often unspecified) in corporate practice. In general, I find these objections persuasive, though they need to be tested and debated in each situation.

One argument in favor of divestment that I find entirely unpersuasive is the claim that a university is obligated to take a stand on any issue of broad social import that individuals—including, not infrequently, the president of a university acting in citizen mode!—regard as highly consequential. This is nonsense. To abstain is both a legitimate and appropriate action when the issue is not central to an institution's educational mission. Universities need to keep control over their agendas and decide for themselves when it is appropriate to take a position. An issue such as affirmative action—which directly affects educational processes and outcomes—has a very different claim on academia than does the conflict between the Israelis and the Palestinians.

Taking an institutional stand on political issues of many kinds threatens the primary educational mission of the university, which is to be avowedly open to arguments of every kind and to avoid giving priority to partisan or other political viewpoints. The university should be the home of the critic—indeed, the home of critics of many different persuasions—not the critic itself.

COMMENTARY

SCOTT WALKER'S TEST OF ACADEMIC FREEDOM

~

William G. Bowen and Eugene M. Tobin
June 22, 2015

CHICAGO TRIBUNE OP-ED

One hundred years ago this month, the Board of Regents of the University of Wisconsin dedicated a bronze plaque commemorating a historic victory for academic freedom. When a distinguished faculty member, economist Richard T. Ely, had been accused of promoting socialism and fomenting disorder through his pro-labor speeches and writings, the regents had cleared him of wrongdoing, even though he had spoken out at a time of violent nationwide industrial conflict. In the words of the tablet:

> Whatever may be the limitations which trammel inquiry elsewhere, we believe that the great State University of Wisconsin should ever encourage that continual and fearless sifting and winnowing by which alone the truth can be found.

In the late 1960s—another period of violent unrest—facsimiles of the "sifting and winnowing" plaque were installed across the state. At a campus dedication in Green Bay, Republican Governor Warren Knowles declared, "These are freedoms that must be fought for and won anew by each generation."

Events have proved that Knowles was prescient. Today, the so-called Wisconsin Magna Carta is being tested as Governor Scott Walker and the legislature move to change the system of tenure. Fortunately, earlier efforts to alter the mission statement of the University of Wisconsin system by deleting references to the search for truth and the creation of knowledge were retracted as "drafting errors." Still, the symbolism of such proposed changes is having a chilling effect on the flagship campus at Madison and across the university system.

At stake is the venerable Wisconsin Idea: the belief articulated by early twentieth- century Republican Governor Robert M. ("Fighting Bob") La Follette that the state should be a laboratory for democracy and that university faculty should use their knowledge and research to solve problems and improve people's lives.

This concept of a social contract between the people of a state and their university system is not unique to Wisconsin. America's public universities were created in general to serve as a great equalizer in an upwardly mobile society and to benefit people's lives beyond the boundaries of the classroom. Precisely because of their social, cultural, and economic role and their preservation of free and open inquiry, our public universities have also been subject to periodic political challenges, as is now happening in Wisconsin.

Wisconsin maintains one of the nation's largest public university systems, whose thirteen four-year universities, including its outstanding flagship campus at Madison, and thirteen two-year college campuses educate more than 180,000 students, employ 39,000 faculty and staff, and provide valuable outreach services for business and community development. The fact that tenure, academic freedom, and the faculty's influence over curriculum and hiring may be affected by the legislative changes championed by Walker and by proposed system-wide spending reductions of some $250 million raises fundamental questions about the relationship of the university system to the state of Wisconsin and its people.

The heart of this relationship, which can save the Wisconsin Idea, is shared governance. It is a system based on the understanding that the governance of public universities is an art that depends on maintaining a balance among regents, administrators, faculty, and elected officials. The agreements and compromises needed to effect this balance derive less from a set of abstract concepts or rules than from a common understanding that decisions should be made by those who have relevant expertise and can be held accountable. In a system of shared governance, it would be an error, for example, to vest too much decision-making authority in the faculty, despite their hands-on expertise, because they cannot really be held accountable if things go badly wrong. Presidents and chancellors, on the other hand, can be fired for the consequences of their decisions.

In our increasingly partisan and polarized climate, it is harder and harder to achieve the balance needed for shared governance, particularly when the university is buffeted by budget cuts and political agendas. We do not believe, however, that efforts to change governance to keep up with the times should move universities toward "divided" governance focusing primarily on identifying which issues "belong" to the faculty and which to the regents, administration, students, legislature, or executive branch.

The transcendent importance of the Wisconsin Idea is the constant reminder that all operations in a university system bear upon one another and rely upon respect for robust academic freedom, and that public higher education exists to serve the needs of the people.

CHAPTER 2

~

EXTENDING OPPORTUNITY

LIFE ON THE *RIVER*

TALKING WITH AMERICANS ABOUT
RACE-SENSITIVE COLLEGE ADMISSIONS

～

William G. Bowen
June 3, 1999

MACALESTER CONFERENCE

INTRODUCTION

Since so many of you have been subjected to earlier presentations of the research underlying *The Shape of the River* and its principal findings, I am going to take a different tack tonight. My plan is to talk not so much about the research itself but about Life on the *River* (or perhaps I should say on the road) following publication of the book. The reactions, both critical and supportive, have been most revealing.

My posture is forward-looking, and I want to spend most of my time on lessons I have learned concerning what more needs to be done to advance the original purposes of race-sensitive admissions. In the last section I will comment explicitly on how I think the case

Editor's note: This talk was originally presented at the conference Diversity and Stratification in American Higher Education at Macalester College. It summarizes and responds to reactions and controversies surrounding the publication of Bill's *Shape of the River: Long-Term Consequences of Considering Race in College and University Admissions*. An abridged version was included in the foreword to the paperback volume of *Shape of the River*.

Author's note: Although I take sole responsibility for the content of this paper and especially for the "editorial" comments, I wish to emphasize that Derek Bok has been a full partner in this research and its presentation from the beginning.

for race-sensitive admissions can be presented more effectively. First, however, I need to "set the table," as it were, by commenting on some recurring themes in the debate over the research itself.

REACTIONS, RESPONSES, AND NON-RESPONSES TO THE RESEARCH

To start with the most basic point, in framing our study, Derek Bok and I tried hard to make important substantive distinctions between very different admissions strategies. In some measure we have succeeded, I think, in helping a broad audience understand that it is possible to be strongly opposed to quotas and set-asides, as both Derek and I have been for over thirty years, while favoring a much more nuanced approach to admissions that involves taking account of race in conjunction with many, many other factors—test scores, grades, recommendations, personal qualities, athletic talent, socio-economic status, geographic origin, leadership potential, and, yes, the characteristics of other candidates. Sadly, however, some commentators (most recently Thomas Sowell in his column in *Forbes*[1]) remain determined to deny the existence of this distinction even though it was central to Justice Powell's opinion in *Bakke* and is today, in most of the country, the line dividing approaches permitted by law from those that are impermissible. Lesson learned: never underestimate the difficulty—or the importance—of defining issues appropriately. And, yes, we need to keep pointing out that we are *not* talking about quotas.

A related point is that a surprising number of people (including several who are in favor of considering race in admissions) fail to understand how the admissions process works at most of the academically selective schools that we studied. We keep being asked to distinguish "special" minority admits from "regular" minority admits, or, in the words of Sowell, "those admitted under lower standards and those who got in like everyone else." Help! We are being

---

[1] See Thomas Sowell, "Lies, Damned Lies and Blurs, *Forbes*, May 31, 1999, www.forbes.com/forbes/1999/0531/6311176a.html.

given an impossible assignment. To be admitted, students of all races had to be above a very high academic threshold. Then, in choosing from this talented pool, race is considered in conjunction with many of the other attributes listed above; the admissions process is a probabilistic one in which judgment is used rather than any rigid formula in deciding, say, which African American students with SATs over 1100 were admitted and which were rejected.

The same multi-faceted selection process applies to every applicant, regardless of race. One of the collaborators in our study grew up in Pakistan as the son of missionary parents and was admitted to Stanford. As he put it, "Growing up in Pakistan surely must have helped my application, but is that why I was admitted?" Another of our collaborators has a father who is a faculty member at the school he attended. Is this why he was admitted? No one can answer such questions, and within the highly selective institutions at least, it is time to abandon the search for some "special," "rag-tag" group of minority students who got in solely because of their race. As our admissions data indicate, considerable numbers of white students were admitted with weaker pre-collegiate records than some African American students who were rejected, even though, overall, the odds of being admitted within a given SAT range were of course considerably higher for minority students than for white students. Each successful applicant had a *composite* of qualities that were weighed together, and each was considered in the context of efforts by the admissions staff to assemble a class whose members, considered individually and collectively, would best serve the educational mission of the school. As one experienced practitioner of the art of admissions put it, "When you are considering so many outstanding candidates, all of them well above threshold, each one is a 'special' admit; there are no 'regular' admits."

While it is impossible, for the reasons just given, to identify particular individuals who were admitted solely because of race-sensitive admissions, it is possible to note the "average" characteristics of that group of people whom we estimate would have been excluded from the class had race-neutral policies been in effect. We performed this exercise by adopting an operational definition of "race neutrality" that assumes that each school had been required, retrospectively, to admit the same percentage of white and African American applicants from within each 100-point SAT range. The result is, as one would have expected, a substantial reduction (more than half) in the number of black matriculants. A more surprising finding is that the average SAT score of the retrospectively rejected group is quite similar to the average SAT score of the "survivors"—1145 versus 1181.

Moreover, when we go on to approximate, very roughly, the subsequent accomplishments of this statistically estimated group of retrospectively rejected students, we find that their graduation rates, fields of study, patterns of advanced degree attainment, earnings, civic contributions, and satisfactions with college are so similar to those of the "surviving" group that no significant differences can be noted. Our analysis suggests that, of the roughly 700 African American matriculants in 1976 who would have been retrospectively rejected, 225 went on to attain professional degrees or doctorates, 70 are now doctors, well over 300 are leaders of civic activities, and so on. In short, these retrospectively rejected students had good academic qualifications by any normal standard and went on to do exceedingly well in what coaches like to call the "game of life." Conclusion: eliminating race-sensitive admissions would not have "purified" the student bodies of these schools by excluding some marginal group of low-achieving individuals.

Our analysis has been more effective in debunking another of the principal arguments used against race-sensitive admissions by its critics—namely, that race-sensitive admissions policies harm the very minority students they claim to help by stigmatizing them and forcing them into harmful competition with white classmates of much greater ability. This "reasoning" withers in the light of the evidence. Far from being stigmatized and handicapped, minority students admitted under race-sensitive policies have, overall, performed very well. Moreover, the more selective the college they entered, the more likely they were to graduate and earn advanced degrees, the happier they say they are with their college experience, and the more money they make in their careers. This important finding holds for students at the lower end of the SAT distribution (of those who matriculated at these schools) as well as for students at the higher end.

Having had to give up the argument that the intended beneficiaries of race-sensitive admissions ended up as victims, some critics now take the somewhat different tack of asserting that ending affirmative action will have no ill effects because there are many other good colleges that minorities can attend if they cannot gain entry to the selective institution of their choice. We agree that many non-selective colleges are excellent educational institutions and may even give more personal attention to students than some of the prestigious research-oriented universities. Many successful Americans of all races have attended colleges that accept almost all those who apply. Ronald Reagan went to Eureka College, and scores of successful African American leaders have graduated—and continue to graduate—from historically black institutions.

It scarcely follows, however, that no harm would be done if selective colleges and universities were to do away with race-sensitive admissions policies. Although attending a selective college is far from essential to achieving success in life, it surely helps. The masses of data assembled in our book provide hard evidence of the benefits of attending such schools. The reality of these findings is brought home by the behavior of applicants and their parents. Why else would people be making such a fuss about the terms of admission to such institutions? As one person asked recently, "Are all those white folks fighting so hard to get their kids into Duke and Stanford just ignorant? Are we supposed to believe that attending a top-ranked school is important for the children of the privileged but shouldn't matter to minorities?" In fact, the data show that the gains associated with attending the most selective schools are, if anything, greater for minorities than for whites.[2] This is not surprising. For individuals who continue to experience handicaps in competing for top positions in the workplace, the advantages of having been educated by the most competitive schools can be especially important.

[2] Stacy B. Dale and Alan B. Krueger, "Estimating the Effects of College Characteristics over the Career Using Administrative Earnings Data," *Journal of Human Resources* 49, no. 2 (Spring 2014): pp. 323–58.

From my perspective, one of the more puzzling responses to the data in the *River* is akin to a non-response. In discussing the consequences of eliminating race-sensitive admissions, which of course would mean dramatic reductions in the numbers of minority students at the most selective colleges, some critics make little if any mention of the putative effects of these cuts in minority enrollment on the education of *all* students on these campuses. In a race-neutral world, white students at the most selective institutions would lose much of the opportunity they now have to learn how to live and work more effectively with members of other races. Our surveys of the alumni/ae of these colleges show that large majorities of whites value their experience on diverse campuses and that almost 80 percent believe that current race-sensitive admissions policies should be retained or strengthened further. Since America's population will be one-third black and Hispanic within the working lives of today's undergraduates, one would surely think that the chance to spend four years on a racially diverse campus would be an increasingly valuable part of a well-rounded education.

If we had more time together tonight, I could tell you many stories of how important interactions across racial lines have been to white students and minority classmates alike. During a recent statewide conference in Colorado, the head of one of the main campuses said that a principal concern of his white students is that their campus is inadequately diverse to prepare them to live in, as they put it, "such exotic places as Chicago and New York." The head of another campus bemoaned her own limited exposure to students of other races as she was going to school and spoke eloquently of how hard it had been for her to overcome what she saw as a real handicap. And I cannot resist retelling one of my favorite post-book stories. Shortly after publication of the book, Vernon Jordan and I had breakfast together in New York to discuss the findings—which Vernon found very interesting. In the course of our conversation, Vernon provided the following vignette:

Let me tell you about my own experiences at DePauw in the 1950s. I was one of four black students at the school in those days and the only black student in my class. When I arrived on the campus I encountered two white roommates (what else). Were they *amazed* to see me! The first month or so was more or less live and let live. Then, one night I returned to my room to find these two white guys talking, and they said: "Vernon, we have been talking about you, and we have made the most astonishing discovery—you are just like us! You fall asleep over your desk at night, your mother sends you cookies, you are just like us."

Vernon then looked at me and asked,

Do you think those white guys learned anything because I was at DePauw? I think they did. Do you think I learned anything? I have spent the rest of my life coping in predominantly white environments, and my ability to do that has been helped so much by my college education.

Much of the recent debate also fails to acknowledge that the practical consequences of imposing race-blind admissions policies may be even greater at the professional school level than among undergraduates. Because there are far more applicants to law schools and medical schools than there are places in the entering classes, ending affirmative action would severely reduce the number of blacks and Hispanics seeking to become doctors and attorneys. For example, it is estimated that admission of both these minority groups to law schools would be cut in half, and the percentage of blacks able to attend the top half of all law schools would decline to about 1 percent. The effect of such massive cuts on the number of minorities in leading law firms, the availability of well-trained minorities for judicial appointments, and the supply of lawyers serving the legal needs of minority communities would be drastic indeed. In addition, the imposition of race-blind admissions policies would mean that white students in leading schools of law, business, and medicine would complete their studies in an environment almost totally bereft of black and Hispanic students. In a recent survey administered with the help of the Gallup organization, large majorities of students at Harvard, Michigan, and other prominent law schools reported that their understanding of subjects such as civil rights law, poverty law, and criminal justice had benefited from the existence of a racially diverse student body.

My final reflection on the discussion of our findings is that little weight has been given to the costs of dashing hope. I am amazed that people can talk blithely about policies that would drive the percentage of African American students at, say, Harvard or Stanford, back to 2 or 3 percent of the undergraduate population (and more like 1 percent of the professional school population), without seeming to care about the symbolic as well as substantive effects of what would be an extraordinary reversal of trajectory. We have made considerable progress these last thirty to forty years in opening up opportunities for minority students in the leading educational institutions in the country. The campuses of these institutions are very different places than they were in the mid-1960s, and the broad "signaling" effect of this dramatic change on the society at large has to be real.

I remember so well the mother of a black student at Princeton in the early days of race-sensitive admissions telling me that she could put up with almost anything as long as she had hope for her children. She said that she had understood from an early age that because of her race and her lack of even a high school education, there was a stark limit on what she could hope to achieve. She was determined, she said, that for her children there would be "no limits." She was so proud that her oldest son graduated from Princeton. Do we really want to contemplate the implications of turning this clock back? Are we unmoved by the potential effects on aspirations, incentives to do well in school, and, yes, our own sense of fair play, our own hope for the future—especially when, according to the evidence in the *River*, these programs are succeeding so well?

LOOKING AHEAD: LESSONS LEARNED—WHAT WE NEED TO DO BETTER

In talking about the generally very positive findings in the *River*, it is also clear to me that there is much that can be done better. And it is important that we not just "stand pat." Let me list four areas in which I think improvement is both needed and possible.

1. First, while continuing to confront up front the present-day realities of existing applicant pools and making the hard choices that are required, we also need to work harder to identify ways of augmenting the pools of well-qualified minority candidates. I am not talking just (or even mainly) about more aggressive recruitment efforts, since much is already being done in this area. Rather, I have in mind several other approaches:

- A talented Harvard graduate student, Deborah Bial, has been experimenting for some years now with an alternative set of rating criteria that allow her to identify inner-city students of substantial promise who nonetheless test poorly. She focuses on a rigorous assessment of personal qualities such as ability to accept criticism, to articulate one's concerns, to persist in the face of adversity, and so on—all of the intangibles that we know intuitively have much to do with success in every kind of endeavor. Ms. Bial then arranges for these students to attend selective schools and observes their performance. To date, her "Posse" program, as it has been called, has achieved remarkably high graduation rates at selective schools such as Vanderbilt.[3]

- Two groups of able labor economists are working to understand better the effects of differential access to information on college-going behavior. We know that minority students are much less likely, on an "other-things-equal" basis, to take the standardized tests that often govern access to selective institutions, and David Card and Alan Krueger are analyzing carefully differences in test-taking behavior, using a new database constructed by the foundation in collaboration with the College Board.[4] Thomas Kane

[3] The Posse Foundation was founded in 1989. According to its website: "The Posse Foundation identifies public high school students with extraordinary academic and leadership potential who may be overlooked by traditional college selection processes. The Foundation extends to these students the opportunity to pursue personal and academic excellence by placing them in supportive, multicultural teams—Posses—of 10 students. The Foundation's partner colleges and universities award Posse Scholars four-year, full-tuition leadership scholarships." Since its founding it has selected nearly seven thousand high school students to be Posse Scholars. The persistence and graduation rate for those selected is 90 percent. See www.possefoundation.org.

[4] See David Card and Alan B. Krueger, "Would the Elimination of Affirmative Action Affect Highly Qualified Minority Applicants? Evidence from California and Texas," [Cornell University] *Industrial and Labor Relations Review* 58, no. 3 (April 2005), pp. 416–34.

and his colleague Chris Avery also suspect that "information gaps" have a considerable amount to do with some of the large differentials in college-going behavior that we observe. They propose to work closely with Boston public schools to see if investments designed to close this information gap can affect college-going behavior in a cost-effective way.[5]

- Another economist, Ernest Bartell at Notre Dame, is focusing on differences among secondary schools in their ability to prepare minority students to succeed at the academically selective schools included in the College and Beyond database. He hopes to learn more about what works and doesn't work at the secondary school level.

As you would imagine, these kinds of approaches resonate well in discussions of the *River*, in part for the best of reasons (we really need these creative approaches), but also in part for reasons that are less praiseworthy. For me it remains a mystery why some people seem determined to think in either-or terms and to consider ways of building larger pools of talented minority candidates as alternatives to race-sensitive admissions. The two approaches are highly complementary, and it sometimes seems as if critics of race-sensitive admissions policies want to "let themselves off the hook" by focusing exclusively on these other approaches. My response to this "let's-find-an-easier, less-controversial-path-to-achieving-diversity" line of argument is that I have two hands, and there is no reason in the world why I shouldn't use my left hand to work hard at building larger pools of talented candidates while simultaneously using my right hand to tap existing pools of minority students as effectively as possible in order to make progress now.

2. Second on my "to do" list is to find ways to improve the in-college academic achievement of the minority students being admitted to academically selective colleges. The most disturbing finding in the *River* is that African American matriculants do less well

---

[5] Thomas J. Kane and Christopher Avery, "Student Perceptions of College Opportunities: The Boston COACH Program," in *College Choices: The Economics of Where to Go, When to Go, and How to Pay For It*, ed. Caroline Hoxby (Chicago: University of Chicago Press, 2004), available at https://sites.hks.harvard.edu/fs/cavery/Student%20Perceptions%20of%20College%20Opportunities.pdf.

academically than their white classmates with comparable SAT scores, high school grades, and socio-economic status (crudely measured). In discussions around the country, many views have been expressed as to what explains this pattern—stereotype vulnerability, as Claude Steele has suggested,[6] wrong kinds of peer effects, insufficiently demanding expectations on the part of both students and faculty, feelings of discomfort on campus, and so on—and we need to continue to try to answer this question.

Fortunately, there are some existing programs that appear to have overcome this "performance gap," and that is good news. For example, students from the College and Beyond database who have participated in the foundation's own Mellon Minority Undergraduate Fellowship [MMUF] Program[7] consistently "overperform" academically, and we don't think this result is simply due to selection factors, though they surely play a role. There is also the highly successful Meyerhoff Scholars Program[8] at the University of Maryland. The foundation is currently supporting major longitudinal studies that will help us understand much better than anyone does now the stages in the educational process at which performance gaps emerge and what factors seem to be associated with them. One thing we know for certain: contrary to much popular wisdom, grades matter—they matter a lot! Moreover, the findings in the *River* demonstrate that the penalty for being in the bottom third of the class is bigger for African American students than it is for white students. So, for every reason, we need to find approaches that will elicit top academic performance from minority students capable of earning As rather than A minuses.

3. *Third, we need to improve the advising and mentoring of minority students.* There is ample testimony in the *River* and in the discussions of the book to the effect that taking an interest in individuals can pay off handsomely. No surprise in that. There is less faculty mentoring of minority students than any of us would think

[6] See Claude Steele, "A Threat in the Air: How Stereotypes Shape Intellectual Identity and Performance," *American Psychologist* 52, no. 6 (June 1997): 613–29, available at http://dx.doi.org/10.1037/0003-066X.52.6.613.

[7] See www.mmuf.org/.

[8] See http://meyerhoff.umbc.edu/.

desirable, and one reason often given is that there are so few minority faculty members. But we should not be too quick to accept that sad reality as justification for inadequate mentoring. One of the strong conclusions to emerge from careful study of the experiences of students in the MMUF program is that white mentors are often very effective in working with minority students. The difference a faculty member can make is illustrated by this recollection of a black woman in the '89 cohort at Princeton who is now in medical school:

> I had a religion professor ... who was a huge influence on me. We disagreed a lot. So in disagreeing, we basically forged a medium through which we could really carry out our conversation and fight it out. We always ended up agreeing to disagree but it was good for me, because it allowed me to understand that it's okay to believe something other than what the professor is saying. In [my] Haitian culture, if you disagree with your elders, you're not supposed to say anything. It was difficult to start in this mode. In class one day early on, he [the religion professor] saw that I wasn't saying anything and he asked me—in French—"What do you think?" So I told him that he knew that I couldn't say anything because I disagreed—he clearly knew about my culture. And he said, "No, this is different. You should say what you believe." Throughout college, he would check on me and say, "Are you remembering to say what you think?" He's the one who ultimately made me realize that at Princeton, you have to talk. Otherwise people won't know that you understand the issue at hand or that you have your own opinion. I'm glad—if I hadn't had his class during the first year, then I probably would have been more quiet in the subsequent years than I actually was at the end.

The lack of minority faculty cannot be an excuse for failing to do better on the mentoring front.

4. *We need to be much more open in talking about race-sensitive admissions and how well these policies have worked.* Let me tell you of a conversation I had in Washington after a presentation to the American Council on Education. A young African American woman came up and introduced herself. She had been an undergraduate at Harvard in the mid-1980s, and she said that she had

studied the *River* carefully and had found it extremely "liberating." She went on to say: "I guess I have been walking around with a kind of cloud over my head, which I didn't really understand was there, and it's gone now.... We did pretty well didn't we?" Yes, I responded, you did very well indeed. She added, with emphasis: "I'm now ready to stand up and fight!" The positive reaction of so many African American graduates to the *River* has been by far the most gratifying response we have received from any quarter.

MAKING THE CASE FOR RACE-SENSITIVE ADMISSIONS

Let me now discuss a final task to which I assign a very high priority: namely, to present the case for race-sensitive admissions more effectively than we have on many occasions in the past. To save time, let me avoid many of the caveats, disclaimers, and the like, and simply "pronounce," if you will allow me that liberty. What do I think we need to do?

1. First, be more direct in talking about the costs of race-sensitive admissions, alternative approaches and their costs, and the trade-offs that people would prefer to ignore. Several of my labor economist friends have reminded me that when places in a class are limited, there is always an opportunity cost associated with every admit: someone else is denied admission, and that "someone else" is likely to be an excellent candidate who may well have benefited from going to the school in question. Having attempted so often in my earlier life as a university president to assuage the pain, and often the anger, of disappointed parents of outstanding applicants, I know full well that there is no way of persuading them that the "last" minority admit may have brought more to the campus community, and offered even better long-term prospects to the society, than the rejected white applicant, who resembled so closely other white candidates who were accepted.

Fundamental judgments have to be made about societal needs, values, and objectives. When a distinguished black educator visited the Mellon Foundation, he noted, with understandable pride, that his son had done brilliantly in college and was one of two contenders for a prestigious graduate award in neuroscience. "My son," the professor said, "needs no special consideration; he is so talented that he will make it on his own." His conclusion was that we should be indifferent as to whether his son or the white competitor got the particular fellowship in question. We agreed that, in all likelihood, both candidates would benefit from going to the graduate school in question and, in time, become excellent scientists or doctors. Still, one can argue with the conclusion reached by the parent. "Your son will do fine," another person present at the meeting said, "but that isn't the issue. *He may not need us, but we need him!* Why? Because there is only one of him."

But it does help, I think, to be clear that a conscious, if difficult, set of choices were made and to be ready to defend those choices in terms of the mission of the institution. I remember well a comment by a participant in a University of Virginia symposium that I addressed. After focusing on the data in our study showing the value to all students of attending a selective institution, she shook her head and said: "There are no easy exits from this debate; we just have to make our choices and justify them." Yes, we do. And, of course, we can emphasize the really quite remarkable record of success in achieving the purposes of race-sensitive admissions policies that is documented in the *River*.

Let me be clear. There is an incorrigible appetite for the painless alternative. Tom Kane has explained, better than anyone else, why attempts to substitute what is sometimes called "class-based" affirmative action for race-sensitive policies are unlikely to produce anything like the numbers of well-qualified minority students that are presently enrolled.[9] There are, of course, many other ways to seek increased diversity on campuses without explicitly considering race, and Glenn Loury at Boston University is now embarking on a major effort to analyze rigorously the trade-offs involved in deciding, for example, to declare eligible for admission all students in the top 5 or 10 percent of their high school classes, or to admit students above some SAT/grade threshold by means of a random

[9] See Thomas J. Kane, "Misconceptions in the Debate over Affirmative Action in College Admissions," in *Chilling Admissions*, ed. Gary Orfield and Edward Miller (Cambridge, MA: Civil Rights Project, Harvard Education Publishing Group, 1999), pp. 24–25.

process, and so on. Needless to say, each such approach entails costs, and Glenn intends to quantify them by running simulations using real data. He suspects that his research will show that in fact willingness to consider race explicitly is a more "efficient" approach (in the economist's jargon) than any of these alternatives.[10] Politicians may not want to hear the results of this kind of analysis, but they should not be permitted to ignore them.

2. *Drive the discussion back to the fundamental missions of these colleges and to the values of a democratic society.* Nothing annoys me more than the suggestion that the advocates of race-sensitive admissions policies are somehow arguing solely from a pragmatic, rather mindless "practical perspective" that stresses the needs of the society (which heaven knows are real, as business leaders, in particular, will attest) while the opponents are arguing from some higher ground of lofty principle. Nonsense. Educational institutions, in my view, are obligated *by principle* to do two things: (a) create as rich a learning environment as possible for everyone on their campuses and (b) contribute to meeting the needs for larger numbers of exceptionally well-prepared students of color in a society that is far too stratified by race. If someone disagrees with those objectives, so be it. But let us not be reluctant to state them and argue for them.

3. *Emphasize that race is but one aspect of diversity, and that we should be interested in all aspects—including, of course, socio-economic status.* It is not true that the academically selective colleges and universities care only about race. Not at all. The focus of so much of the discussion has been on race because it is the use of race, alone among dimensions of diversity, that has been under political and legal challenge.

4. *Confront directly the question of whether it is legitimate to consider race at all.* We need to ask why people accept so readily the legitimacy of considering other dimensions of diversity but pause, and often feel uncomfortable, when race is used. The answer, surely, is to be found in our history. For over three hundred years, racial

[10] See Roland G. Fryer Jr., Glenn C. Loury, and Tolga Yuret, "An Economic Analysis of Color-Blind Affirmative Action," *Journal of Law, Economics, and Organization* 24, no. 2 (2008): 319–55.

classifications have been used in the most odious ways, to put people down, to deprive them of basic rights, and so on. It is only within the last half century that we have ruled out explicit discriminatory treatment of minorities by public entities. But this progress hardly means that we can now operate as if some color-blind nirvana has been reached. Race continues to matter in American society, make no mistake about that. As Ronald Dworkin has put it, "The worst of the stereotypes, suspicions, fears, and hatreds that still poison America are color-coded."[11] I also agree with Dworkin when he goes on to suggest how ironic it would be, how perverse, if we were now to be prevented from considering race when, at last, it is finally possible to use a nuanced consideration of race to make real progress in overcoming the differences in opportunity and influence that are still so much a part of the American heritage. If the ultimate goal is, as a wise undergraduate friend of mine said nearly thirty years ago, to allow everyone to feel "*unselfconsciously included*," we are a long way from that destination.

5. *Stress the importance of allowing institutions to make their own judgments—subject to the discipline of accountability.* One of my most conservative friends, Charles Exley, former chairman and CEO of the NCR [National Cash Register] corporation, makes this point very strongly and very eloquently. In a conversation that I will long remember, Exley explained that, somewhat to my surprise, he held essentially the same view of the admissions question that I hold. "If I were in charge of one of these colleges (heaven forbid!)," he said, "I would probably not admit the same class that you would admit, even though I don't know how different the classes would be." "You will certainly make mistakes," he went on to say, "but I would much rather live with your errors than with those that will inevitably result from the imposition of more outside constraints, legislative and judicial interventions, and pages on pages of regulations." And then, with the nicest smile, he concluded: "And, if you make *too* many mistakes, I can always fire you!" Right. The wise approach, I am persuaded, is to combine a

[11] Ronald Dworkin, "Affirming Affirmative Action," *New York Review of Books* 45, no. 16 (October 22, 1998): 99–100.

reasonable degree of institutional autonomy with acceptance of a clear obligation to monitor performance.

6. *Finally, speak out!* One of the most discouraging aspects of my experience in talking with Americans about race-sensitive admissions is the number of times I have encountered individuals who say something like, "I agree entirely with these policies" (as do, let me remind you, 80 percent of the white graduates whom we surveyed), "but I am just not comfortable going on record." Why not? What is there to be afraid of? Are we going to allow ourselves to be intimidated by controversy? Fortunately, not everyone is, or has been. Let me tell you about a recent visit to St. Louis. What struck me most forcefully was the broad and deep support in that community for the kinds of policies we have been discussing tonight— support that appeared to be particularly strong in the business community. What accounts for this? I kept asking myself. The answer, I believe, is the extraordinary leadership that one individual, Bill Danforth, has provided in St. Louis. He has been concerned with race and opportunity in that city for over forty years. He *has* spoken out, he adopted forward-looking policies both at the Danforth Foundation and then as chancellor of Washington University, and he and his wife have lived their values through children they have adopted. In short, if you live in St. Louis and you want to argue about the role of race in admissions, you have to argue with Bill Danforth.

We need many more Bill Danforths, and I hope that this conference and other gatherings will sustain the momentum that has been built through the hard and effective work of people like him. We have made progress. There is, as another earlier proponent of these policies, Frank Thomas, likes to remind us, much to celebrate. But we still have miles to go before the river empties finally into the sea.

EXTENDING OPPORTUNITY

"WHAT IS TO BE DONE?"

William G. Bowen
June 21, 2005

MACALESTER COLLEGE AND SPENCER FOUNDATION FORUM

Tonight I thought that I would organize my remarks around what I see as important tasks ahead for those of us who believe that education should be an important engine of opportunity in America. Progress—significant progress—has been made in the last forty years in opening up opportunity, but barriers aplenty remain, including barriers related to race and socio-economic status.

RACE IN AMERICA

Race remains the most deep-seated and intransigent barrier to opportunity. That was, is, and will remain the reality in this country for the foreseeable future.[1] I was recently asked about the prospects for race-based affirmative action in higher education in light of the Supreme Court decisions in the University of Michigan cases.[2] My one-word answer was "Bright." I am bemused by speculations

---

Author's note: With apologies to Vladimir Lenin, who gave this title to his famous 1902 pamphlet in which he argued that "while capitalism predisposes the workers to the acceptance of socialism, it does not spontaneously make them conscious Socialists." See Marxists Internet Archive, www.marxists.org.

[1] For an exceptionally clear-headed examination of why this is true, see Glenn C. Loury, *The Anatomy of Racial Inequality* (Cambridge, MA: Harvard University Press, 2002).

[2] This part of my remarks draws heavily on a talk I gave at a University of Michigan Symposium on April 14, 2005.

to the contrary in articles with titles such as "Michigan: Who Really Won?"[3]

Taken together, the *Grutter* and *Gratz* decisions tell us these things about the legal status of race-based affirmative action in the United States:

1. In the words of Sandra Day O'Connor's opinion in *Grutter*: "Today we hold that the [University of Michigan] Law School has a compelling interest in attaining a diverse student body.... The Equal Protection Clause does not prohibit the use of race in admissions decisions to further a compelling interest in obtaining the educational benefits that flow from a diverse student body."[4]

2. At the same time, in rejecting the admissions policy used by the undergraduate College of Literature, Science, and the Arts, *Gratz* makes clear that the use of mechanical approaches such as "bonus points" for being from an underrepresented minority group is not permitted; schools must consider all candidates on an "individualized" basis.

Having always believed strongly in the nuanced consideration of each candidate, this outcome seems just right to me. I believe that individualized approaches to admission decisions are both better on the merits and much more defensible politically.

The power of the majority opinion in *Grutter* was summarized well by Linda Greenhouse: "The result of today's rulings was that Justice Powell's solitary view that there was a 'compelling state interest' in racial diversity, a position that had appeared undermined by the court's subsequent equal protection rulings in other contexts and that some lower federal courts had boldly repudiated, has now been endorsed by five justices and placed on a stronger footing than ever before."[5]

[3] Jeffrey Selingo, "Michigan: Who Really Won?," *Chronicle of Higher Education*, January 14, 2005. For a far less equivocal position, see Roger Clegg, "Time Has Not Favored Racial Preferences," *Chronicle Review*, January 14, 2005.

[4] Quoted in William G. Bowen, Martin A. Kurzweil, and Eugene M. Tobin, *Equity and Excellence in American Higher Education* (Charlottesville: University of Virginia Press, 2005), p. 148. Much of the rest of this part of my remarks is based on chapter 6 of this book.

[5] Linda Greenhouse, "The Supreme Court: Affirmative Action: Justices Back Affirmative Action by 5 to 4, but Wider Vote Bans a Racial Point System," *New York Times,* June 24, 2003, p. A1.

This "stronger footing" reflects two principal conclusions stated emphatically in the majority opinion in *Grutter*. First, the court expanded dramatically the rationale for enrolling a diverse class to include not only the on-campus educational benefits of diversity but also the preparation of larger numbers of well-educated minority candidates for leadership positions in the professions, business, academia, the military, and the government. "Democratic legitimacy" is introduced as one of the principal societal needs that race-sensitive admissions address, and an extraordinary coalition of *amici* argued—eloquently—for this rationale. Second, the court was clear that "narrow tailoring does not require exhaustion of every conceivable race-neutral alternative." The claim that there exist race-neutral means to obtain the educational benefits of diversity was greeted with a high degree of skepticism if not outright disbelief.

Against this backdrop, what are we to make of the evidence of declines in minority enrollment at certain schools in the aftermath of the Supreme Court decisions—in the undergraduate programs at the University of Michigan and Ohio State, for example? My answer: "Not much." Should it surprise anyone that elimination of bonus points for minority group membership and addition of essay requirements apparently discouraged some minority applicants from applying? Of course not. For minority candidates, the cost-benefit ratio of applying changed fairly significantly. Moreover, the enrollment data collected by the *Chronicle of Higher Education* for twenty-nine colleges with competitive admissions found that minority enrollment declined at only seven of them; it increased at eleven and was mixed or ambiguous at the other eleven. Longer-term, there is no reason why minority enrollments at most places should not increase. And preliminary data for the class that will enter in the fall of 2005 suggest that minority enrollments will in fact rebound at schools such as the University of Illinois at Urbana-Champaign, the University of Michigan, and the University of Georgia.[6]

---

[6] See Robert Becker, "Black Enrollment at U of Illinois Rebounding from Last Year," *Chicago Tribune*, June 7, 2005, p. C3.

So the first thing that I believe we should do, looking ahead, is re-emphasize to one and all that race-sensitive admissions policies are on a firmer legal footing than ever before and should be actively promoted, not just defended. At the same time, we should of course do all we can to hasten the day, even if it proves to be more than twenty-five years from now, when race-sensitive policies will not be needed.

The second thing that we should do is listen to what the Court said, heed the principles that the Court established, and give careful consideration to modifying "enrichment" and other programs that were racially exclusive to eliminate the exclusivity without harming—and sometimes even strengthening—the ability of such programs to achieve their purposes. This approach is both sensible and practical, as I believe the foundation's experience with what is now called "The Mellon-Mays Undergraduate Fellowship [MMUF] Program" demonstrates. I regard the modifications that were made in MMUF and in MIT's exceptionally well-regarded summer program, to mention only those two, as "aggressively thoughtful" responses to a changed legal environment. From all indications, these programs will continue to enroll very large numbers of minority students. One reminder that I take away from this experience is that just getting mad is rarely, if ever, an effective response to a challenge—in this instance, a challenge to end racial exclusivity. Rather, we need to respond by reaffirming the basic objectives we are seeking to serve and by finding the most effective ways of achieving them. We definitely need to "stay the course," but not by being foolishly confrontational.

Third, we need to resist assaults on race-sensitive programs that are based on inadequately documented critiques of existing policies. We should reaffirm the results of soundly based research and not be too quick to allow others to call into question well-established findings by reference to new work that has yet to be properly vetted. I refer to the renewed discussion in the law school context of the so-called mismatch hypothesis, which argues against affirmative action on the ground that it entices minority students into programs that are too demanding for them, with bad results (low graduation rates) for the minority students in question. Others are in the process of challenging the methodology of Sander's law school study, and I have nothing specific to contribute to that debate.[7] But I can report that my colleague Nirupama Rao has just completed an analysis of recently compiled data for the 1995 entering cohorts of undergraduates at twenty-nine academically selective colleges and universities in the expanded College and Beyond database, and her findings reaffirm the flat rejection of the mismatch hypothesis reported in *The Shape of the River*.[8] There is no evidence to support the mismatch conjecture. Indeed, the general implication of the earlier analysis and of these new results is that, in choosing among undergraduate institutions, minority students are well advised to attend the most selective institution that will admit them.[9]

[7] Richard Sander, "A Systemic Analysis of Affirmative Action in American Law Schools," *Stanford Law Review* 57 (November 2004): 367–483. A collection of responses to Sander's article, by authors including David B. Wilkins, William C. Kidder, David L. Chambers, Richard O. Lempert, Timothy T. Clydesdale, Ian Ayres, and Richard Brooks, can be found in the May 2005 issue of the *Stanford Law Review*. Economists Jesse Rothstein at Princeton (now at University of California–Berkeley) and Albert Yoon at Yale (now at the University of Toronto), who contend that Sander's conclusions are unsupported by his analyses, are embarking on a study that will use the same data—principally the Bar Passage Study (BPS), based on the Law School Admissions Council's survey of students who entered law school in 1994 plus data about the respondents who passed the bar exam—to analyze with greater empirical rigor the effect of attending a selective law school on black students' academic outcomes.

[8] William G. Bowen and Derek Bok, *The Shape of the River: Long-Term Consequences of Considering Race in College and University Admissions* (Princeton, NJ: Princeton University Press, 1998), pp. 59–68.

[9] Using raw, unadjusted data, Rao finds that graduation rates for both black and Hispanic students with SATs in specified ranges increase with school selectivity overall but that the pattern is not entirely consistent. However, once controls are added for gender, socioeconomic status, and characteristics of individual schools, the results become entirely consistent. Otherwise comparable black students in every SAT range graduate at higher rates the more selective the schools that they attend. When she studies rank-in-class, Rao finds that, as one would expect, both white and black students pay a "rank-in-class" penalty for attending more selective schools where they have to compete with large numbers of exceptionally well-qualified classmates. Interestingly, black students pay a somewhat higher price than otherwise comparable white students in moving from the least selective Sel-3 to the more selective Sel-2 schools, but they pay a smaller price than the white students in moving from Sel-2 schools to the most selective Sel-1 schools. We should also recall that survey data reported in *The Shape of the River* demonstrated that even if minority students earn, on average, lower grades than their high-achieving classmates at selective schools, they earn advanced degrees at high rates and go on to do well in later life in terms of earnings, life satisfaction, and civic participation.

Nevertheless, there is a real issue here, even though it has nothing to do with the mismatch hypothesis. In his study of law school results, Sander is right to call attention to the disappointing academic performance of minority students. Indeed, our recent work shows that, in general, minority students in undergraduate programs continue to underperform academically (by which we mean that academic outcomes for minority students lag academic outcomes for other students with similar observed characteristics). Underperformance appears to have declined somewhat between the '89 and '95 entering cohorts, but it still exists—at all kinds of schools and in all SAT ranges.[10] Thus, as a fourth "to do," I conclude that we should focus on the roots of this troubling problem of underperformance and find ways of attacking it—of the kinds pioneered by Freeman Hrabowski at the University of Maryland and by our colleagues in South Africa.[11] Some of the lessons to be learned by studying the academic experiences of students from modest socio-economic backgrounds may also turn out to be highly relevant to our interest in improving the academic outcomes of minority students.

[10] Some people confuse the mismatch hypothesis with underperformance. They are two entirely different concepts. The mismatch hypothesis could be one explanation for underperformance by minority students if these students underperformed at schools where average SAT scores were appreciably higher than their own scores but did not underperform at schools where school SAT scores and their SAT scores "matched." But this is not what the evidence shows. As we point out in the text, underperformance exists *at every SAT range within every selectivity range*. It is an endemic phenomenon that does not correlate with the relation between an individual's SAT scores and the average SAT scores at the school the student attends; underperformance cannot be explained by claiming that minority students are attending schools where they are over-challenged.

[11] Ian Scott, Nan Yeld, Janice McMillan, and Martin Hall, "Equality and Excellence in Higher Education: The Case of the University of Cape Town," pp. 261–284, in *Equity and Excellence in American Higher Education*, ed. William G. Bowen, Martin A. Kurzweil, and Eugene M. Tobin (Charlottesville: University of Virginia Press, 2005); Freeman Hrabowski, "Supporting the Talented Tenth: The Role of Research Universities in Promoting Higher Achievement among Minorities in Science and Engineering," David Dodds Henry Lecture, University of Illinois at Urbana-Champaign, November 5, 2003; Freeman Hrabowski, Kenneth I. Maton, and Geoffrey L. Greif, *Beating the Odds: Raising Academically Successful African American Males* (New York: Oxford University Press, 1998); Freeman Hrabowski, Kenneth I. Maton, Monica L. Greene, and Geoffrey L. Greif, *Overcoming the Odds: Raising Academically Successful African American Young Women* (New York: Oxford University Press, 2002).

SOCIO-ECONOMIC STATUS

My most recent research has focused on socio-economic status, college enrollment, and educational attainment. It should be no surprise to anyone that in today's world, America's premier colleges and universities, including the great public universities, serve mainly the children of the privileged classes. At the nineteen selective colleges and universities we studied, only about 10 percent of the students come from low-income families, and an even smaller fraction are first-generation college-goers. Very high fractions come from well-educated families with substantial incomes.

In considering what to do about this discomforting reality, my first suggestion is that we work harder to explain convincingly why such disproportionate access to educational opportunity is a serious problem for the country. There is, to be sure, an issue of fundamental fairness to be confronted, and there is a corresponding need in a democratic society for social mobility. This is, as it were, the moral/social/political rationale for extending opportunity more broadly. But there is also a more mundane, economic rationale. Increasingly, economies, and certainly the US economy, are driven by what Sir Arthur Lewis called "reliance on brain" (or, if you prefer, trained intelligence). Yet the United States can no longer simply assume that its educational system, and its educated workforce, will be preeminent. Incremental educational attainment in the United States (measured, for instance, by the percentage of the US population 25–29 years old who have completed college) is no longer increasing at a steady rate, as it did for so many decades. At the same time that educational attainment is plateauing in the United States, it is continuing to rise rapidly in many other parts of the world. The United States is no longer at the top of the world tables in educational attainment of those 25–34 years of age, and it is far below a number of other countries in the ratio of first university natural science and engineering degrees to the 24-year-old population.[12]

---

[12] In 2002 the percentage of the 25- to 34-year-old population in the United States that had attained tertiary education was 39 percent, close to that of South Korea, New Zealand, Norway, Finland, Sweden, and Belgium. With attainment levels at or just above 50 percent,

What is happening? There is ample evidence, we believe, that America today confronts a major supply-side block in college preparedness that limits our country's ability to increase educational attainment. How else are we to explain the plateauing of educational attainment in the United States at the same time that the returns to college education are so high? Put another way, the question is this: why do we observe a pronounced lack of market response to such a compelling economic opportunity? The ability to pay for education, and the existence of credit constraints are, as economists always note, surely part of the explanation, but no one seems to think that they are anything like the whole story—or even the main part of the story. More consequential factors include college preparedness in all of its dimensions (health, attitudes at home, motivation, the availability of information, the quality of elementary and secondary education, out-of-school enrichment opportunities, and residential and social segregation). College preparedness varies dramatically with socio-economic status, as we have documented in our recent book [*Equity and Excellence in American Higher Education*, written with Martin A. Kurzweil and Eugene M. Tobin (Charlottesville: University of Virginia Press, 2005)]. Students from the bottom income quartile are only *one-sixth* as likely as students from the top income quartile to be in what we define as the credible pool of candidates for admission to academically selective colleges and universities; students who lack a parent with some experience of college are *one-seventh* as likely as other students to be in the credible pool.

The connections, on the one hand, between socio-economic status and educational attainment and, on the other hand, between

Canada and Japan were at the top of the list. Organisation for Economic Co-operation and Development (OECD), *Education at a Glance 2004* (Paris: OECD, 2004). In 2015 the percentage of the 25- to 34-year-old US population that had attained tertiary education was 46.5 percent. This was behind behind Korea (69 percent), Japan (59.6 percent), and Canada (59.2 percent), as well as Lithuania (54.8 percent), Ireland (52 percent), and the United Kingdom 49.2 percent). OECD, *Education at a Glance 2015* (Paris: OECD, 2015). In the United States, the ratio of first university degrees in the natural sciences and engineering to the 24-year-old population is 5.7. The ratio exceeds 10 in a number of countries in Europe and Asia. National Science Foundation (NSF), *Science and Engineering Indicators 2004* (Arlington, VA: NSF, 2004), appendix table 2-33, available at https://www.nsf.gov/statistics/seind/.

educational attainment and economic competitiveness are crystal clear, and there is a crucially important political reason for emphasizing this nexus. One of my most knowledgeable friends, at a discussion of the findings in *Equity and Excellence*, expressed pessimism at the prospect of mobilizing society to address disparities in opportunity because, he said, only a small fraction of people in the United States today really care about "liberal" goals such as fairness and social mobility; he believes that most (he suggested 80 percent) care mainly about how they themselves are doing. That may or may not be correct, but in any case it is surely a political mistake to base the case for addressing inequalities in access to a high-quality education on moral or social considerations alone. Why be so single-minded? The most conservative, market-oriented American should see that unless the United States does better in educating more students from low-income, out-of-the-mainstream families to a high standard, we will lose out, over time, to other countries in the world-wide competition for talent. That brute fact alone should make it clear *across the political spectrum* why we cannot afford to accept supply-side blocks on educational attainment. Looking ahead, demographic trends only reinforce what I have been saying. Reliance on children of well-educated high-income (mostly white) families to fill the educational pipeline will not suffice. Check out the numbers.

Let me now assume that we succeed in marshalling at least some number of troops, conservatives and liberals alike, who will support efforts to augment opportunity for students from modest backgrounds. What programs and policies will do the job?

At the most fundamental level, the only way, in the long run, to solve the college preparation gap is to attack it directly, through improvements in the schools that disadvantaged young people attend, in the neighborhoods in which they live, and in the health-care and other services on which they, like everyone else, depend. In terms of schooling, recent results achieved by fifth graders in some of New York's poorest districts offer some grounds for hope. Both math and reading scores have improved dramatically, and it appears to have been good organization, and a lot of hard work, that did the job—no magic wands were in evidence.[13] The Gates Foundation is mounting a major, highly ambitious, effort to see if investing in smaller schools will make a large, measurable difference in high school completion and college preparedness.[14] And there are other initiatives in many states and communities. But these "bedrock" programs, essential as they are, will require years to affect college enrollments, and we do not want to lose more generations of promising candidates from modest circumstances in the interim.

Governmental programs and policies, at federal, state, and even municipal levels, clearly have a major role to play "in the here and now," and we catalog a number of opportunities to do better in these realms in our *Equity and Excellence* book. But my own knowledge of these programs is very much second-hand, and I would not serve you well by simply repeating propositions regarding incentives and cost-effectiveness that many in the audience can assess much more knowledgably than I can. (I cannot resist, however, saying that I think *completion*, not just starting out, matters enormously, and that policy-makers need to focus more on attainment, and on reducing attrition, not just on first-year enrollments.) Please do not, in any case, misinterpret my failure to discuss governmental initiatives tonight as implying that they are anything less than tremendously important. My focus will be on educational institutions, and especially on the academically selective colleges and universities that I know fairly well (public and private), even as we all understand that if Harvard's enrollment profile were to "look like America" tomorrow, the needle that tracks national numbers would move hardly at all. There would be consequences,

[13] See David M. Herszenhorn and Susan Saulny, "What Lifted Fifth-Grade Scores? Schools Say Lots of Hard Work," *New York Times*, June 12, 2005, p. A1.

[14] This initiative was met with difficulties and received criticism. However, some view the initiative as less of a failure than others. See Valerie Strauss, "How Much Bill Gates's Disappointing Small-Schools Effort Really Cost," *Washington Post*, June 9, 2014, www.washingtonpost.com/news/answer-sheet/wp/2014/06/09/how-much-bill-gatess-disappointing-small-schools-effort-really-cost/?utm_term=.d29774b234fa. See also Jack Snyder, "Small Schools: The Edu-Reform Failure That Wasn't," *Education Week*, February 9, 2016, www.edweek.org/ew/articles/2016/02/10/small-schools-the-edu-reform-failure-that-wasnt.html.

nonetheless, that transcend aggregate numbers. The leading colleges and universities continue to be important pathways to opportunities of every kind, and, as admired institutions, to play leadership roles within American higher education. They send strong messages (for better or for worse), and such "signaling" effects should not be underestimated.

Looking at the question of "what is to be done" from the perspective of the gatekeeping function of leading selective institutions,[15] there are three intersecting levers that can be used.

First is the admissions process itself, and the criteria used to "craft a class." In *Equity and Excellence* we point to a surprising disjunction between the rhetoric used to describe institutional commitments to diversity of all kinds and present-day realities. The rhetoric regularly includes language like "Admissions officials give special attention to ... applicants from economically and/or culturally disadvantaged backgrounds ... and those who would be the first in their families to attend any college."[16] What is striking is the juxtaposition of this clear statement of intent with the equally clear empirical finding that, for the '95 entering cohort at the selective schools in our study, there is absolutely no admissions advantage associated with coming from a poor family and only a very small advantage (about 4 percentage points) associated with being a first-generation college-goer. These estimates are all based on an "other-things-equal" analysis. It is instructive to compare the corresponding admissions advantages enjoyed by the typical recruited athlete (about 31 percentage points), a member of an underrepresented minority group (27 points), and a legacy (19 points).[17] We do not believe that admissions officials are dissembling when they suggest (or even insist) that their results are different from the em-

---

[15] In focusing on how the gatekeeping function is to be managed I set aside the question of what these institutions can do to improve pre-collegiate preparation through programs of every kind, ranging from the activities of schools of education in preparing teachers to tutoring and mentoring services provided by faculty and students.

[16] The quotation is from the amicus brief submitted to the US Supreme Court in *Grutter v. Bollinger et al.* and *Gratz v. Bollinger et al.* by Harvard University, Brown University, the University of Chicago, Dartmouth College, Duke University, the University of Pennsylvania, Princeton University, and Yale University.

[17] These numbers are based on new logit probabilities calculated by Nirupama Rao; they differ slightly from those in *Equity and Excellence* (p. 166).

pirical findings that we have assembled. In most cases, admissions offices lack the data needed to compare rigorously the characteristics of those offered admission and the characteristics of all those in the applicant pool (an important observation, we think, in its own right). Moreover, there is a natural human tendency to live in "the anecdote range"; these schools do enroll many wonderful students from poor families, and we like to talk about them. The empirical findings are also affected significantly, we think, by the presence in the admissions process of "champions" for the other special groups who enjoy sizeable admissions advantages—and the lack of similarly visible champions for applicants from modest backgrounds. Finally, it is entirely possible—likely, in fact—that applicants at given SAT levels from well-to-do families will present more impressive non-academic credentials than applicants from poor families, who are less likely to have had opportunities to be outstanding musicians, leaders of clubs that have traveled the world, social activists, and so on. These other qualifications surely deserve some weight, but we wonder how fully people recognize the effects on the socio-economic profile of the class of taking these wealth-related qualifications into account.

In any event, one (purely hypothetical) approach to doing more in the admissions process for students from modest backgrounds would be to put what we have called a "thumb" on the scale when considering their applications. By this we mean simply using individualized assessments in the case of these poor students analogous to the assessments used, for example, in considering legacy applicants; the goal would be to seek a rough equivalence between poor students and legacies in the odds of being admitted at any given SAT level. Heuristically, there is, it seems to us, a nice symbolism to giving the same "break" to those who have overcome so many obstacles that schools give to the most privileged applicants with the same observable credentials. This approach would give the biggest admissions break to those from modest backgrounds who have really excelled, since this is the approach used in considering legacy applicants. Simulations suggest that this approach would raise the percentage of students from low-income families from about 10 percent of the class to about 18 percent. Any number of other algorithms could of course be employed, and schools should use whatever size or shape of thumb makes sense to them. All that we are suggesting is that high-achieving students from modest backgrounds deserve at least some break when being considered for admissions—it would be splendid if rhetoric and reality were brought into closer balance.

Before moving on, I want to mention an important political point made by Amy Gutmann (president of the University of Pennsylvania) at a discussion of this topic held at Brookings in April. Amy said (and I paraphrase): "Let's not focus solely on the bottom income quartile. Students from the second and third quartiles are also underrepresented, and we should avoid 'dissing' the middle class." Amy is right about the underrepresentation of the broad middle class, and her political sensitivity is also right on point. We are certainly not opposed to making greater efforts to admit more applicants from these middle income groups. But everyone needs to recognize that it is students from the bottom quartile who have leapt over the highest hurdles in getting into the credible pool of applicants and that, for example, applicants from the third quartile are 2.5 times more likely to get into our "credible" pool than are those from the bottom quartile; those from the second quartile are also more likely to be in the pool, but their advantage over the bottom quartile is much less pronounced. Perhaps the best place to draw some kind of line is between the bottom and top halves of the income distribution.

The second lever is the provision of generous financial aid, and I presume that all of you are aware that some of the wealthier private schools (such as Princeton, Harvard, and Yale), and some of the more aggressive public universities, have replaced loans with full grant aid for students below some income threshold. We applaud this initiative, if the funds are available to sustain it, but we wonder if this is the most cost-effective use of available resources. The admissions yields for low-income admittees are already high, and we do not know how much difference, on the margin, the more generous aid packages really make. One heretical idea would be to redeploy some of the grant aid in the by now very generous basic grant packages (expecting some parental contribution and/or some use of loans) in order to free up funds that could be used to cover the additional financial aid costs associated with enrolling the modestly increased number of applicants with need who might be admitted by means of the "thumb" approach.

The third lever is a more aggressive effort to provide information that would, for example, help students and their families get over "sticker shock" and appreciate the extent to which need-based financial aid is available. Additional investments in recruitment, designed to enlarge applicant pools, are highly desirable, and we have nothing but praise for them. What remains to be learned is which approaches are most effective, and whether additional investments should be made in multi-institutional recruitment/enrichment efforts of the kind being tried out by Gary Simons and his Leadership Enterprise for a Diverse America (LEDA) program.[18]

More generally, we are strongly in favor of monitoring and assessing the growing range of initiatives of this kind. It is important to acquire a sharper understanding than I think anyone has today of what really works and what doesn't work, in different settings. As much as the "missionary" individual is to be applauded, what we need are systematic strategies that are not dependent on the charisma of particular individuals. Public policy research must identify interventions that are replicable. It is not enough to assume that good intentions will necessarily produce good results—or, put more accurately, will produce results good enough to justify the particular investment as compared with other possible investments of scarce resources.

Having suggested several approaches worth considering, individually and in concert with one another, I want now to voice a few cautions.

- We should be very careful not to overvalue numerical goals such as raising the percentage of students in the class who come from the bottom income quartile to some arbitrarily set threshold. This caution mirrors the warning that Sarah Turner and others have

[18] See http://ledascholars.org/.

voiced about overweighting the value of Pell Grant data in assessing how particular schools are doing in extending opportunity.[19] So much depends on the location of a particular school, on the demographics of the surrounding region, and on institutional history. Pushing too hard to reach a numerical goal can also lead to admissions decisions that put the likely success of a student too much at risk.

- A related concern is that in seeking to reach pre-set goals, or just in trying to do everything one can to increase socio-economic diversity, schools may not think hard enough about their real objectives. At the risk of being misunderstood, and annoying large numbers of friends, let me ask, for example, if we really believe that a state university should view as equivalent enrolling Student A, who is an out-of-state applicant from an immigrant family that is poor but advantaged culturally, and Student B, who is from a family in a poor rural region of the state that has been poor for decades and has no experience of higher education. Sympathetic as I am to both of these students, I am even more taken by the case of Student B, since I think that some emphasis should be placed on achieving real inter-generational mobility. To generalize further, I am increasingly skeptical that family income per se is the right measure of disadvantage. We can all think of cases of individuals from families that do not earn a great deal of money, but that have had other advantages (the children of missionaries may be the classic example). We certainly want to enroll such students, but we will need to work even harder to enroll students from culturally deprived backgrounds that have somehow made it into the credible applicant pool—through the efforts of a special teacher, the determination of a mother who would insist that for her children there would be "no limits," or sheer grit.

- The last caution I want to mention has to do with issues of social discomfort and isolation. In thinking about obstacles to the enrollment of more students from non-mainline backgrounds, we

---

[19] See Jeffrey Tebbs and Sarah Turner, "College Education for Low Income Students: A Caution on the Use of Data on Pell Grant Recipients," *Change*, June 2005.

need to take into account not just academic considerations (and fears), and not just worries about being able to pay bills and stay out of debt, but also concerns about the prospect of social isolation—of feeling entirely out of place and uncomfortable on a campus where BMWs are much in evidence and socially exclusive social systems affect campus life. These considerations tend to be more serious barriers at schools in bucolic settings than in urban institutions, but they are real and cannot be dismissed. In many discussions of our book, we were reminded over and over again of how acutely students from modest backgrounds feel about these kinds of social issues. And how often, in the past, discomfort led to attrition or disappointing performance.

Let me now put some "clothes" on these rather abstract observations by quoting from a letter I received a few weeks ago from Rhonda Hughes, a faculty member at Bryn Mawr who had read part of our book and wanted us to know of her personal odyssey. She is a professor of mathematics, and she thought (rightly) that her own experiences might highlight some of the continuing challenges that we face in promoting opportunity. Here is part of what she wrote:

My [Chicago] high school was populated primarily by the children of Polish, Lithuanian, Swedish, Greek, and German immigrants, most of whom held blue-collar jobs. Gage Park was the last all-white high school in the city. I was one of about three or four Jewish students in the school, a minority among minorities. Although I was ranked first in my class for four years, I do not recall receiving any encouragement to attend college. In fact, I was in a secretarial track until I realized that I could not take shorthand, and that my grades would suffer accordingly. I asked a counselor to allow me to switch into a physics course, in order to protect my grades; the change inadvertently placed me in the college preparatory track.

In our senior year, a few of my girlfriends announced that they were applying to the University of Illinois at Urbana-Champaign, and I followed suit. Most of the girls in my class would either become secretaries (an avenue closed to me for obvious reasons), or go to other state schools to study elementary education. Only a few of the boys I knew went to college; those who did not were drafted and went to Vietnam. My friends and I started college in February, thoroughly naïve about the profound culture shock that awaited us. I can only imagine what would have happened to us at an Ivy League institution, or an elite liberal arts college.

At Urbana, we encountered relatively sophisticated suburban kids who, compared to us, had a great deal of money and privilege. I was terrified that I would not do well academically, since I had no idea how my education had prepared me for college. The academic challenges proved far easier to navigate than the social ones. Despite my 4.0 GPA, I dropped out by the middle of my second year. Another Gage Park student, a brilliant scientist and artist who had finished second in the Illinois State Science Fair, left before the end of the first year. After working for six months, I applied to the University of Illinois at Chicago Circle, where I completed my bachelor's degree. The diversity and anonymity of a commuter campus suited me well. Thanks to the encouragement of a particular professor I encountered in my junior year, I stayed at Chicago Circle and went on to earn MS and PhD degrees in mathematics. Although my parents ultimately were very proud of my achievements, at the time they were frustrated by my insistence on becoming what they viewed as a "professional student," and were relieved to see that eventually I could earn a living doing what I loved.

Through a University of Illinois connection, I landed a tenure-track job at Tufts University, where I remained for five years before moving to Bryn Mawr.... From the moment I began teaching, I was struck by a sense of injustice and unfairness on behalf of my fellow Gage Park students. Before, I had no metric by which to gauge how bright they really were. However, teaching well-prepared students, I realized that many of my friends would have excelled academically at the elite institutions where I now taught.

I want to end by repeating an injunction that I take very seriously. In making the case for enrolling—and graduating—more students from families of modest background, there is also one thing (among many, no doubt) that we should *not* do: namely, suggest that paying more attention to socio-economic status will eliminate the need for race-based affirmative action any time soon. Recognition of the most obvious demographic proposition—that minority families are heavily concentrated at the bottom of the income distribution—has led some to suggest that the way to get past the need for race-sensitive admissions is to give more preference to applicants from poor families, white or minority. Again, we should check out the numbers. Simulations for the nineteen schools in our study demonstrate that giving low-income students the same admissions preference that is given today to legacies would increase the percentage of enrolled students from underrepresented racial minorities above what it would be in the absence of *any* racial or socio-economic preferences by only about 2 percentage points; the overall result would be to cut minority enrollment at the undergraduate level to about *half* what it is today. At graduate and professional levels, the impact would probably be even greater.

In short, paying attention to class and background, which we strongly favor, is, at this juncture in our history, no substitute for paying attention to race. As I have said before, Americans always seek the painless alternative, and it is much easier for most people to be sympathetic to economic disadvantage than it is for them to understand and address the more deeply rooted and emotionally challenging issues that are due in such large part to what Glenn Loury has called the "unlovely history" of race in America. But surely it ought to be possible to think about opportunity from more than a single perspective—to recognize that the river of opportunity has tributaries of many hues and many kinds. There is also the matter of attitude. It is clearly necessary to focus on the difficulties and the challenges involved in helping this river wind to the sea, however measured its progress. But we should also be grateful for the privilege of addressing such fundamental questions, and we should be permitted to take some satisfaction from trying to do the right things for the right reasons.

APPALACHIAN COLLEGE ASSOCIATION

~

William G. Bowen
June 8, 2008

REMARKS

In thinking about what to say today, I decided to stress two themes:

- First, the enormous importance of doing a far better job than America has done to date in increasing educational attainment—and especially improving educational outcomes for minority students and students from modest backgrounds, whatever their race or ethnicity.
- Second, the power of collaboration in working to achieve educational goals of every kind—especially for small colleges and universities.

EDUCATIONAL ATTAINMENT: DOCUMENTING DISPARITIES

I begin with some sobering facts, many of which will be known to most of you.

Editor's note: These remarks were delivered at an event to honor Alice Brown, the longtime and exceptional president of the Appalachian College Association (ACA), who was retiring. The ACA grew out of a program that was originally funded by the Mellon Foundation in 1979. In 1991, a grant provided by the foundation when Bill was president helped to create the current organization, which is composed of thirty-five colleges and universities.

1. There has been a pronounced slowdown in the rate of increase in educational attainment in the United States (receipt of BAs) over the last several decades, *in spite of high rates of return to investments in college education.* Figure 1 highlights the very modest progress that has been made in recent years and the failure of the college completion rate to rise at all. I should add that it is only dramatic increases in the educational attainment of women that have prevented the trend from being even more discouraging. Moreover, time-to-degree at the undergraduate level has been steadily increasing—a trend that is extremely worrisome.

2. The United States is now behind a number of other OECD [Organisation for Economic Co-operation and Development] countries in the percentage of the 25- to 34-year-old population that has attained tertiary education.

3. The United States is even farther down the rank order of countries when we examine the ratio of first-university degrees in the natural sciences and engineering awarded to the 24-year-old population: the United States ranked fifteenth out of nineteen OECD countries included in a recent study.

These troubling trends are in no small measure a reflection of the continuing disparities in educational outcomes at the college level related to socio-economic status and race in America—disparities that are much greater and much more important than many of us seem to appreciate. The NELS [National Educational Longitudinal Study] data for 1992 high school graduates are a good point of departure for examining national patterns. I want to emphasize BA *attainment* (getting a degree) rather than just enrollment, since the payoff to completing one's studies—for the individual and the nation—is so much higher than the payoff simply to enrolling. In my view, too much discussion of educational opportunity focuses on initial access (enrollment).

Figure 2 shows that *both* family income and parental education (considered separately) have an enormous impact on educational attainment. What is striking is not only the regularity of the relationship between family income and BA attainment but the power of parental education. Within each income category, students from

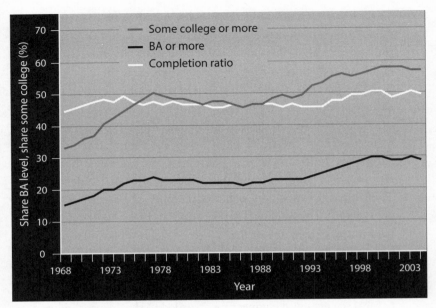

Figure 1. Educational Attainment of 25- to 29-year olds, 1968–2004

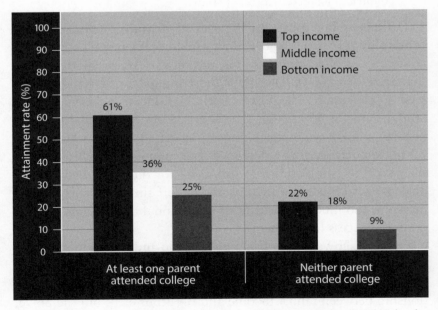

Figure 2. Bachelor's Degree Attainment by Socioeconomic Status (High School Class of 1992). Source: National Educational Longitudinal Study.

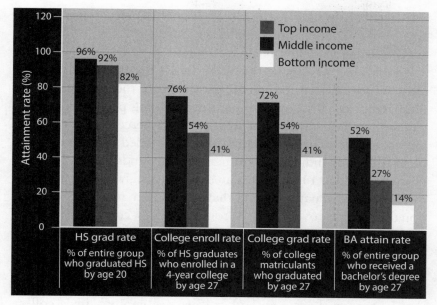

Figure 3. Educational Attainment by Family Income (High School Class of 1992). Source: National Educational Longitudinal Study.

families with some prior experience of higher education (i.e., second-generation college-goers) had at least *twice* as great a chance of earning a BA as did first-generation college-goers.

Figure 3 charts the falloffs in progress toward a degree at each stage of the educational process in relation to family income. These figures are all rates of achievement for successive sub-populations who surmounted the previous hurdle. (And please note that high school graduates include both those who earned a high school diploma and those who earned a GED.) As is evident, disparities exist at each stage and build steadily. The greatest difference is in the odds of starting college—76 percent of high school graduates from upper-income families enroll in a four-year college or university, as compared with 54 percent of high school graduates from middle-income families and 41 percent from low-income families. But these differences in initial access are by no means the end of the story. There is also a pronounced difference in "finishing" among those who did enroll: 72 percent of those from high-income families who started college graduated (by age 27) versus 54 percent of the "starters" from middle-income families and just 41 percent of the starters who came from low-income families.

The final set of bars on the figure shows the combined effect of these successive "falloffs" on the percentage of the base group who ultimately earn BAs: over 50 percent of young people from high-income families earned BAs versus just 14 percent of those from low-income families. In a nation that has prided itself historically on encouraging individuals from all backgrounds to climb the opportunity ladder, 14 percent is an embarrassingly low percentage.

The last set of national data that I will summarize tracks educational outcomes over time. A comparison of college graduation rates for students from the high school classes of 1972, 1982, and 1992 is very sobering. The proverbial bottom line is that the BA attainment rate rose appreciably over this twenty-year period *only among students at the top of the socio-economic status pyramid*: that is, among those who had at least one parent with a college education *and* who were from high-income families. Attainment rates were essentially stagnant for all other groups, the high return to a college education notwithstanding.

Lest you think that these data are dominated by outcomes at colleges and universities of modest quality, let me mention briefly outcomes within a very different population that my colleagues and I are now studying intensively—namely, approximately 125,000 members of the '99 entering cohort at twenty-one leading public universities across the country. These are great universities, and the sector of higher education that they represent—different as it is from that represented by the Appalachian colleges—is extremely important quantitatively, qualitatively, and symbolically. The students at these flagship universities are, by any measure, a special group. They have very strong pre-collegiate preparation, and over 40 percent come from the top quarter of the income distribution. As you would expect, their graduation rates are appreciably higher than the rates among students attending all four-year colleges and universities.

Still, there are serious grounds for concern about patterns of educational attainment within even this far more selective student group. I won't show you more figures, but I will report that here too graduation rates correlate relentlessly with family income—a pattern particularly evident when we focus on four-year graduation rates, which rise from 37 percent to 55 percent as we move from the bottom to the top income quartile. We also find that here too parental education matters greatly, and not just because it correlates with family income. (Interestingly, close inspection of these data teaches us that it is college *graduation* among parents—not merely some college *attendance*—that is most strongly associated with differences in children's graduation rates.)

Differences in graduation rates by race and gender are also substantial. Particularly noteworthy is the four-year graduation rate for black male matriculants at these flagship public universities: *it is only 25 percent!* Time-to-degree is obviously much longer for black men than for white men, and this difference has a big impact on subsequent educational and career opportunities. Black women do appreciably better, but their four-year graduation rate of 44 percent is 12 points lower than the corresponding rate for white women.

The conclusion to be drawn is that pronounced disparities in educational outcomes (graduation rates in particular, but other outcomes as well, which I do not have time to discuss today) are endemic. They are substantial, and there is no evidence that they are diminishing. Moreover, we find that even after controlling for background characteristics and the university the student attended, there is still a relationship between a student's probability of graduating and the student's race, gender, family income, and parents' education. The patterns are remarkably consistent, and each indicator of socio-economic status appears to have an "independent" effect on graduation rates, as does the student's race and gender.

WHY DO THESE DISPARITIES MATTER?

Why should we care that these disparities exist? Why not just let markets and "normal processes" allocate places in college and determine outcomes? There are, in my view, three reasons for being more proactive.

First, there are serious labor market concerns. The country needs trained brainpower, now as never before, to compete worldwide—and unfettered operation of markets seems unlikely to produce a sufficiently well-educated workforce. Lack of information and financial constraints are especially serious problems for individuals from modest backgrounds. These problems will become increasingly serious as demographic changes reduce the share of potential matriculants from the traditional upper-class white population, which has relatively high graduation rates. Census projections suggest that by 2050, white Americans will represent just half the population compared to approximately 70 percent today. A recent set of projections by the WICHE [Western Interstate Commission for Higher Education] suggests that the annual number of Hispanic public high school graduates will increase by 315,000 (68 percent of the base-year number) between today and 2021–22. Over this same fourteen-year span, white non-Hispanic graduates will *decline* by almost exactly the same number (a 16 percent drop from the number in 2007–08).

Another consideration is that at the graduate level the United States has benefited for many years from a large flow of highly qualified students from foreign countries—many of whom have stayed to provide much of the science and engineering talent on which we rely (38 percent of doctoral-level science and engineering workers are foreign-born). It is far from clear that we can continue to import so much talent. Visa issues are one factor, and we also need to recognize that there is a substantial (continuing) growth in educational opportunities in other countries, including China. Foreign students have many more choices as to where to study than they did earlier. And the demand for highly educated individuals is increasing rapidly in Europe and other parts of the world.

The conclusion is that, on labor market grounds alone, we must do a better job of educating US students from families of moderate circumstances and from racial/ethnic minorities. In the South African phrase, we have to "grow more of our own timber." That is important in Appalachia—for the future of this region—as it is important all over the United States.

But it is not only narrow labor force worries that should concern us. As the arguments in the University of Michigan affirmative action case demonstrated persuasively, there is educational value to the presence in classrooms and on campuses of a diverse student population, with diversity measured along many dimensions (including race, gender, geography, and socio-economic status).

Finally, issues of equity and social mobility are, to my mind, of over-riding importance. The long-term health of our country depends on the existence of a widely shared confidence that racial minorities and students from poor families have a real opportunity to move ahead. The growing gaps in income that are so much in the news these days highlight the importance of using educational opportunities to close rather than widen disparities in access to the most powerful as well as the most highly remunerated positions in society. And, truth be told, we are not doing all that well.

THE CHALLENGE: HOW TO REDUCE
THESE DISPARITIES

The consistency and persistence of these patterns, across colleges and universities of every size and every kind, and over time, reminds us that it will be anything but easy to reduce these damaging disparities in educational outcomes. Those of you who know me will not be surprised to learn that in thinking about how to do better, I start out by emphasizing the importance of the research agenda before us. We have to understand, at a deep level, what is producing these patterns. This involves, among other things, looking much more closely at the relationships between different aspects of pre-collegiate preparation and college outcomes (not just treating high school graduation rates and test scores earned by graduating seniors as "the" measures of how high schools are doing). Similarly, more attention needs to be given to the effects of different methods of paying for college, including reliance on work, and the forms, amounts, and allocation of financial aid. Finally, universities need to consider aspects of their curricular and residential arrangements that facilitate or inhibit completion.

I cannot resist pointing out that this kind of outcomes-driven research requires the courage and creativity needed to find ways of coping with well-intentioned policies designed to protect the privacy and well-being of individuals. It is mildly ironic that at the same time that the Department of Education emphasizes the importance of outcomes-based research, the FERPA [Family Educational Rights and Privacy Act] requirements are sometimes interpreted in ways that discourage careful research of this kind, much of which depends on our ability to link records from different sources. The research that the Stinebrickners (father and son) have done with data provided by Berea is an excellent example, within the ACA, of the kinds of studies that need to be encouraged.

Required too is a willingness to face up to the results, good and bad, of policies and practices currently in place. As I have said on other occasions, it is essential that we look with a cold eye at the actual evidence concerning outcomes, that we avoid defensiveness, and that we be willing to make adjustments, or even to shift directions entirely, if something is not working. It will not do simply to assume that what appears to be a good idea is in fact a good idea. Missionary zeal is highly desirable, but it has to be accompanied by a willingness to look carefully at results. Colleges and universities need to develop a culture that distinguishes finding that an experiment failed to produce the desired result from declaring the designer of the experiment to be a bad person. Accountability works best when sensible objectives are clearly articulated at "the front end" and results are then scrutinized in an open-minded way at "the back end"—preferably by someone other than the person who designed the program

More substantively, I want to say how important I think it is, in addressing disparities, to be concerned about *both* race and socio-economic status. (Remember that 25 percent four-year graduation figure for black men at leading public universities.) Some seem to believe that focusing admissions and enrollment efforts solely on socio-economic status would simultaneously, as a kind of by-product, address the need for racial diversity. Since it is true that a far larger fraction of blacks than of whites come from the bottom income quartile, is easy to see why someone might be intrigued by this way of avoiding the issue of race. Americans have an insatiable appetite for the painless solution, and—as we have seen in various polls—considering race continues to be both offensive and painful to many people. Still, evidence deserves respect. A great many studies have demonstrated that taking account only of socio-economic status would result in a dramatic reduction in the number of minority students on campuses across the country.

Next, before turning to my second theme, collaboration, I want to emphasize what I see as the important role to be played by the Appalachian colleges in what has to be a national effort to address—to reduce—these disparities. There are many steps that the leading flagship universities, the leading private universities, and the wide range of other educational institutions nationwide can take to improve educational outcomes. But, as those of you here today know so well, there are regional and local needs—and opportunities—that present themselves to colleges such as those in the ACA. Hard as I (and others) will work to encourage progress at places such as the University of Michigan and Chapel Hill, these universities will never serve your natural constituency as fully or as well as you will serve it. In short, your traditional role as providing opportunity for aspiring students from Appalachia takes on even greater importance as we look to a future in which the national (as well as the regional) need for your graduates is of ever-increasing importance.

Allow me a personal reminiscence. I grew up in Southern Ohio and was the son of a lower-middle-class cash register salesman and a traditional housewife. Neither of my parents was a college graduate, and in fact neither of them had more than the most passing acquaintance with college. I was, then, a prospective first-generation college student. My situation was also affected by the fact that my father died when I was a senior in high school and my mother had no source of income. Even though I was the valedictorian of my class in a small but good suburban high school, it was unthinkable for me to consider a college outside Ohio. Fortunately, I won several scholarships which permitted me to go to Denison University, where I also worked all four years. Denison, I should add, was a much less selective college in the early 1950s than it is today, and its small scale, close faculty-student interactions, and lack of anything resembling an elitist student body made me much more comfortable there than I would have been at, for example, Yale (which had expressed an interest in me). Denison was an extremely good "fit" for me, and I continue to give thanks for my good fortune in having ended up there.

The question of "fit" is an important one for students from modest circumstances, no matter how well they have done in high school, and my own educational experience makes it easy for me to see the critical importance of the Appalachian colleges. You are educating many students who would have had no other educational opportunity, certainly within the universe of four-year institutions. Even for those who might have gone elsewhere, your colleges provide settings in which the transition from a home environment to college can be achieved successfully.

COLLABORATIONS

Valuable as I know the small-college setting can be (hearkening back, again, to my own experience at Denison), it is also clear that scale matters. There are so many opportunities to economize on resources and to provide better educational opportunities when we work together—whether in the context of making purchases, encouraging the sharing of faculty, recruiting students, or managing leave programs. I am so pleased that the Mellon Foundation made several major grants designed explicitly to foster collaborative activities within the ACA. In addition, Mellon supported library and technology initiatives, both of which are inherently collaborative efforts.

Collaboration is never (or almost never) easy. The reality is that educational institutions, including the most prominent colleges and universities, often have a hard time working together. They are just so competitive. Of course, competition for students, faculty, and research support can have positive effects. I am increasingly persuaded, however, that competitive juices can be too strong and can get in the way of progress. When I was at the Mellon Foundation, I was always grateful that it had no football team, and that, perhaps in part for that reason, it was able to broker important initiatives such as JSTOR (which I discuss in more detail later) that have proved beneficial to higher education worldwide. To rise at least some distance above one's immediate institutional concerns is a challenge in every setting, but it is a challenge that has to be accepted.

My argument in favor of looking for good collaborations, and taking a system-wide approach, has particular force, I believe, when we consider the increasingly digitized world in which we live. JSTOR, the digital archive of the back issues of scholarly journals that now contains over 20 million pages of content, drawn from over six hundred journals, is an excellent case in point. It is used today by students and scholars at more than three thousand libraries in well over a hundred countries. In 2006, there were more than 375 million significant accesses, and usage continues to grow at an annual rate in excess of 25 percent.

JSTOR illustrates dramatically what it is possible to accomplish through collaborations in a digital era—in this instance, collaborations among publishers of scholarly literature, libraries, staff at the University of Michigan (where JSTOR was born), the Mellon Foundation, and JSTOR itself, which is now an independent nonprofit organization. It would have been insane, and totally unworkable, for any individual university to attempt to build a digital archive of this kind, and it was the enthusiasm for the "sharing" concept by the early participants in the project that gave us the courage to press ahead and create what is today a highly cost-effective "community resource" that trades on extraordinary economies of scale.

Our capacity to disseminate the basic building blocks of knowledge in digital form has broken down walls of every kind, between nations as well as between institutions and individuals, and the nature and speed of communication have been changed profoundly and forever. An enterprise such as JSTOR serves students and scholars at leading colleges and universities such as Michigan, first, by improving dramatically access to "older" journal literature, and then, in addition, by being truly interdisciplinary and encouraging scholars to make connections "horizontally" across fields of study. But the value of JSTOR extends well beyond the resource-intensive universities. Especially gratifying to me has been the impact of JSTOR on, for example, the under-resourced colleges represented at this gathering, which now have access to much the same core journal literature as students at Michigan—and without having had to build libraries, hire staff, and so on. (I am, let me inject, enormously proud to be associated with the central library of the Appalachian colleges, which provides the glue enabling effective use of JSTOR and similar digital resources.)

There is of course also an international dimension to all of this. JSTOR is now made freely available and is used in Africa and other developing countries, where access to this scholarly resource gives faculty and students a point of connection to mainstream scholarship. In short, JSTOR has, if you will, "democratized" opportunities to learn.

The JSTOR example connects to our earlier discussion of disparities in educational opportunity in another way. Not only do students of modest means at institutions with small libraries now have much greater access to content, but students at all places, large and small, who may be shy, even somewhat intimidated by their surroundings, can work in more anonymous and less "social" ways than they could have otherwise. I am reminded of a favorite *New Yorker* cartoon which shows a large dog at a computer keyboard, looking down at a smaller dog at his feet; the large dog says, "On the Internet, nobody knows you're a dog."

The full implications of this ongoing technological revolution for teaching, learning, and scholarship are impossible to foretell, but there is no denying the need for collaborations of many kinds if we are to take full advantage of the unfolding opportunities before us. The economies of scale are irresistible, and in time, with the benefit of strong leadership, will overwhelm the all too real problems posed by legal issues associated with copyright and by the seemingly even more intractable challenges that are strategic, organizational, and managerial.

One of the big challenges that will face leaders of the academic community is to develop sustainable business models for digital initiatives of various kinds that, on the one hand, respect the implications of very low (though not zero) marginal costs, and, on the other hand, recognize the need to pay the bills (no, knowledge is not "free," even in the digital age). It is essential that we find reliable sources of revenue that are sufficiently diverse to provide some real protection, some real sense of security, to users being asked to make the irreversible decisions needed to realize the cost-savings promised by many of these resources—decisions reflected, for example, in building plans for new libraries and in judgments about the preservation and storage of print content. It will not be easy to resist the temptation to pursue ideologically driven models that are attractive in terms of their stated objectives (to allow everyone to have "free" access to everything) but that do not represent long-term solutions to the critical need for assured sustainability.

These inevitable tensions between a deeply felt desire to serve the widest possible audience and the need to build sustainable business models are being experienced in other digital entities with which I have some personal familiarity. The success of JSTOR led to the creation of ARTstor (a digital repository of art images and associated scholarly materials) and of organizations such as Portico (which is dedicated to archiving electronic journal content so that it will always be available and so that libraries can move more quickly to restructure the ways they handle journal literature), NITLE (which addresses the need of small colleges for shared access to new developments in information technology), and Aluka (which is busily engaged in assembling a digital repository of valuable materials, including many primary source materials, from and about Africa, including Timbuktu manuscripts highlighted in a recent *New York Times* article[1]).

I am persuaded that nonprofit organizations such as ITHAKA/ Aluka can be catalysts of initiatives that eventually will require high-level collaborations throughout higher education and beyond.

---

[1] See John Noble Wilford, "Project Digitizes Works from the Golden Age of Timbuktu," *New York Times*, May 20, 2008, www.nytimes.com/2008/05/20/science/20timb.html.

CONCLUDING THOUGHTS

Let me end with two concluding thoughts. First, the pressing nature of the very practical problems and issues of the day, combined with recognition that the world in which we live, both at home and abroad, is far from any state of perfection, should not prevent us from devoting at least a few moments to larger visions. Just about six weeks ago, I had the privilege of participating in a memorial service for my predecessor as president of Princeton, Robert Goheen, who was born to medical missionary parents in India and spent his life serving other people, worldwide. In typical fashion, Bob designed his own service, and he included in it a hymn titled "Finlandia," which was a special favorite of his because it speaks to the common aspirations of people everywhere—to the fact that, divisions and disputes notwithstanding, we live in one world. Please be assured that I am not going to sing (heaven forbid!), but I am going to read two stanzas from this hymn.

> This is my song, oh God of all the nations,
> A song of peace for lands afar and mine.
> This is my home, the country where my heart is;
> Here are my hopes, my dreams, my sacred shrine.
> But other hearts in other lands are beating,
> With hopes and dreams as true and high as mine.
>
> My country's skies are bluer than the ocean,
> And sunlight beams on cloverleaf and pine.
> But other lands have sunlight too and clover,
> And skies are everywhere as blue as mine.
> Oh hear my song, oh God of all the nations,
> A song of peace for their land and for mine.

CROSSING THE FINISH LINE

COMPLETING COLLEGE AT AMERICA'S PUBLIC UNIVERSITIES

~

William G. Bowen
May 30, 2010

ASSOCIATION FOR INSTITUTIONAL RESEARCH

I am delighted to have this opportunity to meet with this very important group of stalwarts, dedicated to analyzing carefully and objectively how our institutions of higher education work, and how they can be helped to work better. All of us interested in promoting the effectiveness of our institutions of higher education are indebted to you. Beyond that, I am personally indebted to legions of talented institutional researchers for having provided me with the data that I had to have in order to complete a by now embarrassingly large number of studies of outcomes in higher education.

Perhaps I should back up and say that when I moved from Princeton University to the Mellon Foundation I was struck by how many grant-seekers believed that they understood things that were in fact obscure. There is a terrible tendency in higher education (and in other spheres as well) to assume that we know more than we do and to trust impressions that are vague at best. Too often we live in the anecdote range. Evidence is truly important, and I have spent the last two decades trying to persuade all sorts of

Editor's note: This keynote address was delivered in a plenary session at the fiftieth annual Association for Institutional Research (AIR) Forum in Chicago. It is the nation's largest institutional research conference.

people that they need to find the facts before announcing sweeping conclusions. It is so easy to fool yourself, never mind others.

So, once again, my thanks to all of you for the important behind-the-scenes work that you do in providing the basis for judgments that are often highly consequential.

My topic today is educational attainment in America. The good news—and it is very good news—is that the Obama administration clearly understands the critical need to raise levels of degree completion at both two-year and four-year institutions. The less-good news is that major progress needs to be made in the face of severe fiscal constraints—we need to make progress in both increasing overall levels of educational attainment *and* reducing disparities in outcomes related to race/ethnicity and socio-economic status.

In suggesting ways in which we may attempt to "square this circle," I will draw on the results of the study of completion rates that Matt Chingos, Mike McPherson, and I published last September [*Crossing the Finish Line: Completing College at America's Public Universities* (Princeton, NJ: Princeton University Press, 2009)]. In focusing our empirical work on outcomes at four-year public universities (twenty-one flagship universities and all forty-seven state-system universities in four states), we certainly did not mean to denigrate the importance of the private sector or of community colleges. But, for reasons explained at length in the book, we are convinced (a) that the number of BA degrees attained—the number of students crossing that particular finish line—needs to be increased substantially and (b) that the public universities have to do the heaviest lifting. It is these institutions that have the clearest historical commitment to educational attainment for all, as well as the scale, the cost-price structure, and the greatest extant opportunities to do better.

Since the book has received such extensive coverage, I am not going to say more about its contents or organization, but I will be glad to try and answer any questions you may have. Toward the end of my remarks, I will also add more recent impressions of what needs to be done to combat "the cost disease" in higher education at the same time that we seek to improve educational outcomes.

FRAMING THE PROBLEM

To sum up the challenges we face, the twin problems before us are, first, an unacceptably stagnant level of overall educational attainment [Figure 1] in spite of historically high returns to degree completion and, second, persistent disparities in BA completion rates by socio-economic status [Figure 2]. The two are, as it were, linked at the hip because we can't achieve significant increases in the overall level of educational attainment unless we do a better job of graduating students from poor families and from Hispanic and African American populations. The demographics and the extant disparities leave us no choice other than to do a much better job with these populations.

There is also a third problem that deserves much more attention than it has received—namely, the long time-to-degree. At the flagships in our study, slightly less than half the entering students earned their BA in four years (49 percent) from the institution they first attended; at the universities in the four state systems, only 38 percent graduated in four years. The total six-year graduation rates from institutions first attended is 77 percent, and the figure for state systems is 62 percent; thus, roughly a third of all those who graduated in six years took more than four years to finish. Among black men at the flagship public universities, just 26 percent graduated in four years—the total six-year graduation rate was 59 percent, so well over half of all those who graduated took more than four years. [Transfer graduation rates are about 4 percent for everybody.]

The situation has been steadily worsening. In an important recent paper,[1] John Bound, Michael Lovenheim, and Sarah Turner have found that for students at all colleges and universities, the percentage finishing in four years dropped from 58 percent in the National Longitudinal Survey of the High School Class of 1972

[1] John Bound, Michael F. Lovenheim, and Sarah Turner, "Increasing Time to Baccalaureate Degree in the United States," [MIT] *Education Finance and Policy* 7, no. 4 (September 2012): 375–424.

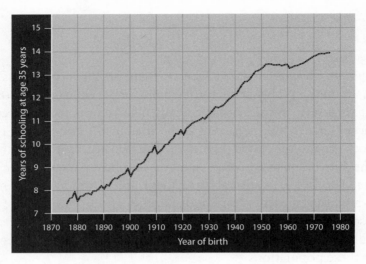

Figure 1. Years of Schooling by Birth Cohorts, US Native Born: 1876–1975. Source: Claudia Goldin and Lawrence F. Katz, *The Race between Education and Technology* (Cambridge, MA: Belknap Press of Harvard University Press, 2008), fig. 1.4, as rendered in William G. Bowen et al., *Crossing the Finish Line: Completing College at America's Public Universities* (Princeton University Press, 2009), fig. 1.1.

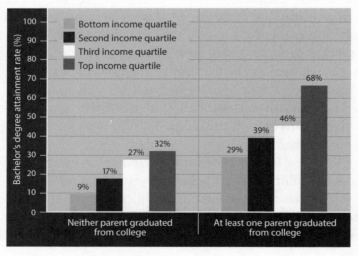

Figure 2. Bachelor's Degree Attainment by Socio-economic Status. Source: National Educational Longitudinal Study 1988/2000, as rendered in William G. Bowen et al., *Crossing the Finish Line: Completing College at America's Public Universities* (Princeton University Press, 2009), fig. 2.2.

(NLS72) to 44 percent in the National Educational Longitudinal Survey of 1988 (NELS88). Falloff is much greater among less selective publics than elsewhere and is especially pronounced among low-income students. This result is not due to changes in college preparedness or to demographic shifts; rather the explanation lies in the students' having access to fewer collegiate resources in less selective places and having to spend more time working.

The consequences of long time-to-degree for both individual students and institutions are obvious. The longer it takes to graduate, the lower the odds that the student will ever finish—and future career opportunities, including especially opportunities for graduate study, are harmed by long time-to-degree. For institutions, long time-to-degree increases costs substantially. We find it ironic that some legislators are calling today for more three-year BA programs; it would be much wiser, we think, to find ways to raise the fraction of graduates who complete their work in four years rather than taking five or six, which could well become the new norm. Part of the problem here is institutional rigidities (lack of places in gateway courses, for example). But student assumptions are also relevant. One student at a leading flagship university said that graduating in four years is like leaving the party at 10 pm!

A final general observation: attrition (withdrawal) occurs all along the path to BA completion and is much less heavily concentrated in the first two years than is commonly assumed. At the flagships, nearly half of all withdrawals occurred *after* the second year. The obvious implication is that, while it may make sense to front-load some efforts to reduce attrition, focusing only on the first two years is a mistake.

WHAT TO DO? FIRST, ADDRESS THE UNDERMATCH PROBLEM

One of the biggest surprises to us was the extent of what we have come to call "undermatching"—by which we mean situations in which high-achieving secondary school students who are presumptively eligible to attend a strong four-year institution attend a two-year college, a four-year college that is less demanding than places for which they are qualified, or no college at all. In North Carolina (where we have the best data), over 40 percent of all SAT-test-takers who were presumptively qualified to attend one of the state's most selective universities failed to do so—they "undermatched." Undermatching is a serious problem because students who under-match pay a big graduation rate penalty: they are appreciably less likely to graduate, and to graduate on time, than comparable students who attend the more selective universities for which they are qualified. This is, in one sense, counter-intuitive, in that one might expect students with given qualifications to have a better chance of graduating if they go to a "less competitive" school. But that is not what the data show. I will return later to the causes of this per-sistent and pervasive pattern, which we think is rooted primarily in peer effects and expectations.

Here let me add only that, not surprisingly, undermatching is far more prevalent among students from poor families and from un-derrepresented minority groups (especially Hispanics) than it is among the children of more affluent families [Figure 3]. The data also demonstrate that undermatching occurs primarily at the appli-cation stage of the college-going process: astonishingly large num-bers of well-qualified students do not even apply to colleges and universities that might be excellent "matches" for them—a pattern evident both in our work and in the rich data assembled by the Chicago Public School Consortium. With the strong support of the Chicago Public School system, we are now working with colleagues at MDRC on a pilot project intended to test out, rigorously, cost-effective ways of "rationalizing" the submission of applications and subsequent college-going experiences. There is here, we believe, a real opportunity to increase social mobility and simultaneously in-crease overall levels of educational attainment.

Next, in an effort to put a sword through the heart of a recurring myth that is highly damaging, let me state that the new data in our study demonstrate unequivocally, once again, that there is *no* prob-lem associated with "overmatching." Opponents of affirmative ac-tion have often claimed that race-sensitive admissions policies harm the very minority student they purport to help by inducing them to

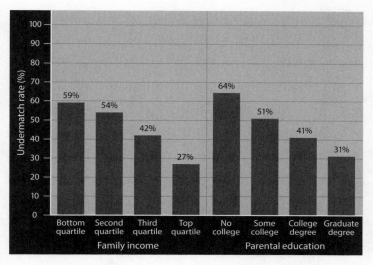

Figure 3. Undermatch Rates by Family Income and Parental Education. Source: North Carolina High School Seniors Database, as rendered in William G. Bowen et al., *Crossing the Finish Line: Completing College at America's Public Universities* (Princeton University Press, 2009), fig. 5.5.

attend colleges that are too demanding, thrusting them into harmful competition with white classmates of greater ability, demoralizing them, and harming their outcomes. In our extensive new dataset, there is absolutely no support for this hypothesis. On the contrary, we find that black men who went to more selective institutions graduated at *higher*, not lower, rates than similarly prepared black students who went to less selective institutions [Figure 4].

WHAT TO DO? IMPROVE SORTING BY COLLEGES AND UNIVERSITIES AND SEND BETTER SIGNALS TO HIGH SCHOOLS ABOUT THE IMPORTANCE OF HIGH SCHOOL GRADES AND ACHIEVEMENT TESTS

We are not at all opposed to testing, which is helpful when used in right ways and in right settings to predict what you want to predict. Still, our findings on the predictive power of standardized tests surprised us. The evidence is clear that high school grades are far better

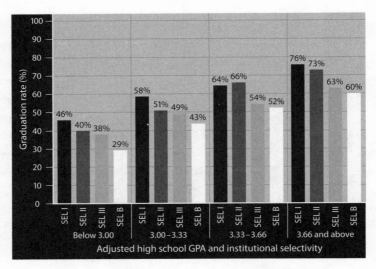

Figure 4. Graduation Rates of Black Men by Adjusted High School GPA and
Institutional Selectivity, 1999 Entering Cohort. Note: SEL stands for selectivity
cluster. Source: Flagships Database and State Systems Database, as rendered in
William G. Bowen et al., *Crossing the Finish Line: Completing College at
America's Public Universitie*s (Princeton University Press, 2009), fig. 11.1.

incremental predictors of graduation rates, and especially four-year
graduation rates, than are SAT/ACT scores [Figure 5]. The reason:
grades measure not just cognitive skills but perseverance, motivation, and time-management skills. High school grades matter even
when a student comes from a poor high school. There is a strong
case for weighting grades very heavily, especially at less selective
universities eager to improve their graduation rates.

High school grades are also less correlated with socio-economic
status than are "aptitude" tests, and so putting more weight on
grades should increase diversity as well as improve graduation rates.
Finally, we find that achievement tests, and especially scores on AP
tests, are strong predictors of graduation rates, and it is encouraging to learn from the College Board that more and more students
are taking AP tests. As Richard Atkinson has argued for many
years, admissions criteria send strong signals to secondary schools,
and there is much to be said for encouraging the schools to concentrate on teaching content.

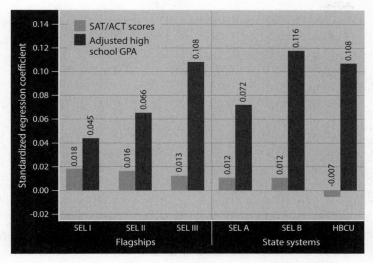

Figure 5. Predictive Power of SAT/ACT Scores and High School GPA on Six-Year Graduation Rates, Standardized Regression Coefficients. Note: SEL stands for selectivity cluster. Source: William G. Bowen et al., *Crossing the Finish Line: Completing College at America's Public Universities* (Princeton University Press, 2009), appendix tables 6.1 and 6.2, as rendered in fig. 6.1.

WHAT TO DO? PUT MORE EMPHASIS ON NEED-BASED AID AND LESS EMPHASIS ON MERIT AID

Money matters. Our study is full of evidence showing that family income is a powerful predictor of graduation rates and time-to-degree even when we control for parental education and everything else. We should do everything possible to simplify financial aid forms and increase aid available to students from poor families.

One new piece of evidence from our work shows that *net price* (tuition less grant aid) has a clearly measurable effect on completion rates of low-income students—but essentially no effect on completion rates of high-income students. These results reinforce other concerns about how much student aid money is distributed on the basis of "merit" rather than "need." Some reallocation of these funds could have a considerable impact on both disparities in outcomes and overall graduation rates.

WHAT TO DO? UNDERSTAND BETTER WHY INSTITUTIONAL SELECTIVITY IS ITSELF SUCH A POWERFUL PREDICTOR OF GRADUATION RATES

Let me highlight one last finding from our research, related to institutional selectivity, that raises a series of intriguing questions. We would of course expect that the more selective public universities would have higher graduation rates than less selective places, simply because they enroll larger numbers of students with strong academic preparation [Figure 6]. The much more interesting finding is that institutional selectivity is strongly correlated with graduation rates (and time-to-degree) *even after we control for differences in the entering qualifications and other characteristics of students* [Figures 7 and 8].

We cannot be sure of all the factors affecting this persistent pattern—which of course is what explains the conclusions concerning undermatching and overmatching stated earlier—but we think

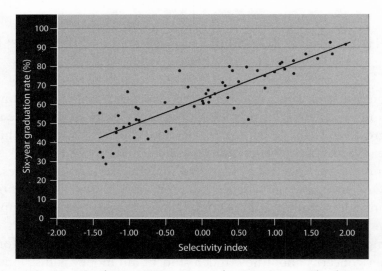

Figure 6. Six-Year Graduation Rates versus Selectivity. Source: Flagships Database and State Systems Database, as rendered in William G. Bowen et al., *Crossing the Finish Line: Completing College at America's Public Universities* (Princeton University Press, 2009), fig. 10.1.

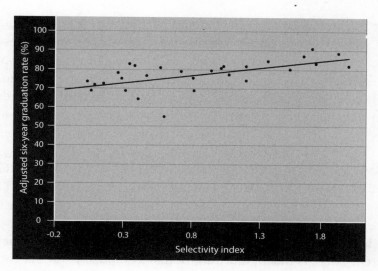

Figure 7. Adjusted Six-Year Graduation Rates versus Selectivity, Flagships and State-System SEL As. Note: SEL stands for selectivity cluster. Source: Flagships Database and State Systems Database, as rendered in William G. Bowen et al., *Crossing the Finish Line: Completing College at America's Public Universities* (Princeton University Press, 2009), fig. 10.3a.

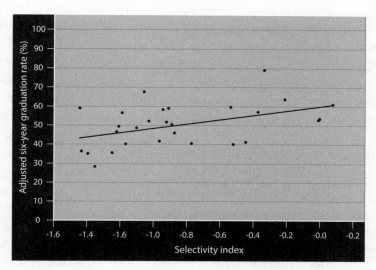

Figure 8. Adjusted Six-Year Graduation Rates versus Selectivity, State-System SEL Bs. Note: SEL stands for selectivity cluster. Source: State Systems Database, as rendered in William G. Bowen et al., *Crossing the Finish Line: Completing College at America's Public Universities* (Princeton University Press, 2009), fig. 10.3b.

that the factors involved include (a) peer effects; (b) expectations; (c) financial aid and access to academically related jobs; (d) access to abler graduate students and other teaching resources; and (e) some unobservable selection effects. Understanding better what is going on here might yield valuable clues as to how to improve graduation rates across the board.

WHAT TO DO? EXPERIMENT WITH WAYS OF USING ONLINE LEARNING TECHNOLOGIES TO INCREASE PRODUCTIVITY AND IMPROVE OUTCOMES

Well, that concludes my sampling of highlights of our recent research. There is much, much more that I could say—about topics such as transfer patterns, outcomes at two-year versus four-year institutions, and lasting effects of parental education on the graduation rates of children—but instead I want to end by speculating briefly on a very different approach to the problems we are considering. As some of you may know, I am a co-author (with William Baumol) of a long-lasting explanation for rising costs in higher education. Writing initially about the performing arts, Baumol and I argued that the costs of labor-intensive activities such as performances by string quartets and standard classroom teaching would inevitably rise faster than costs in general—that is, faster than the general inflation rate. This phenomenon is sometimes called "the cost disease," and its presence in higher education, going back a century or more, is all too well documented.

Now, more than forty years after we first articulated the economic basis for the cost disease, I am wondering if the time is finally at hand when truly sophisticated methods of using online teaching technologies in basic introductory courses might change things. I have been on record for some time in being skeptical about the likely effects on productivity in higher education of various new technologies (see my Romanes Lecture at Oxford in 2000). But some recent evidence has caused me to re-think my position. I won't go into detail today, but I will suggest that this may be an area where what is needed is a modest number of very large investments aimed at producing courses in applicable subjects that do not mimic classroom teaching but rather take full advantage of the new media—of opportunities to provide very rapid feedback, use mini-cognitive tutors, and allow students to move ahead at whatever pace works for them. I am inclined to agree with Bill Gates when, in his annual "letter,"[2] he argued for developing a small number of really well-designed online courses rather than a large number of less effective course offerings. There should be opportunities here to take advantage of big-time economies of scale.

If these more optimistic ruminations prove to have merit—and that is what we must find out—there might be an opportunity to save significant amounts of resources in teaching introductory courses in fields such as math, statistics, and foreign languages while actually improving outcomes. The work of Claude Steele and others suggests that this kind of teaching technology might actually be especially effective in improving outcomes for minority students. It is also conceivable that well-designed approaches of this kind could reduce attrition by helping more students navigate the so-called killer courses such as mathematics that often serve as barriers to timely completion of degrees. Resources saved in this way could be redeployed to teach more students or, conceivably, to teach advanced students more effectively.

I don't know if this is only wishful thinking, but I am increasingly convinced that the fiscal realities of state governments, including intense competition for resources to solve healthcare and other problems, make it unlikely, as a practical matter, that states will provide the resources needed to allow us to continue teaching

[2]See Bill and Melinda Gates Foundation Annual Letter, 2010 (www.gatesfoundation .org/Who-We-Are/Resources-and-Media/Annual-Letters-List/Annual-Letter-2010#Online Learning). "We need to bring together the video and interactive pieces for K–12 and college courses. We should focus on having at least one great course online for each subject rather than lots of mediocre courses. Once we have this material in place, it can be used in many different ways. A teacher can watch and learn how to make a subject more interesting. A teacher can assign subsets of the material to students who are behind and finding something difficult. A teacher can suggest online material to a student who is ahead and wants to learn more. A teacher can assign an interactive session to diagnose where a student is weak and make sure they get practice on the areas that are difficult for them. Self-motivated students can take entire courses on their own. If they want to prove they learned the material to help qualify for a job, a trusted accreditation service independent from any school should be able to verify their abilities."

in the manner to which we have become accustomed over many years. There is tremendous pressure to "do more with less," and I think higher education will be well advised to think as creatively, and as freshly, as it can in contemplating the path ahead.

Let me say, in closing, how much I admire the open-minded way in which so many presidents and other leaders in higher education have been willing to look at problems as they are and to act courageously. To be sure, as a friend of mine is fond of saying, "Not all of our ducks are swans." Still, I am not one of those who blames current leadership for our problems—that is, I believe, scapegoating of the worst kind. The basic problems are all too real, and looking for villains is not going to make them disappear.

CHAPTER 3

~

ATHLETICS, ADMISSIONS, AND CAMPUS CULTURE

RECLAIMING THE GAME

COLLEGE SPORTS AND EDUCATIONAL VALUES

~

William G. Bowen
September 25, 2003

WALTER E. EDGE LECTURE, PRINCETON UNIVERSITY

I. INTRODUCTION

Our topic tonight—college sports and educational values—is one of the most complex, emotion-laden, and contentious issues facing academically selective colleges and universities today. On these campuses it is far more contentious than affirmative action. To illustrate, a colleague of mine, James Shulman (co-author of the predecessor book, *The Game of Life*), was brave enough to speak at a gathering organized by the Harvard athletic alumni group; at the event, he was moved to refer to himself as "the designated piñata." At issue are major questions about our commitment to educational values, the rationing of opportunities—*both* to attend these schools and to play sports—and our truth-telling obligations.

My thinking about this topic is rooted in the straightforward conviction that intercollegiate athletics should enhance the educational experiences of students and, in the process, contribute to the overall quality of residential life. Yet, sadly, the realization of these traditional purposes is threatened today by powerful forces that

Editor's note: The Walter E. Edge Lecture at Princeton University is a public lecture. Distinguished individuals who have given the Edge Lecture include Justice Ruth Bader Ginsburg, Elie Wiesel, Václav Havel, and Chinua Achebe.

create an ever-widening "divide" between intercollegiate athletics and the educational missions of many colleges and universities, *including those that are free of the unique problems of "big-time" sports.* Everyone is aware, from watching TV and reading the daily newspapers, of the recurring scandals at some scholarship-granting schools that are, whether they acknowledge it or not, in the entertainment business. But intercollegiate sports programs at places like Amherst, Bryn Mawr, Columbia, Denison, and Yale, which offer no athletic scholarships and make no money from athletics, face issues that are at least as serious, in terms of educational policy, as those that confront schools in the ACC [Atlantic Coast Conference] and Big 10.[1]

The findings I am going to present tonight are based on new research that Sarah Levin and I have just published in a Princeton University Press book titled *Reclaiming the Game: College Sports and Educational Values.* Thanks to the splendid cooperation of the thirty-three academically selective colleges and universities included in the expanded College and Beyond database (see listing of schools on Figure 1), Sarah and I were able to examine in detail the records of all 27,811 students who entered these highly selective schools in the fall of 1995; we also had access to information about more than 130,000 applicants for places in the fall 1999 entering cohort. These data are more recent and more comprehensive than the data presented in *The Game of Life.* They also incorporate one important new distinction: in this new study we are able to differentiate *recruited* athletes (those who were on the coaches' lists submitted to admissions offices) from both other varsity athletes ("walk-ons") and all other classmates (called "students at large").

One key fact is that intercollegiate athletics programs have a far greater impact on the composition of the entering class (and perhaps on the campus ethos) at an Ivy League university or a small liberal arts college than at most Division IA universities. Whereas Ohio State or the University of Michigan can field awesome teams with only a tiny percentage of their students, a small liberal arts college or a university with a modest-sized undergraduate college

---

[1] It will not be lost on you that Princeton is one such school, but this talk is not about Princeton. Please do not blame President Tilghman for anything I say tonight—or at any other time, for that matter. One president at a time is enough—maybe more than enough!

Ivy League Universities	New England Small College Athletic
Brown University	Conference (NESCAC) Colleges
Columbia University	Amherst College
Cornell University	Bates College
Dartmouth College	Bowdoin College
Harvard University	Colby College
Princeton University	Connecticut College
University of Pennsylvania	Hamilton College
Yale University	Middlebury College
	Trinity College
	Tufts University
University Athletic Association	Wesleyan University
(UAA) Universities	Williams College
Carnegie Mellon University	
Emory University	
University of Chicago	Other Coed Liberal Arts Colleges
Washington University in St. Louis	Carleton College
	Denison University
	Kenyon College
Women's Colleges	Macalester College
Bryn Mawr College	Oberlin College
Smith College	Pomona College
Wellesley College	Swarthmore College

Figure 1. Institutions Included in the Study. Source: Modified from William G. Bowen and Sarah A. Levin, *Reclaiming the Game: College Sports and Educational Values* (Princeton University Press, 2003), p. 4.

cannot (Figure 2). College athletes can easily comprise anywhere from 25 to 40 percent of the class at a liberal arts college and 20 to 30 percent at an Ivy League university—as compared with under 5 percent at a school such as the University of Michigan. And such very different percentages really make a difference.

True, many big-time programs suffer from commercialization, cheating, and other vices that are largely absent at the schools in our study. But there are other issues. Our research shows that, as a group, recruited athletes in the Ivies and in a number of the country's most outstanding liberal arts colleges differ more and more from their fellow students: they enter with weaker credentials and tend to underperform academically; increasingly, they are seen on campuses as a group apart from their classmates. One irony is that

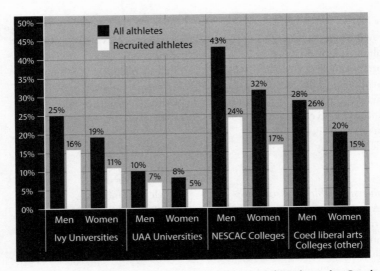

Figure 2. Athletes and Recruited Athletes as a Percent of Students, by Gender and Conference, 1995 Entering Cohort. Source: Expanded College and Beyond Database, modified from William G. Bowen and Sarah A. Levin, *Reclaiming the Game: College Sports and Educational Values* (Princeton University Press, 2003), figs. 1.2 and 4.1.

the far more visible problems of many big-time programs engender a false sense of comparative well-being, and therefore complacency, on many of the campuses on which we are focusing. The "success-by-invidious-comparison" syndrome ("We can't be so bad; just look at what is going on over there") invites a numbing complacency. The issues are different, yes. But they are as consequential at these schools as at the big-time programs—they are central to what these places are all about.

Two final preliminaries.

First, I cannot emphasize strongly enough that we are talking about *policies, not about people*. Students who excel in sports have done absolutely nothing wrong, and they certainly do not deserve to be "demonized" for having followed the signals given to them by coaches, their parents, admissions officers, alumni of their institutions, and admiring fans. Our quarrel is with policies, priorities, and the resulting "system"—not with those caught up in it.

Second, a major purpose of our research has been to "find the facts," and the conclusions we present are heavily data driven. Anyone seeking to find an orderly path through the myths and nostalgia endemic to college sports will recognize the desperate need to move beyond "the anecdote range" and ground conclusions on a solid base of empirical evidence. It is comforting that all major findings from our research easily pass any normal test of statistical significance. Indeed, it is rare to find a set of empirical results as relentlessly consistent. To be sure, what we report are averages, and some individuals will, of course, do far better than the norm for their group—just as others will do worse. As for those who doubt the validity of any statistics, we refer them to Damon Runyon, who once observed: "*It may be that the race is not always to the swift, nor the battle to the strong—but that is the way to bet.*"

II. PRINCIPAL FINDINGS

Those of you with an appetite for detail (who would like to know, for example, whether the academic outcomes for female soccer players in the Ivy League differ, and by how much, from those for female soccer players in the NESCAC [New England Small College Athletic Conference] colleges, or from those for male soccer or football players) will want to peruse the myriad figures, tables, and regression equations presented in *Reclaiming the Game*; you will find, I think, many interesting tidbits. My plan tonight is to give you the briefest of tours through the findings—a kind of (ESPN) *SportsCenter* highlights film, if you will—before commenting on why I believe all of this matters and what might actually be done, at a practical level, to make things better.

Recruitment and Admissions: The Advantage Enjoyed by Recruited Athletes

Over the last several decades, the amount of time spent on recruiting by coaches has increased dramatically. As Richard Rasmussen (Executive Director of the University Athletic Association) puts it: "Recruiting has become every coach's second and third sport." In building a class, there is no counterpart to the time and other re-sources devoted to recruiting athletes.

Having made such an effort to identify top prospects and to encourage them to apply, coaches naturally expect that admissions offices will pay special attention to the names on the lists that they submit, and especially to the names high on the list. We can see how much difference being on the list makes by looking at Figures 3a and 3b (for male and female athletes in the Ivy League and in NESCAC), which show the differences in the odds of admission, at the same SAT levels, for recruited athletes and all other applicants.

As one would expect, acceptance rates rise with SAT scores for all groups of students. *Note, however, the substantial gap at each SAT level between the acceptance rates for the recruited athletes and for all other students.* For example, in the 1200 to 1299 SAT range in the Ivies, the probability of being admitted for a male athlete on a coach's list was about 50 percent, as compared with a probability of about 10 percent for all other male applicants. The corresponding probabilities of admission for recruited female ath-letes and for all other female candidates were just over 60 percent and roughly 10 percent. Similar (but slightly smaller) gaps are present at the NESCAC colleges. Looking across all SAT ranges, the typical male recruit in the Ivies had *more than four times as good a chance of being admitted as did the comparable male appli-cant not on a coach's list.* The odds of admission for the typical female recruit on a coach's list were more favorable yet.

To anticipate one frequently asked question, the admissions ad-vantage for recruited athletes is far greater than the admissions advantage enjoyed by legacies in every group of schools we stud-ied. In the Ivies, it is also much greater for recruited athletes than for underrepresented minorities; in NESCAC and the other liberal arts colleges, the advantages for recruited athletes and minorities are roughly comparable. A related question is how recruitment of athletes affects racial diversity on campuses. The short answer is that, on these campuses, recruited athletes are slightly *less* likely than students in general to come from minority groups.[2]

---

[2] To anticipate another question, the admissions advantages for recruited athletes are affected by Early Decision programs. The existence of Early Decision programs is, however,

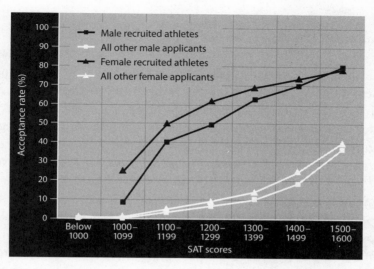

Figure 3a. Acceptance Rates of Recruited Athletes and All Other Applicants, by Gender and SAT Group, 1999 Applicant Pool, Ivy League Universities. Source: Expanded College and Beyond Database, as rendered in William G. Bowen and Sarah A. Levin, *Reclaiming the Game: College Sports and Educational Values* (Princeton University Press, 2003), fig. 3.2a.

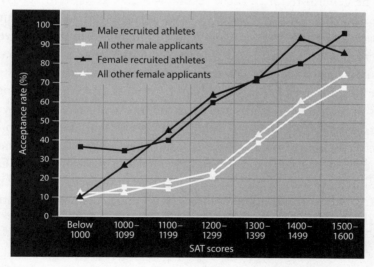

Figure 3b. Acceptance Rates of Recruited Athletes and All Other Applicants, by Gender and SAT Group, 1999 Applicant Pool, NESCAC Colleges. Source: Expanded College and Beyond Database, as rendered in William G. Bowen and Sarah A. Levin, *Reclaiming the Game: College Sports and Educational Values* (Princeton University Press, 2003), fig. 3.2b.

Academic Outcomes: Bunching in the Bottom Third of the Class

On average, recruited athletes earn much lower grades than do other students. Nor is the lower average rank-in-class the product of just a few students doing very poorly. To avoid burying you under rank-in-class distributions, let me show you just one figure (Figure 4). We see that *four out of five of the recruited high-profile athletes in the Ivies (defined as those who played football, basketball, or ice hockey), and nearly three out of four of those in the NESCAC colleges, were in the bottom third of the class.* The corresponding figures for the recruited male lower-profile athletes (those playing all other sports) are only slightly less disappointing: about two-thirds of those in the Ivies were in the bottom third of the class, as were over half of those in the NESCAC colleges. Substantial numbers of the recruited women athletes in the Ivy League also ended up in the bottom third of the class (45 percent), as compared with only a quarter of the female students at large.[3]

The general tenor of these results is highly consistent across individual schools in both the Ivy League and NESCAC. It is human nature to believe that a widely perceived problem applies everywhere but "at home," and this tendency to "look away" is compounded by the fact that internal, one-campus studies often lump together different groups of athletes (recruits and walk-ons, members of high-profile teams and those who row or sail). In any event, if progress is to be made in thinking through what are shared problems, it is important to move beyond the "everywhere but here" mindset. A memorable moment occurred at a meeting of NESCAC presidents to which Sarah Levin and I were invited. After we presented data for individual colleges (with codes disguising the identities of particular schools), one president observed wryly: "The picture is very clear. *There are no outliers—only liars!"*[4]

---

by no means a full explanation for the admissions advantage enjoyed by recruited athletes. Recruited athletes have higher probabilities of admission in *both* the Early Decision round and the "regular" round.

[3] Women students as a group earn higher grades than men students, which is why well under 33 percent of female students at large are in the bottom third of the class.

[4] There is, however, one "conference" outlier. Athletes in the University Athletic Association or UAA (consisting of Brandeis University, Case Western Reserve University, Carnegie

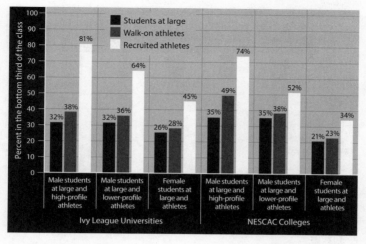

Figure 4. Percent of Athletes and Students at Large in the Bottom Third of the Class, by Recruit Status and Gender, 1995 Entering Cohort, Ivy League Universities and NESCAC Colleges. Source: Expanded College and Beyond Database, as rendered in William G. Bowen and Sarah A. Levin, *Reclaiming the Game: College Sports and Educational Values* (Princeton University Press, 2003), fig. 5.4a.

Academic Underperformance

As a result of the admissions advantage that they enjoy, many recruited athletes enter school with weaker credentials than most other students. But this is by no means the only reason that they earn relatively low grades and seldom graduate with honors (an even more telling measure, in my view). Recruited athletes also *underperform academically*—that is, as a group, they earn markedly lower grades than they would be expected to earn in light of their test scores and high school grades. The amount of underperformance is substantial and highly significant statistically. In the men's high-profile sports, it is roughly 20 percentile points in both NESCAC and the Ivies (that is, a recruited football, basketball, or ice hockey athlete predicted on the basis of his SATs and other attributes to end up in the 45th percentile actually ends up in the

Mellon University, Emory University, New York University, Washington University, the University of Chicago, and the University of Rochester) earn essentially the same grades as all other students—with football players being a partial exception to this finding.

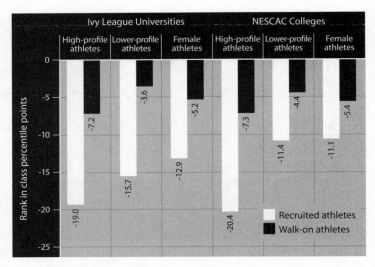

Figure 5. Underperformance of Athletes, by Type of Sport and Recruit Status, Controlling for Differences in Race, Field of Study, SAT Scores, and Institutional SAT, 1995 Entering Cohort, NESCAC Colleges. Source: Expanded College and Beyond Database, modified from William G. Bowen and Sarah A. Levin, *Reclaiming the Game: College Sports and Educational Values* (Princeton University Press, 2003), figs. 6.1a and 6.1b.

25th percentile), and underperformance is also present in men's lower-profile sports and women's sports (Figure 5).

Contrary to what some have suspected, it is not found only among those with the lowest SAT scores; in fact, recruited athletes in the broad middle range of the SAT distribution are at least as likely to underperform as recruited athletes with the weakest incoming credentials. There are sport-by-sport differences (some of them surprising), but the overall pattern is quite consistent.

What is causing this pervasive phenomenon? We believe that persistent underperformance is related primarily to the criteria used in recruiting and admitting athletes—to "selection"—and *not* mainly to "treatment" (the intensity and nature of the athletic experience), differences in race or socio-economic status, or field of study. Time commitments and involvement in an athletic culture are relevant, but they appear to be far less important than selection. Some evidence:

- Highly significant degrees of underperformance persist among *recruited* athletes even when these athletes are *not* playing on intercollegiate teams; clearly, the time demands of the sports cannot account for this result.

- A parallel finding is that *walk-ons* show much less underperformance than recruited athletes even when they *are* playing during a particular year.

Thus, the main story line appears to us to be "selection, selection, selection." We believe that *the interests and priorities of the typical recruited athlete are the key factors in explaining underperformance.* It is hardly counter-intuitive to suggest that, as one president put it, underperformance depends on the extent to which "athletics is the focus of a student's life." Coaches naturally look for candidates who are fully committed to the sport, to the team, and to the coach. It would be useful to think of hypotheses that would permit further tests of this line of reasoning; to date, we have been unable to identify any evidence that refutes it.

Bunching of Majors, Living Together, Disciplinary Issues

Not surprisingly, many recruited athletes also tend to separate themselves from their classmates in ways other than academic performance. They often major in the same fields (especially in the social sciences), take many of the same courses, live together, and spend large amounts of time together apart from practice and competition—in general, they form a "tighter circle" than students interested in activities such as the performing arts and student publications (who do not, in any case, underperform academically). These cultural patterns have an effect on academic performance and the academic ethos of the college, but they also have other effects. For example, disciplinary problems are somewhat more common among athletes, especially men playing the high-profile sports.

Has It Always Been This Way? Some Recent History

The situation was very different in "earlier days." In the Ivies, the typical male athlete in the 1951 entering cohorts had a cumulative grade point average that placed him precisely in the middle of his class; in the coed liberal arts colleges, the typical male athlete actually ranked slightly higher than the average male student at large. There was no concentration of athletes in the social sciences (in the Ivies, for instance, 21 percent of the athletes and 22 percent of the students at large majored in these fields). Athletes in the 1950s were as likely as other students—perhaps more likely—to be campus leaders, not just team captains, and many of these former athletes went on to become prominent in their professions and key trustees of many of these schools. Their own positive experiences as athletes *and as students* on these campuses in earlier days can sometimes make it difficult for those with success stories from yesteryear to realize how much has changed. This is an absolutely key point to understand in discussing the achievements of former athletes, such as (in Princeton's case) George Shultz, Don Rumsfeld, Bill Bradley, and Jim Leach. They attended Princeton in earlier days. Their counterparts today are very different, and there are reasons for doubting that today's linebacker will mimic the after-college performance of his predecessors.[5]

By the late 1970s, the picture had changed markedly. In the high-profile sports, in particular, gaps in academic performance were evident, and athletes were appreciably more concentrated than other students in certain fields of study. Gaps in academic performance were also found among male athletes playing the lower-profile sports. On the other hand, women athletes were indistinguishable from women students at large in their academic performance; in this important respect they resembled the male athletes of the 1950s. By the late 1980s and early 1990s, the women athletes were "catching up" with the men, and the athletic divide was more pronounced for both genders. Whereas women in the '76 entering cohort had done as well academically as other women, women athletes in the '89 cohort, in the Ivies in particular, now fell short of the standard set by their female classmates. Still more recently, as

[5] It is, of course, impossible to know, because current undergraduates still have their after-college lives to live. However, we do know that current athletes are very different from their predecessors in both their academic performance and their involvement in the overall life of their schools. We also know that class rank correlates with subsequent earnings (to cite just that one outcome measure). It can also be argued that analytical or intellectual capacities are becoming more and more important in vocations of many kinds.

we have seen, the academic outcomes for recruited athletes in the '95 entering cohort have departed substantially from school-wide norms. Women athletes from the '95 entering cohort in both the coed liberal arts colleges and the women's colleges now show—for the first time—the beginning symptoms of underperformance that initially appeared only among Ivy League women athletes in the '89 cohort.

The "drift" seems abundantly clear, and it is probably less important to try to date precisely when the divide started to open up (especially since the answer is sure to differ by type of sport, by gender, and by conference) than it is to recognize the unmistakable direction of movement. Because of strong forces within athletics (greater specialization of players and coaches, and general increases in the intensity of competition) and within higher education more generally (increases in academic standards and more emphasis on independent work, for example), the divide has continued to widen from both sides. There is not a single indicator pointing in the reverse direction. The driving forces are not random, do not represent passing shocks, and cannot be wished away. *These forces should be expected to continue to distance the academic side of colleges and universities from the athletic side in which the professionalized model of intercollegiate athletics has become so ingrained.*

III. THE GROWING "COSTS" OF THE ACADEMIC-ATHLETIC DIVIDE: WHAT ARE THEY?

First, at most of the schools we studied, admission of large numbers of recruited athletes entails substantial "opportunity costs." Highly talented students, eager to take full advantage of the educational opportunities a particular college has to offer, are turned away because places have been claimed by recruited athletes who bring with them to college values and attitudes that make them less likely to do well academically—to place a high enough premium on exploiting the educational opportunities of the institution to excel. Underperformance is a serious problem precisely because it suggests that scarce places are going to students whose priorities take them in another direction—who appear to lack the zeal (or commitment) to exploit aggressively the educational opportunities that the institution offers. There is nothing more dispiriting to a faculty member than encountering a student, perhaps a student of high potential, who is inclined to "just get by." Our goal should be to enroll students who will take a passable B+ paper and rework it ... and then rework it some more—who will, in the words of Arthur Lewis, "go from the easy part to the hard part." Nor is it just appetite for demanding academic work that matters. Students should be open to participating in a wide array of activities, to give time to "service" projects, and to meet and get to know well a wide range of fellow students. They should not have a narrow focus on pursuits at some distance from the educational core of the institution— what Woodrow Wilson called "the main tent."

Underperformance can also have serious spillover effects. According to the Ad Hoc Committee Report on athletics at Williams: "When some groups of students habitually underperform, and especially when they are blunt about their own (different) priorities, the combination of their attitudes and their performance can affect the campus ethos. Faculty in economics and history are concerned about 'evidence of anti-intellectualism, of clear disengagement and even outright disdain, on the part of varsity athletes.' "

Heavy reliance on recruited athletes to field teams imposes another kind of opportunity cost on the school: there is relatively little opportunity—less every year, it would seem—for non-recruited students (walk-ons) to play varsity sports. Coaches often form their teams, on paper at least, before the school year even starts. It seems more than mildly ironic that opportunities to play varsity sports—often paid for in substantial measure by tuition payments made by all students—are, in the words of a Middlebury faculty committee that studied that college's athletic program, "the exclusive privilege of those pre-selected by coaches through the recruiting process." Moreover, it may often be the "less fully trained walk-on" who stands to benefit the most from the real educational benefits that competitive sports provide.

College sports, once heralded as a means of unifying the campus and building school spirit, have become much less consequential in this regard as athletes and other students have come to see less and less of each other, and as attendance by students at large at athletic events has declined (in part because these students are less likely to feel a bond with recruited athletes than students of other generations did with their classmates who were star performers on and off the field). The faculty report on athletics at Williams includes this telling sentence: "The claim that athletics unifies the student body collides with evidence that varsity athletics is resented by many of our top students." This kind of cost is difficult to quantify, but it cannot be ignored.

In addition, there are real issues of institutional integrity and truth-telling. Regrettably, there are numerous examples of differences between what schools say about their athletic programs and what really goes on. For example, videos and other pronouncements about the openness of intercollegiate athletic programs to all comers are contradicted by the heavy preference given to recruited athletes when rosters are built. Even among recruited athletes, one regularly hears complaints about coaches who promise a starting position and more playing time to secure the athlete's commitment. Also, claims that athletes, as a group, do just as well academically as other groups of students are usually untrue. More generally, it is discouraging to see the disconnect that exists today between stated principles (for example, the assertion by both the Ivies and NESCAC that athletes will be "representative" of their classes) and present-day realities. It is all too easy to remain in a state of "deep denial." Truth-telling is important, especially for institutions that pride themselves, as colleges and universities should, on standing for the highest level of integrity. One college president put it this way: "We need to change either what we do or what we say."

Looking beyond the campus, we should not underestimate the "signaling effects" of current practices (especially giving substantial admissions advantages to recruited athletes) on secondary schools, prospective students, and their families.

Dollar costs (and fundraising commitments) also need to be taken into account. Today's intercollegiate athletic programs, even at the Division III level, involve substantial financial outlays, especially when we consider the capital costs of facilities alongside rising personnel costs and operating expenses. Colleges face difficult choices among competing priorities, and it is hard to ignore the question of how many scarce resources should be spent on teams that are heavily populated by recruited athletes, especially at a time when financial constraints have become more pressing than they were in the 1990s.

Finally, there is a real risk that failing to reverse the directions now so evident will undermine the enduring values of intercollegiate sports on campuses where athletics is meant to be an integral part of the educational program. From our perspective, the challenge is to re-integrate college sports more fully into the overall life of the college, not to allow athletics to exist in its own space. A well-conceived athletic program offers tremendous benefits. "Games" are, first and foremost, a source of pleasure and satisfaction, and an important way of introducing some balance into a student's life. Competing on intercollegiate teams can be an important learning experience. Countless athletes have testified that one learns "life lessons": teamwork, discipline, resilience, perseverance, how to "play by the rules" and accept outcomes one may not like. As Bart Giamatti, former president of Yale, once put it: "Athletics teaches lessons valuable to the individual by stretching the human spirit in ways that nothing else can."

But realizing these benefits does not require the kinds of "near-professionalized" athletic programs that have evolved over the past three or four decades. The most compelling arguments for college sports are undercut, not strengthened, by fielding teams that are cut off from much of campus life and in significant ways are at odds with the primary educational missions of these institutions. The most basic lessons that sports teach can be learned without compromising academic values.

IV. A REFORM AGENDA FOR DIVISION III COLLEGES

In thinking about how to "reclaim the game," we start with certain basic assumptions.[6]

---

[6] We have chosen to focus our reform efforts at the Division III level rather than at the Division I-AA level (to which the Ivies belong). The main reason is that we think the odds of success, hard to predict in any context, are higher if we work with a set of interested

First, to achieve real reform it is going to be necessary to work simultaneously at both the local (the individual institution/conference) and the national level. Some people ask why it is not sufficient to work only at the level of the individual conference since the conference is generally free to adopt more restrictive practices than the NCAA [National College Athletic Association] prescribes. The rejoinder is that athletic programs are linked in ways that transcend conference borders. Not only do schools need to find "suitable opponents" outside their conferences as well as within them, but they also compete across conference borders in recruiting athletes and coaches. Both the availability of suitable opponents and the ability to compete on even terms for athletes and coaches depend on the willingness of a reasonably large number of schools to follow the same set of rules. In short, the individual conference is not "big enough" to establish the tighter common boundaries that many of us believe are needed.

Second, a "holistic" approach to reform that deals simultaneously with all aspects of the modern-day athletic enterprise is absolutely essential. It is tempting to concentrate one's energies on a particular issue (such as season length or activities permitted in the non-traditional season), but experience indicates that just "tweaking" the system will not accomplish much. The pieces of this complex puzzle are closely connected—with, for example, the emphasis placed on recruiting tied to the aspirations of coaches, with both of these linked to the practices of competitors and to assumptions about success at the national level, and with all of the above tied tightly to admissions policies and the willingness (or not) to accept significant academic underperformance by recruited athletes. It is essential to have clearly in mind a broad framework that is derived from a consistent philosophy of athletics and rooted in core educational values.

Third, it will have to be understood that if athletic programs are to be aligned more closely with educational values (and, for

---

colleges in Division III, where the stated principles of the division are reasonable ones, than if we try to address the issues faced by the Ivies, which are compounded by Division I-AA policies and regulations. Still, much of what is written here applies in one degree or another to the Ivies and to members of the Patriot League, as well as to NESCAC members and the other schools in Division III.

example, athletes are to be truly representative of their student bodies), schools are going to have to accept reductions in skill levels. More "regular students" would earn places on varsity squads. There would be fewer recruited athletes focused primarily on their teams. There would be less "raw (athletic) talent" in a class, and any set of colleges or universities serious about adopting reform measures of the kinds proposed here would have to accept this reality. But intercollegiate athletics need not be any less competitive. Players would be expected to play just as hard as they do now, and to play to win. Varsity teams would continue to be composed of highly accomplished athletes, even though they would usually weigh less, not run quite as fast, and have less powerful serves. At the same time, the athletes on these teams would yield nothing to the more talented athletes recruited by big-time programs in their zeal, drive, energy level, discipline, or understanding of the game or of the lessons to be learned through competing: indeed, they might actually value good sportsmanship more highly.[7]

Fourth, it may be necessary to seek a new grouping of schools within Division III (and, conceivably, within Division I at a later date). At present, a determined effort is being made by the Division III Presidents' Council of the NCAA to alter certain principles and practices, including season length, number of contests, permitted activities in the non-traditional season, eligibility requirements, and the monitoring of student aid practices.[8] We see these proposals as an important first step in achieving a comprehensive set of reforms, and we certainly hope that they will pass at the January 2004 convention. There is, however, much more that needs to be accomplished. In particular, serious attention also has to be paid

[7] As one college president puts it: "Within broad limits, the quality of an athletic contest, whether viewed from the standpoint of the participants or the spectators, is largely independent of the absolute quality of the athletes, and depends much more centrally on how well the competitors are matched. (A dramatic illustration of this point is the fact that millions of fans are drawn to big-time college football and basketball contests, when it is obvious that even the best college team would be decimated by the worst team in the NFL or the NBA.) The striking fact is that there are almost no net benefits to colleges as a group from improving the absolute quality of the athletes on their teams, while the costs of such improvements are becoming increasingly apparent."

[8] See the "Reform Package" recommended by the Division III Management Council of the NCAA (press release, July 25, 2003).

to recruitment/admissions policies, coaching philosophies, and the close monitoring of academic outcomes. If Division III as a whole were prepared to embrace the fuller and more comprehensive set of principles outlined below, that would be a splendid outcome. But Division III encompasses over four hundred institutions that have very different missions and face very different circumstances. It seems unlikely that a "one-size-fits-all" approach is going to work when the underlying institutional population is so diverse.

Given this reality, and taking account of past experience in seeking to achieve even modest changes in a limited number of areas, we think it is highly desirable to define an overall set of principles and practices that might appeal to some number of Division III institutions (and perhaps to some schools now in Division I-AA), if not to Division III as a whole. Ideally, the desire to draw "tighter common boundaries," defined by this set of principles, can be accomplished within the present NCAA structure.

In effort to be more specific, let me now offer a highly provisional outline of certain core principles that we have in mind.

1. *Athletes should be truly representative of the student bodies of their institutions.*

We propose that all schools that wish to operate within a new set of common boundaries commit themselves to the broad principle of "representativeness." Recruited athletes should not enjoy a substantial "admissions advantage" over other applicants. Less emphasis should be placed on rankings of candidates by coaches, and the admissions office should be expected to admit those students, including students recommended by coaches, thought to be qualified *and motivated* to take full advantage of the educational offerings of the college—and not just to be "over threshold" in terms of formal qualifications.[9]

"Representativeness" should not be thought of, however, mainly in terms of entering credentials (SATs, high school grades).

---

[9] In a 1966 faculty report on admission policy, Yale economist James Tobin wrote: "One principle is clear. Extracurricular activity of candidates for admission is important only as it tells us something about their qualities of mind and character. We should *not* count extracurricular activity in a candidate's favor simply because it foreshadows success in similar

Academic *outcomes* are even more important, and enrolled athletes should be expected to perform at roughly the same level as the student body in general. This implies a determined effort to avoid systematic underperformance, with both admissions offices and athletic departments holding themselves accountable for underperformance and expecting to be measured in this regard. Other aspects of "representativeness" include enrolling athletes with a broad range of academic interests and a broad range of other interests, including interests outside athletics. In my view, a commitment to "representativeness," measured by outcomes and carefully monitored, is more important than anything else.

2. *Opportunities to participate in intercollegiate athletics should be expanded for both men and women, and should not be limited to recruited athletes.*

Sincere efforts, including well-advertised open tryouts, should be made by athletic departments to encourage participation by non-recruited students who want to play varsity sports.

3. *The extent and intensity of the athletic program should be regulated so as to make it possible for athletes to participate in a wide range of activities and to be full participants in campus life.*

Season length should be shortened, and caps should be placed on the number of contests in a season. No required athletic activities, including "captain's practices," should take place outside the traditional season. Students interested in competing in more than one sport should be encouraged to do so and should not be limited by out-of-season conditioning expectations.

4. *Coaches and athletic directors should be integrated more fully into the educational life of their institutions.*

A key criterion in the hiring of coaches and athletic administrators should be their understanding of, and commitment to, the primacy of the educational mission of the institution. Once on campus, athletic personnel should be encouraged to involve them-

---

extracurricular activity at Yale. The central business of the university is the mutual pursuit of knowledge by students and teachers. It is not to produce newspapers, singing groups, or athletic teams.... [Evidence of character can be provided] just as well by those light in weight and short in stature as by the physically well-endowed, ... just as well by those whose Yale athletics will be only [intramural] competition as by those who will play in the Bowl."

selves in campus activities beyond their sports, with the explicit understanding that less time would be devoted to recruiting. Schools operating within the new set of "common boundaries" should coordinate workshops and develop a range of ideas and programs that would facilitate this effort to take fuller advantage of what coaches and athletic staff members can contribute to all aspects of campus life. Evaluation procedures should be established that would take account of the full range of a coach's contributions; participants in this evaluation process should include faculty and other individuals outside the athletic department.

5. *National or regional championship competitions should be organized for the schools operating within the new common boundaries but should not be the focal point of a season.*

Only schools committed to the principles outlined here (which define the new common boundaries) would be eligible to participate in these regional and/or national championships. Providing a new outlet for the natural desire to be able to compete for recognition beyond the conference is important; at the same time, it is equally important to eliminate the incentive to recruit students, and organize programs, so that schools can compete against other institutions with different philosophies, objectives, and program definitions. Participation in national championships, in particular, should be viewed as a "rare experience," and should not be the norm. This implies that there would be tight controls on the number of spots in any such championships. Post-season championships should fit within reasonable scheduling constraints, to minimize conflicts with examinations and to avoid extending seasons unduly.

6. *Conference alignments should be made more flexible, with suitable opponents determined on a sport-by-sport basis.*

One goal in choosing regular opponents should be finding institutions with which a school can compete on a reasonable basis, year in and year out. (In the nice phraseology of Rasmussen: "When the ball goes up, the pitch is thrown, the whistle blows, or the gun sounds, the outcome should be in doubt.") Schedules should never result in perennial losers and winners—if this were to prove to be the case, orbits of competition should be realigned.

Some sports may require different conference alignments than others (with football being a prime example), and flexibility in this regard should be encouraged.

V. CAN (WILL) ANY OF THIS HAPPEN?

The history of reform efforts is anything but encouraging. The barriers to any thorough-going reform are formidable. They include inertia; the natural (entirely understandable) resistance to change by players, coaches, and athletic directors committed to the status quo; pressure applied by vocal advocates among alumni/ae and trustees who are in favor of placing still more emphasis on recruiting and competing nationally; and the reluctance of individual schools and their presidents to "go it alone." Presidential survival is an objective with which I can identify!

Still, preliminary conversations with a number of presidents lead us to believe that the time may be right to make a renewed effort to change directions. The willingness to pursue new options is fueled by discomfort with both the rising costs of the academic-athletic divide—which include the rationing of access to *athletic* as well as academic opportunities—and the truth-telling dilemmas that are more and more evident. Recent actions taken within the Ivies and within NESCAC are encouraging. There is more and more recognition that the "divide" is widening and that postponing action will only make the underlying tensions ever harder to address. The present state of affairs is not likely to be sustainable.

In sum, college sports need to be restored to their rightful place in campus life. More regularly chosen students, who have come to highly selective colleges for the right educational reasons, should have the opportunity to play competitively—to learn the lessons that sports can teach, and to have fun in the process.

WHY YOU CAME

~

William G. Bowen
October 13, 2005

REMARKS AT DEDICATION OF COLLEGE CENTRE,
CENTRE COLLEGE

I am delighted to have been asked to participate in the dedication of this splendid new College Centre, which is really a pairing, and, if I may say, an inspired pairing, of two buildings—one the central academic facility of the college and one that is home to fitness, recreation, and indoor athletic programs. I speak of this pairing as "inspired" because of my strong belief that there is truth in extolling the virtues of "a sound mind in a sound body" (cliché-ridden as the phrase has become). Too much of college life, for too many students at too many places, has become one-dimensional, with, as it were, the stereotypical nerds in one corner and the muscle-bound athletes in another. Centre College clearly stands against tendencies rampant in the land to create, or at least accept, an "academic/athletic divide."

In these remarks, I want to return to the subject of the role of sports on campuses, and I also want to talk about the importance of a commitment to social mobility and the challenges of scale facing a small college like this one in today's world. Then, at the end, I will explain the title I have given this talk: "Why You Came." But before turning to any of these topics, I want to comment briefly on

Editor's note: At the invitation of President John A. Roush, Bill was asked to speak at Centre College at a new state-of-the-art academic and athletic complex. He was also awarded an honorary degree.

some impressions of Centre College that I have gained from reading about it. Three themes, in particular, have real appeal to me.

- First, I like very much the commitment to "guided growth of the individual student." This phrase captures both an emphasis on the individual and the college's obligation to provide guidance, and not simply to assume that each soul will find his or her own star without help.
- Second, I applaud the emphasis on residential life and the value of ideas exchanged and lessons learned in the late-night bull session as well as in the classroom. I still remember the formulation of a former woman student at Princeton, Michele Warman, who recalled with fondness "the evening rap sessions that begin promisingly enough with high flown debates on free will and determinism and descend by dawn to the inevitable indictment of the frailties of the human male." One of the most valuable aspects of my own undergraduate education at Denison was the friendship I formed more than fifty years ago with a classmate, David Bayley, who also became an academic and who continues to this day to be one of my closest friends. We shared an apartment while serving as head residents of a dorm. As you can imagine, we had many memorable experiences. Just last year, my wife and I had the pleasure of establishing a Faculty Fellowship at Denison in honor of my friend, and as a tribute to the lasting friendships that can be formed at residential colleges such as Denison and Centre.
- Third, I admire the evident determination of Centre to avoid complacency. I was struck by the insight of David Grissom, the chair of your board of trustees, in his foreword to one of the college's publications: "Like many others, I have great memories from my student days at Centre College. But we must never allow our memories—wonderful as they are—to be greater than our dreams for Centre's future." No educational institution of consequence can stand still, and it is true, as someone once said, that "nothing wilts faster than a laurel rested upon."

Let me now return to the subject of college sports and related fitness and wellness programs. There is absolutely no question about the value of these activities. There are clear health benefits, of course, which society at large understands more and more clearly. Moreover, games are just plain fun and a way of introducing some balance into a student's life. In college I was a highly competitive tennis player, and I used to say, with only a hint of tongue in cheek, that for me competing was a more or less harmless outlet for aggression. Playing sports can also confer "life lessons": teamwork, discipline, resilience, perseverance, and learning how to "play by the rules" and accept outcomes one may not like. But it is also possible to learn from sports, as from other activities, wrong lessons: a "win-at-all-costs" attitude, lack of respect for one's opponents (or even one's teammates), and an arrogance that can lead to abusive and insufferable behavior. I resist giving examples. The newspapers are full of them. Fortunately, there are also "good" stories. At this year's US Open, the two men who played the longest singles match, a five-setter that lasted nearly four and a half hours, managed right to the end to exchange wan smiles. As another professional tennis player, Kim Clijsters, said recently: "You don't have to hate your opponent to play hard."

Especially at the college level, so much depends on getting program objectives right, doing everything possible to inculcate the right motivations in students, and having coaches and teachers who provide outstanding leadership. In my tennis-playing days at Denison, I was fortunate to have as my coach an outstanding professor of folklore who is another life-long friend. How much I learned from him—both when we won, which, fortunately, we did much of the time, and when we fared less well. How to think about winning is a perennial source of debate. Of course, competitors should always want to win, and should play hard to win. I know I always did. But we should guard against overemphasizing winning records and over-professionalizing in college what must remain a game. I was amused when an irate Princeton alumnus, angered by some blunder or other on the football field, was heard to yell: "They're playing like amateurs!" That would be simply a funny remark, if it had been so intended. But of course the alumnus was not at all trying to amuse, and his remark says more than he meant it to say about the attitudes of many of us toward college sports.

In big-time programs, the premium associated with winning has become so great that it skews the entire nature of the athletic enterprise. The sad reality is that some of the same assumptions and attitudes have percolated down to the Ivy League and some Division III programs. I am persuaded that the right mantra is one articulated by Richard Rasmussen of the University of Rochester: "When the ball goes up, the pitch is thrown, the whistle blows, or the gun sounds, the outcome should be in doubt." It has even been argued that there are virtues associated with losing. During one stretch at Princeton, the football team lost to Yale sixteen times in a row. After one such depressing Saturday afternoon, a colleague of mine who was a minister said: "You know, Bill, Princeton does so many things well that these losses to Yale are really valuable—they give us a healthy dose of humility." I fear I was not entirely persuaded. But life did go on, and we did our best to resist reacting to disappointing won-lost records in inappropriate ways.

The first book that some of us at the foundation published on college sports (called *The Game of Life*) elicited strong responses from alumni passionate about sports—and about winning. A trustee of one college argued that we just didn't get it. "Let's be honest," he said, "Winning is what this is all about. These kids get to learn about winning, and once they get out of school, that's what the whole thing is about, isn't it?" At one level, this view reflects what those of us who love sports love about them—their clarity and simplicity. Fair is fair and foul is foul. The game ends and there is a winner. But my co-author (James Shulman) and I believe that this single-minded focus on winning is fundamentally at odds with the educational values of a liberal arts education. Complexity is an integral part of such an education. Providing definite answers—who won and who lost—is not what the liberal arts do very well, or indeed, what they aim for. What is *Hamlet* really all about? The liberal arts are about teaching complexity rather than reductionism, telling us not simply to accept at face value the Whig view of history, the half-proven hypothesis, or even the teaching of our parents. If one really comes to believe that "winning is everything," then the message of a liberal arts education—appreciation of complexity, rigorous questioning of what seems obvious, and the impulse to learn how to play an active and thoughtful role in a complicated world—may be seen as either empty rhetoric or muddled ramblings.

One aspect of today's college sports scene—at some Division III schools as well as in Division I, I am sorry to say—is that athletic recruiting has gone to such lengths that there is no longer any real opportunity for "walk-ons" to play. Coaches often know before seasons begin who will play what position, and those not on the coach's list are sometimes told, rudely, that they should just stay out of the way. One consequence of this over-zealous recruiting is that recruited athletes are often so focused on their sport that they lose track of what should be first priorities at an educational institution; they then end up underperforming academically (doing less well academically than we would expect them to do on the basis of their incoming credentials). One of the goals of the Mellon Foundation's College Sports Project, in which Centre participates, is to find ways of ensuring that teams are made up of regular students who will be representative of their classmates, as they often are not today, and who will perform academically at the same level as their fellow students. Another objective is to re-integrate athletics into campus life. President Roush has been a real leader among college presidents in the effort to "reclaim the game," and we are grateful to him. Until some of these problems get fixed, college sports will continue to send wrong signals to the world at large, and especially to high school students and their parents who may conclude that, as one young person put it: "If I want to go to college, I should work on my running, not on my chemistry."

Let me make one other comment that relates more directly to the fitness and wellness programs that exist within the College Centre. Having the courage to spend money on such activities, as well as on club sports, is enormously important. A terribly disturbing finding of *The Game of Life* is that, at many colleges as well as universities, spending on intercollegiate athletics dominates spending on these less highly publicized pursuits to an embarrassing degree. Centre is leading the way in getting its priorities straight.

Giving every student who is so inclined the opportunity to participate in sports, at one level or another, says much about the values of a college. But the concept of "opportunity" has of course a much deeper and even more consequential meaning in a country that cares about social mobility and equal opportunity. In America today, and for that matter all over the world, a young person's life chances depend increasingly on the individual's educational attainment. Yet access to educational opportunity is conditioned heavily on how one grows up: specifically, on family income and on parental education, which together are so influential in providing both preparation and motivation. In a recent book, *Equity and Excellence in American Higher Education*, my colleagues and I found that students from the bottom income quartile are only *one-sixth* as likely as students from the top income quartile to be in what we define as the credible pool of candidates for admission to academically selective colleges and universities; students who lack a parent with some experience of college are *one-seventh* as likely as other students to be in the credible pool. These are enormous disparities, which can be eroded over time only by determined efforts to improve pre-collegiate educational opportunities and by related efforts to improve health and environmental conditions that also affect college attendance. The challenge is enormous, and it would be naïve to expect major changes in anything approaching the near term.

Right now, colleges and universities have to live with the unequal distribution of preparedness that is so evident. But even in the face of these troubling realities, there are four things that colleges like Centre that care about opportunity can do to help.

- First, colleges can continue to be aggressive in recruiting promising students from modest circumstances, taking advantage as well of programs such as Posse.
- Second, colleges need to be sure that in making admissions decisions they are taking full account of the barriers that some applicants have had to surmount in presenting their credentials.

In *Equity and Excellence* we point to a surprising disjunction between the rhetoric used to describe institutional commitments to diversity and present-day realities. The rhetoric regularly includes language like "admissions officials give special attention to ... applicants from economically and/or culturally disadvantaged back-grounds ... and those who would be the first in their families to attend any college."[1] What is striking is the juxtaposition of this clear statement of intent with the equally clear empirical finding that, for the '95 entering cohort at the nineteen selective schools in our study, there was absolutely no admissions advantage associated with coming from a poor family and only a very small advantage (about 4 percentage points) associated with being a first-generation college-goer. We believe that there is a strong case to be made for putting at least a modest-sized thumb on the scale when consider-ing applicants from low-SES backgrounds.

- Third, colleges can redouble their efforts to find financial aid for such students. And I know that Centre has fundraising in support of financial aid high on its list of priorities.
- Fourth, colleges can also make even more determined efforts than they make today to be sure that those students from low-SES backgrounds who are enrolled persist in their studies, enjoy academic success, and obtain degrees.

I believe that a liberal education in the arts and sciences at a place like Centre College has very practical payoffs, especially in a world in which the ability to analyze, to communicate, and to keep on learning count for more and more. There is, however, much more involved here than merely acquiring tools and skills that will prove invaluable (as they will). The indirect consequences of this kind of learning can be profound. There is, I would argue, a direct connection to another concept perhaps as elusive as "truth." I am referring to "character," and since Centre College continues to quote a predecessor of mine, Woodrow Wilson, who was a great admirer of Centre, I hope you will allow me to quote what Wilson said to the Princeton Class of 1909 at a time when he was being criticized by some alumni for not teaching character. He urged the

[1] The quotation is from the amicus brief submitted to the US Supreme Court in *Grutter v. Bollinger et al.* and *Gratz v. Bollinger et al.* by Harvard University, Brown University, the University of Chicago, Dartmouth College, Duke University, the University of Pennsylvania, Princeton University, and Yale University.

undergraduates (all men, at that time) to be aware that character is not something easily acquired:

> I hear a great deal about character being the object of education. I take leave to believe that a man who cultivates his character consciously will cultivate nothing except what will make him intolerable to his fellow men. If your object in life is to make a fine fellow of yourself, you will not succeed, and you will not be acceptable to really fine fellows. Character, gentlemen, is a by-product of a life devoted to the nearest duty: and the place in which character would be cultivated, if it be a place of study, is a place where study is the object and character is the result.

In concluding these remarks, I want to observe that much of what we have been saying today is value laden—having to do with the reasons we play sports, why the pursuit of equality of opportunity matters so much, and how we approach our studies. I am now going to tell you the origin of the title of this talk, "Why You Came." It will help if I refer us back to our earlier discussion of athletics and athletic recruitment. One of the reasons, I believe, so many heavily recruited athletes underperform academically at excellent colleges and universities is that they came to college with a different set of motivations and expectations than many other students. I regret the loss in educational opportunity that a student experienced who went to a certain university because she was, as she explained to me, "a catcher," and the school in question had an excellent softball team. Not, I would have thought, a compelling reason for occupying a scarce place at a prestigious academic institution. Similarly, when I taught Economics 101 (as I did every year I was in the president's office at Princeton), I was saddened to encounter the occasional student who thought that the purpose of my instructing him or her on the mysteries of supply and demand was to prepare the student to thrive on Wall Street—and who foolishly believed that I could actually teach someone to do that. So much depends on what you, as students, want to accomplish, and on what you think you will gain from your college days—on why you came to Centre College.

Adlai Stevenson was another Princeton graduate, who, like Wilson, was interested in public service, and who, like Wilson, had a lofty sense of why there are colleges and universities and of what students should take from them. Stevenson gave a talk to the members of the Princeton Class of 1954 in the spring of their senior year, and while this is the fall and not the spring, and while only some of you are seniors, I hope the conclusion of his comments on that occasion will resonate with you as they always have with me. Here is what Stevenson said:

> Your days are short here; this is the last of your springs. And now in the serenity and quiet of this lovely place, touch the depths of truth, feel the hem. You will go away with old, good friends. Don't forget when you leave why you came.

PLAYING THEIR WAY IN

~

James L. Shulman and William G. Bowen
February 22, 2001

NEW YORK TIMES: THE OPINION PAGES

It's almost March, a month of games and meets that decide college winter sports championships. Soon afterward comes another kind of final—the weeks in April when many 17-year-olds who applied to selective colleges will open thin envelopes containing the disappointing news that they are not being offered places at schools like Bowdoin, the University of Michigan, or Columbia. These two emotionally charged events of spring are far more closely connected than most of us probably suspect—even at the most selective colleges.

After looking at records of 90,000 students who entered thirty selective schools in 1951, 1976, and 1989, we found that sports today have a significant impact on the schools' admissions and the academic performance of their students. That impact is even more significant at small liberal arts colleges and Ivy League universities than at the large universities, simply because athletics directly affect a higher proportion of their students. Athletes in intercollegiate sports make up less than 5 percent of the male student body at a large school like Michigan but 32 percent at the liberal arts colleges in our study.

Athletes who were actively recruited for teams at the thirty schools in our group—those on "the coach's list"—had a great ad-

Editor's note: James Shulman was a colleague of Bill's at the Mellon Foundation and co-author with him of *The Game of Life: College Sports and Educational Values.* This op-ed summarizes and highlights key points made in the book.

vantage in admissions over others with similar SAT scores, whether high-scoring, low-scoring, or in between. The advantage was greater for athletes than for minority students or children of alumni.

All athletes at the thirty schools—whether recruited or not— entered college with appreciably lower test scores and high school grades than their classmates, and they ended up disproportionately low in their classes: among those we studied who entered in the fall of 1989, the proportions falling in the bottom third at graduation were 58 percent of all male athletes; 72 percent of the male athletes in the high-profile sports of football, basketball, and ice hockey; and 39 percent of female athletes.

The academic performance was not only worse than that of classmates, but worse than what would have expected on the basis of the athletes' test scores. Time pressure does not seem to be the only reason: classmates who participated in other time-intensive extracurricular activities, like editing the student newspaper, tended to overperform academically.

What does distinguish campus life for these athletes is their membership in what might be called an athletic culture. They are highly concentrated in certain fields of study and in certain campus residences. In this atmosphere, athletics are naturally emphasized, and the upcoming game might easily get more attention than the term paper. The evidence of disappointing academic performance is found not only in football and basketball but also in lower-profile sports like tennis and swimming, and among both women and men.

In the 1950s, male athletes at the schools we looked at did well academically and were likely to be leaders of their classes as well as of their teams. In the 1970s, female athletes showed a similar pattern, excelling at athletics and academics, but the recruited male athletes were underperforming academically. By the 1990s, significant gaps in academic performance had appeared for women as well as men athletes. The directional signs are unmistakable.

The great emphasis placed on intercollegiate athletics is often attributed to a desire to please alumni, but when we surveyed alumni, we found that in general they favored decreasing their schools' emphasis on intercollegiate competition, not increasing it. Those who made the biggest donations assigned lower priority to inter-collegiate athletics than to nearly every other aspect of college or university life that they were asked to rank.

Of course, sports are and should be fun and healthy and a positive way to build community spirit on a campus. But trustees, parents, faculty, and society should consider what role specialized sports talent—as opposed to participation in sports as one part of a well-rounded application—should play in admission. Does it make sense for a liberal arts college or university to assign a large share of its scarce admissions places to students who, on average, fail to take full advantage of academic opportunities?

The root question is broader: with intellectual capital ever more important, how great a role should hand-eye coordination play in deciding who is given educational opportunity?

UNTIE THE KNOT BINDING COLLEGE SPORTS AND EDUCATIONAL VALUES

∼

William G. Bowen
April 7, 2014

CHRONICLE OF HIGHER EDUCATION

As most of us are well aware, important challenges to today's existing order in athletics are under way, from the court system and through the widely discussed National Labor Relations Board ruling that Northwestern football players are employees of the university and have the right to unionize. Regardless of their final outcomes, these challenges are long overdue. I believe they represent an inevitable recognition that the oft-acclaimed "amateur" status of big-time college sports is a sham.

We need only look to the example of the University of Kentucky's basketball team, which finished as runner-up yesterday in the NCAA [National Collegiate Athletic Association] tournament, and the number of its star players who opt for "one and done." These are student-athletes? As NFL [National Football League] commentators are wont to say, "C'mon man!" In too many instances, the very term "student-athlete" has become nothing less than an oxymoron; a cynical attempt to put clothes on the emperor. Many of us

Editor's note: In this op-ed, written a little more than a decade after *Reclaiming the Game*, Bill's previous book on the topic, he returns to questioning the balance between college sports and educational values. The catalyst for this piece was the 2014 National Labor Relations Board (NLRB) ruling that initially cleared the way for football players at Northwestern University to unionize. The ruling was appealed, and ultimately the NLRB declined to exercise jurisdiction.

hate to have cherished memories of the joys of real college sports, played in the right way for the right reasons, tarnished in this way.

Many deep-seated factors are at work producing this situation, but chief among them is the huge appetite for high-grade TV entertainment by those who enjoy watching sports played at a high level—and I include myself among that number. The dollars flowing into the system at the top of the big-time-college-sports pyramid are staggering, including multimillion-dollar salaries paid to coaches. However, the crude dollar figures mask a couple of crucial facts: most of the big-time college programs lose money when proper account is taken of generally overlooked capital outlays and other hidden subsidies, and a very small percentage of aspiring-pro players make it big—or make it at all.

More generally, the pernicious effects (creating temptations for leaders to cut corners, if not simply to lie about what is going on) of big-time college sports on fundamental values are evident—and dismaying. Never mind the corrupting effects on the once-cherished notion of what it means to be a serious student who loves playing sports as an integral part of education.

Sports are supposed to support education, not the other way around. This problem is far from confined to the highly publicized programs. As others and I have argued, a misplaced emphasis on new-style college sports is having harmful effects on the educational programs of institutions up and down the competitive landscape, including the Ivies and the Division III colleges.

A problem at many selective colleges and universities (especially the smaller ones) is that admission opportunities are limited for the outstanding all-rounder, who loves sports but is primarily in college to get an education. Highly recruited athletes, focused heavily on their sports, take up too many valuable places. The fact that such places are doing so much better than the high-flying scholarship schools in avoiding the worst excesses means only that their deficiencies are easily overlooked.

In any case, it is high time to untie the knot that, in this country alone, binds what have become largely distinct activities: higher education and what is unmistakably entertainment, served up nightly in the guise of TV-quality college sports. (A historical footnote: this odd "knot" had its beginnings in the nineteenth century, when college students in the United States were notoriously unstudious and colleges were desperate for ways to channel their energies, as well as engage the interest of alumni.) It is a mystery to me how, today, and in good conscience, the big-time programs can claim tax-exempt status in the name of "education."

This is not about individual bad behavior, although we can surely find examples of that. This issue is much bigger than any individual program, coach, or college president. That the labor-board case involves Northwestern is telling. Northwestern is an excellent university with great leadership and, among its peers, one of the football programs most concerned about graduating its players and maintaining the right values. But it is significant, from a social-policy standpoint, that even as principled a university as Northwestern has been taken to task, not for being a "bad employer" (on the contrary, as the NLRB official said, it may be a "good employer"), but for being an employer nonetheless.

Thus the root problem here is not "villains" or "bad people" but *the system* that creates an incentive structure that captures even fine people. It would have been easy, had the object of the NLRB case been a less-principled program, simply to blame the bad guys. That easy way out has been taken away.

Surprisingly, many well-intentioned and highly capable people in education, including many high up in the NCAA, seem not to understand that they have a clear choice. They can either summon up the will to change direction on their own, or they can have changes in direction imposed by outsiders (courts and regulators) that almost surely will prove highly unpalatable—and quite possibly ill-conceived—the unionization of college athletes, for example.

It would take more space than I have here to even start outlining what needs to be done. But the place to begin, surely, is with a broad-based acceptance of the problem and an understanding of its seriousness. One can imagine any number of complex scenarios going forward (including many negative ones), but a hallmark of all sensible scenarios must be a scaling back in the intensity of college sports—perhaps by doing more to control season length, the size of coaching and training staffs, and the reward structure for big-time coaches and athletic directors. There are any number of ways in which we could, collectively, begin to "untie the knot."

Some people believe it may be too late to have any hope of making real progress, but I would not like to think that. I remain an unabashed enthusiast when it comes to the potential of competitive college sports. Properly understood, and in the context of educational programs, intercollegiate competition has an enormous amount to be said for it—from the perspective of participants who could learn life-long lessons of value rather than how to "game the system," and from the perspective of institutions that care about providing real education, inculcating right values, promoting healthy bonding experiences for students and alumni, and protecting themselves from reputational risk. All at a time when public suspicion of higher education is at close to an all-time high.

CHAPTER 4

TECHNOLOGY AND
SCHOLARLY COMMUNICATIONS

JSTOR AND THE ECONOMICS OF SCHOLARLY COMMUNICATION

~

William G. Bowen, President, Andrew W. Mellon Foundation
September 18, 1995

REMARKS, COUNCIL ON LIBRARY RESOURCES CONFERENCE,
WASHINGTON, DC

I am delighted to have this opportunity to discuss "JSTOR" (our acronym for "journal storage"). This denizen of the world of electronic databases began life as one of several demonstration projects funded by the Andrew W. Mellon Foundation, moved rapidly from infancy to adolescence, and now enjoys an independent existence, having been incorporated as a separate nonprofit entity within the last few months.

Editor's note: The Council on Library and Information Resources (CLIR) is an independent nonprofit organization that forges strategies to enhance research, teaching, and learning environments in collaboration with libraries, cultural institutions, and communities of higher learning. Bill gave this talk at a meeting of CLIR representatives to introduce the concepts behind JSTOR, which at that point was incubating as a project at the Mellon Foundation. He delivered almost the same talk one month later, on October 18, 1995, in a plenary session at the fall meeting of the Association of Research Libraries in Washington, DC.

Author's note: In preparing this talk I have been helped by many people, including Kevin Guthrie and Ira Fuchs of JSTOR; Richard Ekman, Dennis Sullivan, and Harriet Zuckerman of the Andrew W. Mellon Foundation; Wendy Lougee and Sarah Turner of the University of Michigan; Hal Varian of the University of California–Berkeley; Elaine Sloan and Kristine Kavanaugh of Columbia University; and William Walker and Heike Kordish at the New York Public Library.

BACKGROUND: A BRIEF HISTORY AND A SUMMARY OF OBJECTIVES

In its original incarnation, JSTOR was conceived to be an electronic database containing "faithful replications" of all pre-1990 issues of ten core scholarly journals in the fields of economics and history (including the *American Economic Review* and the *American Historical Review*). While the foundation's long-term interests in the field of scholarly communications are broad, in this instance we wanted very much to be practical and to test concepts and general approaches by working with a manageable set of well-defined materials within a circumscribed terrain. Hence, the narrow definition of the initial content of JSTOR. In creating JSTOR, we set out to serve three objectives simultaneously: (1) to improve dramatically access to journal literature for faculty, students, and other scholars by linking bitmapped images of journal pages to a powerful search engine; (2) to mitigate some of the vexing economic problems of libraries by easing storage problems (thereby saving prospective capital costs involved in building more shelf space) and also by reducing operating costs associated with retrieving back issues and reshelving them; and (3) to address issues of conservation and preservation such as broken runs, mutilated pages, and long-term deterioration of paper copy.

I will not take time today to explain why we chose to start with the fields of economics and history (or the ten specific journals with which we are working), but I will anticipate another frequently asked question: why did JSTOR initially include in its database only issues of journals published before 1990? Why were current issues excluded? In making the decision to focus on back issues, we knew that we were swimming against the proverbial tide and "challenging marketplace solutions" (or at least assumptions). Consistent with Willy Sutton's explanation of why it was banks that he chose to rob, most publishers and other vendors have been interested primarily in current issues because "that's where the money is." Current issues generate revenue streams; back issues rarely do.

Since it is "contrarian," our emphasis on back issues has surprised many people. Early on, we explained our plans to the head of one widely known commercial enterprise, who was quick to comment: "No sane person would do what you propose." We were undeterred. We thought that we had an opportunity, and perhaps even an obligation, to make upfront investments that could have long-term social value for the scholarly community at large. Unlike commercial entities, the test of success for us is not any "bottom line" but how well we facilitate teaching and scholarship by improving the mechanisms of scholarly communication.

At the same time, we recognize that such broad statements of good intentions often mean little—as one of my friends likes to put it, "Good intentions randomize behavior."[1] Fiscal discipline is needed, and we have always believed that JSTOR would have to be self-sustaining eventually. Perpetual subsidy is both unrealistic and unwise: projects of this kind must make economic sense once they are up and running. If users and beneficiaries, broadly defined, are unwilling to cover the costs, one should wonder about the utility of the enterprise. In this important respect, we *are* strong believers in "market-place solutions"—provided that what the economist calls "externalities" can be captured.

Given our objectives, there were strong pragmatic reasons for focusing on back issues. After all, they comprise that part of the journal literature that is (a) least readily accessible; (b) most in need of preservation; and (c) most avaricious in its consumption of stack space (our ten journals run to some 750,000 pages). Also, from our perspective, the fact that back files do not generate much revenue for publishers has been a plus, not a minus. To launch this project, we needed to obtain copyright permissions, and we knew that this would be much easier if the project offered no threat to basic revenue streams. We wanted to work in concert with publishers as well as with libraries, to advance the common interests of both. It is only by adopting what might be called a "system-wide"

[1] Marion J. Levy Jr., *Ten Laws of the Disillusionment of the True Liberal* (Princeton, NJ: M. J. Levy, 1981), Law 1.

perspective, which recognizes the legitimate needs of *both* the providers of scholarly materials and their users, that socially optimal arrangements can be put in place.

Let me now summarize a great many intervening developments in relatively few words. First, following much discussion, we were able to obtain copyright permissions from all ten journals to bitmap their back issues. Second, we arranged for colleagues at the University of Michigan (working closely with Ira Fuchs, chief scientist of JSTOR) to oversee the technical aspects of the project. Third, we selected several liberal arts colleges to serve as test sites, along with the University of Michigan. If all goes according to plan (almost too much to hope!), the full back files of four of the ten journals will be accessible at these test sites by the end of September, and the remaining journals will be available by the end of the year.

CHARACTERISTICS OF THE ARCHIVAL "PRODUCT" (OR "SCHOLARLY TOOL")

In getting to this point, we made several key decisions about the archival "product" that deserve to be highlighted.[2]

- First, we elected to set a high bitmapping standard of six hundred dots per inch. The objective was to produce images of exceptional clarity, with every shading, every subscript in every equation, and every figure or photograph clearly visible. In short, we wanted to create something of archival quality, with print-outs so good that readers would regard these copies as equivalent to the originals—and superior in many instances to yellowed or soiled pages. This objective is being achieved, and we have sample pages for those of you interested in seeing them.

[2] Terminology is a problem. The word "product" may seem too commercial to some, and it is certainly true that our objective is the development of more than just another "widget." JSTOR is intended to be a major "scholarly tool" with benefits that extend well beyond calculations of costs and revenues that may seem mundane to some. But it is also important that lofty ambitions and high hopes not distract us from the need to provide a "product" that is economically viable.

- Second, we decided to create and include in the electronic file a searchable Table-of-Contents Index. This feature permits readers to obtain bibliographic references to all articles, book reviews, and other components of the database by a specified author, containing a key word or words in their title (such as "Council of Economic Advisors" or "human capital"), or published in a certain journal or in some particular set of years—and then to call up the articles themselves on the screen.

- Third, although the user will see only page images on the screen, this database is linked to a text file created using optical character recognition (OCR) software that will enable users to search not only the Table-of-Contents Index but also the actual text pages of all the journals. Specifications provide that the OCR version of the text will be accurate at the 99.95 percent level; in other words, it will contain no more than one error in two thousand characters.

- Fourth, our colleagues at Michigan have joined these elements to a sophisticated search engine that allows the entire database to be accessed online, via Internet connections, by authorized users. This online feature has obvious advantages, including both ease of access and the minimization of storage problems for libraries (since the database is stored centrally). The software also includes printer applications for MACs and PCs that permit authorized users to print exceptionally high-resolution copies of pages or entire articles at their terminals.

In seeking to translate these concepts into actual electronic files, progress has been slower than envisioned in our original schedule—which, we admit, was aggressive, to say the least. The firm responsible for the bitmapping and OCR work, and our friends at Michigan responsible for technical aspects of the project, have encountered all (it seems like *all*) of the inevitable problems associated with creating any new tool of this complexity from scratch. Still, as I have said, we expect the back files of four of the ten journals to be up and running at the test sites within a few weeks. By now there has been enough preliminary experience with parts of the database, and enough "demos," to convince us that JSTOR is real, and to give solid grounds for believing that it will perform as advertised.

No decisions have been made concerning pricing and controls over access, but I can outline our provisional thinking:

- We anticipate that JSTOR would ask libraries to make two types of payment for access: (a) a one-time capital charge for acquisition of permanent rights to the base archive and (b) an annual fee to cover the recurring costs of maintaining and updating the database and associated software. The one-time charge would be related to the amount of material in the archive and would be significantly lower than the costs associated with storing and maintaining the equivalent set of materials in paper. Hypothetically, this charge might be set at, say, a penny or two a page. The annual charge would probably also be related to the size of the base archive and to whether the library wanted new material added each year. It might be in the $25 to $35 range for a typical journal and would certainly be significantly less than the recurring costs of processing, binding, storing, and retrieving new as well as old issues. Alternatively, JSTOR might offer libraries the option of combining the capital and annual charges into a single stream of "lease payments."
- We anticipate that JSTOR would also offer individual subscribers direct access to the archive (so that they would not have to depend on their home institution making access available on a campus network). Charges to individuals could be very modest (for example, perhaps $10 per year in the case of a single journal). Every dollar contributed by individuals would represent additional revenues for "the system" and would lessen the financial burdens on publishers and libraries, thereby reducing the risk that electronic publication might lead to substantial cost-shifting from individual subscribers to institutions.[3]

[3] I am reminded of analogous issues associated with charging students to attend college. In the United States, students customarily pay tuition to offset part of the cost of their education, at the same time that public and private sources also provide subsidies. In many European countries, direct payments by students are less common (though there are still opportunity costs to be borne), and much more of the burden of paying for education falls on the state. This is one reason, I have always suspected, why the United States has been

I want to emphasize again that these are initial thoughts and purely illustrative numbers. No commitments or decisions have been made by anyone. But I thought it would be easier for you to think with us about the prospects for JSTOR if we gave you some hypothetical reference points that had dollar signs attached to them.

Could this kind of model work economically? What levels of charges would be required for JSTOR to break even? Since there are tremendous economies of scale involved in creating and distributing a new electronic tool of this kind, much depends on the interest demonstrated by libraries and individuals. Our GUESS (it is nothing more than that) is that at least half of the current subscribers—libraries and individuals—would elect to participate. Under that assumption, and making another set of guesses concerning costs, we think that the project is viable. But no one can know for sure.

As at least partial protection against the risks associated with ignorance, we have developed a mechanism that should provide reasonable safeguards for all concerned. Our starting point is the concept of a partnership between JSTOR and participating publishers. Since the proposed experiment is a novel one, and no one can predict with confidence either costs or revenue streams, we are contemplating an "upside" sharing of any "net funds available" that remain after costs have been covered. Also, while experience is so limited (non-existent, really), we plan to provide a "downside" protection for an initial set of publishers that choose to cast their lot with JSTOR in its earliest days. JSTOR might guarantee a publisher that, for a period of two years, its gross subscription revenue would not fall below an agreed base level because of any declines in individual subscriptions attributable to the experiment.

The "upside" sharing might involve a commitment by JSTOR to rebate half of any "net funds available" to the publisher and

---

able to channel larger total amounts of resources into higher education. Dividing the costs between direct beneficiaries (students) and society at large is, I believe, both fairer and more effective as a system of educational finance than a regime that relies much more heavily on state support alone. For similar reasons, I think it makes sense to seek ways whereby individual subscribers can make *some* contribution to the costs of JSTOR—provided that the effect is not to discourage access to the database by impecunious users. There are pricing and access mechanisms that can work to serve both objectives in a balanced way.

another one-quarter to participating libraries. JSTOR might itself retain the remaining one-quarter for development purposes. By committing itself in advance to give rebates to both publishers and libraries out of any "net funds available," JSTOR protects everyone against the risk that any one party would benefit disproportionately. At the same time, since it is understood that JSTOR must be self-sustaining, charges would have to be renegotiated if JSTOR's revenues were insufficient to cover its costs. We believe the partnership concept to be the best—and perhaps only—way of handling the uncertainties inherent in a new initiative of this kind.

As a nonprofit entity, JSTOR is not permitted by law to accumulate funds beyond its legitimate needs, and, in any case, would have no interest in doing so. Its sole purpose is to serve the scholarly community by increasing the availability of scholarly journals and enhancing their usefulness, while concurrently reducing library costs. For this reason, the posture of JSTOR differs fundamentally from that of commercial vendors. In creating the "founding" board of trustees of JSTOR, care was taken to assemble a group of individuals who would be known and trusted by the scholarly community— in part to assure credibility from the outset.[4]

INSTITUTIONAL SUBSCRIBERS: LIBRARIES AND CAMPUS NETWORKS

Let us now consider in more detail how the economics of JSTOR might work for institutional subscribers. Conversations with a number of presidents, provosts, and librarians have persuaded us that there is considerable interest in the historical archive. We anticipate that, as one person put it, faculty and students will find JSTOR

[4]The founding trustees of JSTOR include Richard De Gennaro, librarian of Harvard College; Mary Patterson McPherson, president of Bryn Mawr College; Cathleen Morawetz, professor of mathematics, New York University, and president of the American Mathematical Society; W. Taylor Reveley III, partner, Hunton and Williams, and trustee of the Andrew W. Mellon Foundation as well as other nonprofits; Gilbert Whitaker, retired provost of the University of Michigan and professor of business at Michigan; and Elton White, former president of the NCR computer company and trustee of Berea College. William G. Bowen also serves on the board of JSTOR (as its chairman) to ensure continuity.

"irresistible" and will urge their institutions to acquire this resource. In addition to creating new search capacities, JSTOR solves one of the most vexing problems faced by readers and librarians alike—the unavailability of a particular volume because someone else is using it, it has been misfiled, the library is closed, and so on. JSTOR provides predictable access to multiple users at every hour of every day (assuming the continuing cooperation of the gods of cyberspace).

The positive case for acquiring this valuable new scholarly resource will be convincing across a broad spectrum of institutions, including

1. large research universities with faculty and graduate students who make considerable use of back issues and expect to have at their disposal the most up-to-date mode of access, even though their library may already have all of the back issues in paper format, available in open stacks;
2. libraries using a closed-stack system that requires the retrieval and reshelving of large numbers of journals by staff members; and
3. the many colleges and universities, in this country and abroad, that lack complete files of back issues in paper format.

For this last set of institutions, JSTOR offers a unique opportunity to acquire complete runs of journals, in pristine condition, for a small fraction (perhaps 10 percent) of the cost of acquiring paper copies—and without having to incur all the associated costs of building and maintaining library space. To illustrate, if JSTOR were able to offer the archive at a one-time capital charge of as little as one or two cents per page, an institution with limited library resources could obtain the entire back file of *Ecology*, from 1921 through 1994, for something like $750 to $1,500 (there are 77,000 pages). What a bargain!

In other situations, where the back issues of *Ecology* are already available in paper format, JSTOR allows the library to save valuable shelf space on the campus by moving the back issues off campus or, in some instances, by discarding the paper issues altogether. (The natural fear of "losing something" will be minimized if, as we expect, arrangements are made for regional collections of paper copies. As another "fail-safe" mechanism, JSTOR would be able to provide CD-ROMs.)

What are these savings in storage costs worth? Much depends, of course, on local circumstances. Utilizing a methodology devised by Malcolm Getz and cost data assembled by Michael Cooper, we estimate that the one-time capital costs for storing a single volume of a journal in open stacks, excluding the cost of land (hardly negligible for libraries in major metropolitan areas, such as New York), to be anywhere from $24 to $41.[5] It follows that the capital costs associated with storing the complete seventy-six-volume run of *Ecology* could range from $1,800 to $3,100. This cost is roughly twice the hypothetical capital charge for *both acquisition and storage* of the JSTOR electronic archive. One key reason for this large disparity is that JSTOR centralizes the storage function at off-site locations while retaining all the advantages of browsing and providing readers with more or less instant access.

There also appear to be large savings in operating costs associated with the "circulation" function—retrieving and then reshelving paper copies of journals. The New York Public Library (NYPL), which is a non-circulating closed-stack library, reports that it spends an average of $1.94 to retrieve and reshelve a journal volume. We recognize that costs in New York will be higher than average and that closed-stack libraries are more expensive to operate from this standpoint than open-stack libraries. Michael Cooper has estimated the staff-only costs of circulation from open stacks in the University of California–San Diego library to be roughly sixty cents per volume.[6] Of course, as Cooper, Getz, and others who have written

[5] See Malcolm Getz, "Storing Information in Academic Libraries," mimeo, October 17, 1994, and Michael Cooper, "A Cost Comparison of Alternative Book Storage Strategies," *Library Quarterly* 59, no. 3 (1989): 239–60. Getz postulates that shelving ten volumes per square foot is typical for bound volumes of serials (as contrasted with twelve volumes per square foot for monographs. Because Cooper's data for construction costs pertain to the late 1980s, we have assumed (conservatively) that costs have risen 15 percent in the interim. As Getz, Cooper, and many others explain, construction costs are *much* lower for other types of shelving, but then browsing capabilities are sacrificed and circulation costs increase dramatically. Open stack shelving is most comparable to JSTOR, and even then JSTOR remains much more convenient to use.

[6] Cooper, "A Cost Comparison of Alternative Book Storage Strategies," pp. 251–52. Cooper's figures are for the late 1980s, and again we have raised his figure of $.53 to $.60 to adjust very roughly for inflation since then.

on this subject recognize, open-stack systems save operating costs by, in effect, relying on users to do much of the "leg work" involved in retrieving volumes. The time-costs for users are of course considerable, and dwarf staff-only costs.[7]

We cannot hope today to be at all precise in suggesting the right figures, and we certainly do not want to exaggerate the potential savings; but it seems reasonable (actually very conservative) to use $1.00/retrieval as a reference point—*half* the actual cost incurred by NYPL. The implications of using even this modest figure are staggering. As part of the research associated with the introduction of JSTOR, staff at the University of Michigan have tallied usage on their campus of the ten economics and history journals in their paper formats. Also, we have surveyed experiences at the five college test sites. Weighting each institution equally (and thus giving the much heavier usage at Michigan only one-sixth the overall weight), we find that library users request volumes from each of these core journals an average of 45 times per year (the comparable average at the University of Michigan considered separately is 180 times per year). Using the cost figure of $1 per volume, the annual cost of circulation is estimated to average $45 per journal for this set of six schools and $180 per journal at the University of Michigan. And these estimates should probably be doubled for libraries which operate like the New York Public Library.

In addition, use of paper copies involves recurring costs of preservation and conservation. The way library patrons use this literature, often spreading bound volumes on copy machines, subjects the paper to substantial wear and tear. Older journals must be mended, deacidified, and sometimes rebound. While electronic archives are not subject to these "handling" costs, they do entail costs of other kinds—especially maintaining computer equipment and answering questions posed by users. We expect to estimate these expenditures at our test sites this fall, but we find it hard to imagine that they can be close to comparable to the operating costs associated with paper formats.

[7] Cooper estimates user costs at roughly three times staff-only costs, or about $1.80 per volume; Getz suggests a figure of $4.00 for the time-only costs to the user of retrieving a volume.

Libraries participating in JSTOR might be able to lower their on-going costs even more if the historical Archive were linked to an electronic version of Current Issues. Acquisition and processing costs, estimated by one university librarian to be more than $20 per journal, would be substantially reduced. Also, it would no longer be necessary to bind individual issues into volumes, a process that can cost anywhere from $15 to $30 depending upon how one allocates the staff costs associated with preparing the journals for the bindery.

We recognize that we are enthusiasts, and no doubt our excitement about "our child" should be discounted somewhat. Still, the purely economic case for JSTOR, seen from the perspective of the institution, seems overwhelming. The highly favorable economics are driven by powerful scale effects, since JSTOR permits tasks (especially storage and retrieval) that are now done repetitively at thousands of libraries to be done once—centrally—and to be done far more effectively, as well as at much lower cost. Combining capital and operating costs, and expressing both on an annual basis, we estimate that the continuing costs of storing, retrieving, conserving, processing, and binding one journal, such as *Ecology*, in paper format are at least twice (and perhaps three times) greater than what they would be if the library contracted with JSTOR to provide what we are convinced would be far superior access.[8]

[8] The estimates are based in part on methodology suggested by Getz, including his assumptions for amortizing capital costs (25-year life, 7 percent discount rate). Some of the components of these estimates are rough (especially the figure for average circulation of journals from 1990 forward). Still, the overall level of costs seems reasonable and is, we believe, conservative.

For *Ecology*, these annual costs would appear to be in the range of $350 to $400 for our test-site libraries. (The comparable estimate for a large research library such as Michigan's would be much higher because of greater circulation and thus greater retrieval costs.) In all likelihood, JSTOR would be able to provide the electronic database described here for one-third to one-half as much.

Richard Lemberg at St. Mary's College in Moraga, California, has done a most elaborate and most impressive study of the potential cost savings nationally of digitizing "non-unique" materials already owned by libraries. See Richard Lemberg, "A Life-Cycle Cost Analysis for the Creation, Storage and Dissemination of a Digitized Document Collection," PhD diss., University of California–Berkeley, 1995.

INDIVIDUAL SUBSCRIBERS

How would an individual subscriber gain access to the electronic Archive? Our presumption is that individual subscribers would be given PIN numbers which would entitle them to access the database from any location. "Personal" access would be restricted to those individuals who had PIN numbers. Of course, those individuals who work on campuses that have purchased site licenses for the Archive and/or for Current Issues might have a reduced incentive to take out individual subscriptions. They would no longer have to trek to the library to browse; they could use the campus network.

This "fact of life" in an electronic world is a legitimate source of concern to the publishers of journals with significant numbers of individual subscribers and to professional associations that link membership to the provision of journals. At the same time, it is easy to exaggerate the risks. Apart from the power of inertia (not to be underestimated), publishers need to recognize that by no means all individual subscribers will have ready access to JSTOR files by means of a campus network. Many will not. In addition, publishers could consider giving individual subscribers "something extra," and a number of creative ideas have already been proposed.

At present, of course, individual subscribers have no personal access to any historical Archive except in those situations in which they happen to have accumulated an entire back run of a journal in their office or home. (And, as one colleague observed, it should be easy to demonstrate that a full run of even a few core journals in a field such as economics or history could "bury someone alive in his/her office—perhaps even before the person got tenure.") Since, in almost all instances, individuals must go to the library to peruse back issues, we expect the availability of an electronic Archive to be exceedingly attractive to a number of individual faculty members, who might well be willing to pay a modest annual charge (say, $10) for personal access.

We also suspect that there will be strong synergies between purchase of electronic access to Current Issues and purchase of electronic access to the Archive—which would be regularly updated if the individual subscribed to both. For this reason, demand for individual subscriptions might actually increase, rather than decrease, as a result of JSTOR. If it proves possible to include several core journals from a field (or sub-field) in JSTOR, the appeal of electronic access to a "collection" might be greater yet. We just do not know anything, at this stage, about the elasticity of demand for what would be a totally new scholarly tool. This is an important subject for future research, as experience begins to accumulate. Also to repeat the presence of such large unknowns is strong justification for the "partnership" concept, whereby the interests of publishers, libraries, and JSTOR are aligned.

BROADER CONSIDERATIONS

The behavioral consequences of JSTOR (and other initiatives of a similar kind) also deserve careful thought. One question of great interest is how JSTOR will affect patterns of research and teaching. Our assumption is that dramatic improvements in ease of access, combined with the advantages of a powerful search engine, will cause students and faculty alike to make more use of back issues than they do today. We are told, and anecdotes abound, that students sometimes fill papers with what they perceive to be their quota of citations by relying heavily on recent literature, since current issues of journals are easier to find and use than back issues. Yet it would surely be better if all of us—students, faculty and research staff alike—were able to mine the full range of scholarly literature with less difficulty than present arrangements impose. For instance, one would hope that students writing about the end of World War II would consult articles written by scholars in the immediate postwar years to gain a sense of how the world looked then, rather than relying on more recent compilations of opinion. Similarly, current discussions of welfare reform might be helped by more study of writings in the 1930s about the New Deal.

Thinking about JSTOR also causes this observer to consider a number of aspects of budgeting and decision-making in higher education:

- First, JSTOR emphasizes the importance of considering various budget categories together when making allocation decisions. Specifically, capital costs, which are often neglected by colleges and universities,[9] must be taken into account in calculating the net effects of subscribing to JSTOR. For this reason, it is important that provosts and others with campus-wide budgetary responsibilities be involved in deciding whether an institution should (or should not) start down the JSTOR path. Compartmentalized decision-making, focused solely on acquisition budgets, for example, would not permit a proper assessment of the costs and benefits of JSTOR.

- Second, JSTOR reminds us that too narrow and compartmentalized a view of economic self-interest can be harmful in other ways. For example, if libraries refuse to worry about the effects of their subscription practices (such as purchasing site licenses through consortia) on the number of individual and library subscribers, they may inadvertently inflict considerable economic harm on publishers—who may in turn respond by raising the prices of library subscriptions.[10]

- Third, JSTOR also warns us that attempting to charge for journal literature "by the drink" can lead to results that are far from optimal socially. As the just-cited article by Lieberman, Noll, and Steinmueller emphasizes, the marginal costs of including another user are exceedingly modest, and this is one reason why it is so

---

[9] See Gordon C. Winston's call for "global accounting" and his examination of the importance of capital costs in the setting of a liberal arts college in "The Capital Costs Conundrum," *NACUBO* [National Association of College and University Business Officers] *Business Officer*, June 1993.

[10] See Lisa Lieberman, Roger Noll, and W. Edward Steinmueller, "The Sources of Scientific Journal Price Increase," mimeo, March 23, 1992, which lays out very well the basic economic characteristics of this unusual industry: high fixed costs (the importance of "first-copy cost" for journal publishers), the forces making for proliferation of journals, declining circulation, and its attendant impact on subscription rates. This pattern leads to a socially undesirable and economically inefficient widening of the spread between the marginal cost of a journal and its price.

important that the product be offered on a subscription basis. It would be undesirable, from the standpoint of resource allocation, to discourage an impecunious student from using JSTOR because of a per-use pricing model.[11]

- Fourth and last, JSTOR is unusual in that it violates the usual axiom about the importance of forcing choices between "more" and "cheaper." Let me explain. When new technologies evolve, they offer benefits that can be enjoyed either in the form of more output (including opportunities for scholars to do new things or to do them better) or in the form of cost savings. It is my experience that in universities electronic technologies have almost always led to greater output, and rarely to reduced costs. Yet, it is imperative, if tight resource constraints are to be observed, as they must be, that technological gains lead to at least some cost savings. I make this speech regularly to my colleagues at the Foundation, as well as to my one-time colleagues in academia. In the case of JSTOR, however, it is hard to press for this version of the "discipline of choice" because JSTOR offers *both* great advantages to potential users *and* cost savings.

My Puritanical tendencies cause me to worry about the potentially debilitating effects of such an unlikely product on the will to choose; but I will acknowledge that it is also nice, if only occasionally, to be confronted with an opportunity to argue on behalf of an innovation that is both better *and* cheaper. At least that is what I hope that our experimentation with JSTOR will demonstrate to be the case.

As a wise friend of mine said on another occasion (when contemplating the impeachment of Richard Nixon, to give the exact situation), "We'll know more later." So we will, and the JSTOR

---

[11] A recent article in *Investor's Business Daily* (August 29, 1995, p. A9) quotes the chairman of the Securities and Exchange Commission (SEC) as saying that "a library that charges people by the page or by the minute is no longer a library." The comment was made in response to a proposal that would have provided 10 minutes free browsing time on "Edgar," the SEC's electronic database of corporate filings and other records, and then charged for downloading information.

contingent will undertake to keep all interested parties posted on what we learn (including what mistakes we make). At the same time, we encourage you to give us your suggestions and best thinking as all of us contemplate the murky but exciting future of scholarly communication in an electronic age.

FUNDING THE LIBRARY
OF THE FUTURE

HARVESTING PRODUCTIVITY GAINS AS A
PARTIAL ANSWER

~

William G. Bowen
April 27, 1996

NEW YORK PUBLIC LIBRARY CENTENNIAL

It is a privilege to participate in the celebration of the centennial of one of this country's foremost centers of learning, the New York Public Library. While much has been said and written about this stellar institution, I like the simple elegance of the opening line in the entry in the *Encyclopedia Britannica*: "one of the great libraries of the world." So it is.

Any leading institution has the responsibility to stimulate useful conversations among those with whom it shares aspirations, and I congratulate Elizabeth Rohatyn, Paul LeClerc, and their colleagues for convening this "Summit." It is especially gratifying to see in attendance the leaders of so many of the world's most important libraries. Increasingly, I believe, there are opportunities to learn from each other, to share resources that are both tangible and intangible, and to function more effectively by functioning together.

I have been asked to talk about "funding," perhaps because I am a sometime economist—or perhaps because the grantmaking Foun-

Editor's note: The New York Public Library hosted a symposium that included many leaders from research libraries in the United States and from around the world to celebrate its centennial. At the invitation of the library's president, Paul LeClerc, Bill gave this talk on the future of libraries in a digital age from an economic perspective.

dation with which I am now associated has a longstanding interest in the welfare of the great libraries. (Please do not expect me, however, to say much about foundations in this talk, though I will return to their role at the end.) In any case, I welcome this opportunity because I have a message I want to try out on you. It is this: in a time when traditional funding sources are increasingly inadequate, there is real potential for libraries to make better use of existing resources under their own control—in effect, to create "almost new sources of funding" by taking advantage of potential improvements in productivity permitted by electronic technologies.

CONTEXT AND MINDSET

First, some context. Great libraries have always had to cope with ever more demanding responsibilities, owing in no small measure to the exponential increases in books, serials, documents, and library materials of other kinds—as well as to exponential increases in the numbers of students, scholars, and others who rely on the great libraries. There is no discernible slowdown in either the flood of new materials that "belong" in libraries or in the escalating numbers of potential users. Pressures to find the funds to acquire these materials, process them, store them, provide access to them, and preserve them are, therefore, unremitting. In your world, resource constraints are ever present—it will always be so—and anyone who tries to wish them away is in need of a very cold shower.

Traditionally, the additional funding required to meet at least some of these burgeoning needs has come primarily from external sources, principally agencies of the state, private benefactors, and in certain instances universities. This pattern will continue, and I would be aghast if anything I say this morning were interpreted as relieving these traditional patrons of any part of their ongoing responsibility to meet these needs. But we are all realists. The resource constraints faced by patrons, and thus by libraries, are real. They must be respected, and they have, as we all know, already taken a toll. The Mellon Foundation published a study in 1992 that documented a number of ominous trends within research libraries in this country, including the fact that for several decades now these libraries have been spending more to acquire less.[1] One surprising finding was that, starting in about the mid-1970s, the share of total university expenditures going to their libraries began to decline rather sharply. What happened, I suspect, is that universities concluded that there was simply no hope of maintaining previous acquisitions policies; having had to abandon that reference point, it became easier to impose budgetary ceilings, even arbitrary ones—cutbacks in purchases of monographs, cancellations of serials subscriptions, and other retrenchments followed. Just a few weeks ago, I received a copy of a newer study by the Association of Research Libraries which documents the dramatic decline in acquisitions by U.S. and Canadian libraries of books and serials published abroad.[2]

Is there a ray of light? In company with many others, I am now persuaded, as I was not before, that electronic technology offers real possibilities for simultaneously improving performance *and controlling if not actually reducing costs*. I have underscored the key phrase "controlling if not actually reducing costs," because heretofore advances in technology have served mainly to increase overall expenditures.

Let me backtrack for a moment, put on my hat as a sometime teacher of Economics 101, and provide a simple conceptual framework. When new technologies evolve, they offer benefits that can be enjoyed either in the form of more output (including opportunities for scholars to do new things or to do existing tasks better) or in the form of cost savings. It is my experience that in universities electronic technologies have almost always led to greater output, and rarely to reduced costs. (An important exception to this generalization is the kind of online cataloging service provided by OCLC.)

Given the resource constraints I cited a moment ago, this proclivity for enjoying the fruits of technological change mainly in the

---

[1] Anthony M. Cummings, et al., *University Libraries and Scholarly Communication* (Washington, DC: Association of Research Libraries, 1992).

[2] Jutta Reed-Scott, *Scholarship, Research Libraries, and Global Publishing* (Washington, DC: Association of Research Libraries, 1996).

form of "more and better" cannot persist. Technological gains must generate at least some cost savings. I make this speech regularly to my colleagues at the Foundation, and we have become very reluctant to support technology projects that promise "only" to allow grantees to do something better—projects must also assist grantees to do things cheaper. If this injunction is accepted (no small "if"), we are now at a point when electronic technology can become a more important source of funding for libraries by freeing up funds that otherwise would have been spent on doing things in established ways.

THE JSTOR EXAMPLE

Let me illustrate what I am saying by describing briefly an important project that has been supported by the Mellon Foundation, and to which I personally have devoted more hours and more emotional energy than I (or my colleagues) ever imagined possible. It is called "JSTOR" (an acronym for "journal storage"), and it now lives, as an independent not-for-profit entity that is still emerging from adolescence, right here in the new SILS building of the New York Public Library. The executive director of JSTOR, Kevin Guthrie, and I could not be more pleased by the warm welcome we have received from our many friends at the Library.

JSTOR began modestly enough as an effort to ease the increasing problems faced by libraries seeking to find appropriate stack space for the long runs of back issues of scholarly journals. The basic idea was to convert the back issues of paper journals into electronic formats that would allow savings in space (and in capital costs) while simultaneously improving access to the contents of the journals and addressing preservation problems. We started out with ten journals in two core fields, economics and history, and we have now converted all 750,000 pages in the pre-1990 issues into the JSTOR electronic database, which resides on a server at the University of Michigan. High-resolution bitmapped images of every published page are linked to a text file generated with optical character recognition (OCR) software which, along with newly constructed Table-of-Contents indexes, allow for complete search and retrieval of the published material. The page images are of truly archival quality (600 dpi), and even the most complicated figures and equations can be printed beautifully. Authorized users are able to access the journals using standard PC equipment at any time and from any networked location (this "library" never closes). Issues of journals are never "out;" they are always available, and in pristine condition. In sum, the addition of powerful search and printing capabilities makes the JSTOR system more than just a way for libraries to save capital costs; it has become a scholarly tool of enormous value.

Claims for the "revolutionary" promise of new technologies are often wildly exaggerated, but this seems to be one instance in which the well-orchestrated application of technologies that are now broadly available, and far from esoteric, can make a real difference. Initial users of JSTOR have been enthusiastic, and we are now adding fields of study and journals. We hope to make the JSTOR database available to charter subscribers sometime during the fall or winter of 1996. Having demonstrated that the archival concept works, we are also beginning to experiment with linking current issues to the backfiles (initially in partnership with the Ecological Society of America and the American Economic Association).

The benefits of the database to users are, I think, self-evident. The potential benefits to libraries, large and small, here and abroad, also seem clear. But what about the economics of the project? Is it viable? The Trustees of the Foundation have always believed that JSTOR would have to be self-sustaining eventually. Perpetual subsidy would be both unrealistic and unwise: projects of this kind must make economic sense once they are up and running. If users and beneficiaries, broadly defined, are unwilling to cover the costs, one should wonder about the utility of the enterprise.

No firm answers to this set of questions are in hand. While the Foundation has had to make a large upfront investment to launch JSTOR, the potential economies of scale involved are enormous, and much depends therefore on the interest demonstrated by libraries and individual subscribers. Preliminary calculations we have made (guesses, really) are, nonetheless, encouraging. They suggest that relatively modest charges for both initial acquisition of the database, with permanent access guaranteed, and annual operating/upgrading expenses, should generate sufficient revenue to cover the ongoing costs—which is all that is intended, since JSTOR is, of course, a nonprofit entity whose mission is to serve the scholarly community.

Asking libraries to pay for anything new is, however, no small matter. Fortunately, however, there are potential savings which could more than offset the incremental costs. These include not only the potentially large savings, long run, in space and capital costs, but also savings of many kinds in operating costs: the New York Public Library estimates, for example, that it spends an average of $1.94 to find, retrieve, and then reshelve a single journal volume. In addition, use of paper copies involves recurring costs of preservation and conservation. Ultimately, libraries participating in JSTOR may be able to lower on-going costs even more if the historical archive is linked to an electronic version of current issues. Acquisition and processing costs, estimated by one university librarian to be more than $20 per journal, would be reduced substantially, as would the costs of binding individual issues into volumes, which can easily amount to another $15 to $20 per volume. These illustrative numbers, and others, persuade us that there is a strong possibility of realizing real economies at the same time that the user is offered far better access to scholarly literature than exists at present.

As I have suggested, these highly favorable economics are driven by scale effects associated with technology, since JSTOR permits tasks that are now done repetitively at thousands of libraries to be done once—centrally—and to be done far more effectively at lower cost. As watchers of various trials in the United States are fond of saying, "the jury is still out"; still, in concluding my discussion of JSTOR, I cannot avoid saying that those of us most intimately involved with it are more convinced than ever that it offers great promise.

EARNED INCOME OPPORTUNITIES?

As we consider the future funding of libraries, another question to ponder is whether they will obtain significant amounts of revenue from individual (or corporate) purchasers of services. This is, after all, the age of privatization. Even so, we do not expect—certainly I do not expect—libraries to begin charging entry fees to students or the public at large, or to begin charging for each book or journal consulted by one user or another. As Carla Hesse has said in a recent paper, "These aspects of digitization promise to help us to continue to realize one of the most cherished ideals of modern democratic polities and the libraries they have created—universal access to all forms of human knowledge."[3]

A number of us in this country are concerned about a tendency by some purveyors of scholarly literature to want to charge "by the drink"—that is, to expect students or other users to pay "x" dollars to obtain a copy of a particular article. As Lieberman, Noll, and Steinmueller have emphasized, the marginal costs of including another user are exceedingly modest, and this is one reason why subscription pricing is much preferred.[4] We certainly don't want to see the adoption of pricing rules that exclude impecunious users from access to literature, whether that literature be in paper or electronic form.

At the same time, it is unnecessary—indeed, inappropriate—for great public libraries to subsidize the activities of commercial entities that depend on a library for information vital to their business pursuits. Ways have been found, and should be developed further, to levy proper charges on such commercial users so that they can make a fair contribution to the costs of the information base that

---

[3] Carla Hesse, "Humanities and the Library in the Digital Age," in *What's Happened to the Humanities?*, ed. Alvin Kernan (Princeton, NJ: Princeton University Press, 1997), 107–11, quote on 110–11.}

[4] Lieberman, Noll, and Steinmueller, "The Sources of Scientific Journal Price Increase." Similarly, an article in *Investor's Business Daily* (August 29, 1995, p. A9) quoted the chairman of the SEC as saying that "a library that charges people by the page or by the minute is no longer a library."

serves them. In the case of JSTOR, for example, we expect to have a different level of charges apply to for-profit subscribers.

A final point under this heading: much as I believe in the virtues of subscription pricing, and unfettered access to information, I am not in favor of interpreting these principles in a simplistic way. There will be situations, particularly in the electronic world we have entered, in which it makes excellent sense to provide some special services ("enhancements") to those who are willing and able to pay for them. Scholarly associations and publishers are wrestling with such questions now as they seek ways to make their journals broadly accessible over campus networks without killing off individual subscriptions. The challenge is to find a sane balance between the need to make the "basics" equally available to all and the desirability of assigning some costs, and especially the costs of "extras," to those who can and should help to cover them. Libraries have an important stake in the outcome of these discussions, since costs to libraries can be moderated to the extent that individual subscribers contribute some revenue to the publishing entity.

COLLABORATION AND SYSTEM-WIDE ISSUES

Everyone seems agreed that new technologies make it much easier to collaborate and to share scarce resources. The Mellon Foundation has invested considerable sums of money in assisting libraries in Eastern Europe to develop integrated library automation systems. Similarly, we have been pleased to support the development of network information centers for (and in) Latin America. We are now exploring the possibility of connecting what have been separate libraries in key regions within South Africa.

It is easier, however, to understand how collaboration will make things better than it is to understand how collaboration will make things cheaper *for the overall system of scholarly communication.* Providing better information concerning the holdings in neighboring libraries is obviously a good thing to do, and integrated or coordinated cataloguing systems may also facilitate space savings by making it less necessary for every library to retain all of the same materials. But the calculus becomes more complex when coordinated acquisitions programs are considered. From the perspective of a group of libraries, it makes all kinds of sense to divide up the responsibility for building collections; not everyone needs to subscribe to the same journals, for example. But the implications of such economies for publishers need to be understood. In some situations, the net effect may be simply to reduce revenues for publishers, thereby encouraging higher unit prices. Cost-shifting is very different from genuine cost-saving, from the perspective of the system as a whole.

There is not time today to explore in any detail a host of subtle distinctions along this continuum. Perhaps it will suffice to say that it is important for all of us to seek genuine reductions in costs *for the system*, which then need to be managed conscientiously and shared appropriately. At a time of scarce resources, it is very tempting to pursue "beggar-my-neighbor" policies, and at some level the different sets of institutional actors have to be expected to look out for their own self-interest. But somewhere in the process attention also needs to be paid to the long-term welfare of the entire system of scholarly communication. In this connection, I think it is especially important that libraries insist on "open architecture" and common standards so that the convenience and long-term needs of users are exalted over the narrower interests of those vendors who would seek to market proprietary solutions that may offer short-term advantages to a favored constituency.

THE ROLE OF FOUNDATIONS

This last set of observations brings me to one of the roles that foundations can play. While there is an ever-present danger of arrogance and of trying to impose views, including poorly formed views, on those who in fact know more, it is also possible for foundations to assist well-conceived efforts to advance the common cause. The Commission on Preservation and Access is one example of an entity serving such purposes. Our foundation has also been pleased to support the work of the Association of Research Libraries, and there are many other entities that could be mentioned. Let me mention just one substantive area in which good collaborative work continues to be needed: the world-wide meaning of copyright and fair use in an electronic world.

I want to end these comments by emphasizing another role of foundations as funders of the great libraries. Apart from supporting particular projects in particular libraries which fit within programmatic objectives, foundations have an over-riding obligation, I believe, to think with you about emerging needs that are system-wide and to help design, if we are wise enough, creative ways of addressing them. Increasingly this will involve thinking through opportunities to utilize new technologies and participating ever more actively in collaborations and new partnerships. As in the case of JSTOR, foundations can be expected to make some of the large upfront investments that will be required—and, as a consequence, to be the principal risk-takers for the system. Libraries cannot be expected to assume such a role, but you can be expected to welcome new ideas.

There will always be those who want to wait a bit longer before putting even a toe in swirling water—and there will be times when the voice of caution is exactly the voice that should be heeded. But inertia is a powerful force, and I suspect that more often you will be tempted to want to be too sure of an outcome before taking the proverbial plunge. Unless I am badly mistaken, the traditional funders, on which the great libraries will have to continue to depend for the great bulk of their support, will become impatient with even any appearance of unwillingness to adapt and make changes. One of the many lessons I have learned through my intimate and at times grueling involvement with the JSTOR adventure is that in the field of technology, perhaps especially, we learn principally by doing, and then by correcting our errors. Economists sometimes say that the best is the enemy of the good. I would encourage you, then, if you succeed in resisting the allure of most seemingly crazy ideas, at least to be open to persuasion. At the same time, you should insist, vigorously, on a clear commitment by the proponent of any new approach to assemble real data that can be used to make a fair assessment of what has been tried.

Perhaps above all, we should continue to exchange ideas and experiences, without fear of looking foolish. As one of my great teachers used to be fond of saying: "There is no limit to the amount of nonsense one can propound when one thinks too long alone." In that spirit, I want to thank you again for the opportunity to think out loud with you this morning and to participate, as a colleague and admirer, in the celebration of the centennial of what is truly "one of the great libraries of the world."

MIT OPENCOURSEWARE CELEBRATION

~

William G. Bowen
October 4, 2004

REMARKS

It is a privilege for me to participate in this grand event, which I see as a celebration of a great institution and an opportunity to reflect on a great idea—OCW—and some of the larger questions that it raises.

OPENCOURSEWARE

When the OpenCourseWare initiative was first brought to my attention by your president, Chuck Vest, one morning at breakfast at a simple diner on Second Avenue in New York, I was immediately intrigued by the apparent simplicity of the OCW concept, the boldness of the vision, and the potential for doing good in the world. Subsequent conversations confirmed my early intuition, and I know that I speak for Paul Brest at Hewlett as well as for myself when I say how gratifying it has been to be able to support OCW in its start-up mode. I should add that the commitment of the MIT faculty to this concept has been most impressive, as has the leadership provided by Anne Margulies and many others here at MIT.

Editor's note: Bill spoke at an event celebrating the success of MIT's OpenCourseWare (OCW) initiative at the end of Chuck Vest's tenure as president.

In considering new ideas, one of my friends is fond of asking: "But will the dog eat the dog food?" In the case of OCW, the enthusiastic reaction from around the world is the answer; the response has been truly extraordinary. Users have been identified from more than 215 countries, territories, and city states, including every member of the United Nations. Well over half of all the traffic has come from outside North America. OCW's international reach reflects MIT's broader commitment to the worldwide sharing of knowledge; this institution is, to my way of thinking, *the* most international of all of this country's great universities. Looking at usage from another vantage point, individuals who characterize themselves as "self-learners" make up 52 percent of all users—with students and educators, and especially young educators, right behind. Not surprisingly, content from electrical engineering and computer science courses has been of particular interest, but we should note that roughly two-thirds of the users have accessed material from other fields, including the humanities. One of my colleagues directed my attention to the "Visualizing Culture" course, which uses wonderful images to convey how the Japanese and the Americans saw each other when Perry entered Tokyo Bay in the mid-1800s ("Black Ships and Samurai" is, I believe, a shorthand title for this content). The overall level of satisfaction expressed by users of every kind has been very high. So all of you who have had a hand in developing this remarkable resource have grounds for feeling very good about what you have accomplished. Congratulations!

I certainly do not mean to suggest that all of this has been done easily or without a need to come to grips with tough issues such as the management of intellectual property rights, how to minimize the time commitment of faculty already working at full throttle, and how to standardize the presentation of course materials without being overly rigid (to cite just those three). I can only imagine the hours of discussion and consultation that were required to get OCW where it is today. And all of you appear to be still smiling at one another—remarkable!

As we think more generally about the decision to launch OCW as a "public good," I want to underscore an aspect of the history of this project that should be remembered. Steve Lerman and Shigeru Miyagawa have written an exceptionally informative "case study" detailing the internal process of analysis and institutional decision-making that culminated in the OCW model as we know it today. The study is refreshing in its honesty. It reminds us that in considering the future of what was then called "e-learning," "MIT's core team began with the idea of making its program generate revenue." For at least one brief moment, the team considered launching a for-profit arm of MIT. However, an intensive analysis of preferences of potential "customers," market opportunities, and business scenarios cast doubt on the "the initial idea of a lifelong learning program that would generate net revenue." At the same time, more thought was given to MIT's fundamental educational mission—to advance and disseminate knowledge worldwide. *Thus, the OCW concept was born out of a union of mission-driven thinking and a hard-headed appreciation of business realities.* I will not take the time to list other e-learning initiatives that failed to get beyond easy assumptions about pots of gold at the end of digital rainbows.

In today's environment, when there is much heated debate as to whether it is ideologically acceptable to seek to recover any part of the costs of a digital project by imposing user fees of one kind or another, it is well to recall that the decision about the pricing of OCW (make it free to the world) was not ideologically driven. Rather, it grew out of a careful analysis of the pros and cons of different approaches. Let me suggest to my economist friends at MIT and elsewhere that there is a real need for good analytical thinking about the circumstances in which one distribution/pricing approach or another makes the most sense. In brief, I think that the right pricing structure depends on, among other things, the applicability of the "exclusion principle," the shape of cost curves, the ability to segment markets, and the availability of alternative ways of achieving "fair access" without sacrificing sustainability. A closely related set of questions concerns the mindsets and skill sets needed to make sound judgments in both strategic and operational realms. Kevin Guthrie (founding president of JSTOR and now president of ITHAKA, who is with us today) has pointed out that people in universities are generally more inclined to think about seeking grant support—where they have a lot of experience—than they are to probe revenue-generating options that require entrepreneurial skills and entail market risk.

There is, in any event, "no free lunch"—no escape from the unavoidable question of how best to cover costs and achieve sustainability over the long run. In the case of OCW, I think that MIT made the right call (given its internal culture and its sense of its own mission). I admire MIT's announced institutional commitment to sustain OCW as a "free" resource over the long run. But how are commitments of this kind to be met? This is hardly a trivial question. Projects such as OCW will need ongoing support from philanthropically minded individuals and institutions that possess an understanding of both the social value of the enterprise and its basic organizational and economic characteristics.

My second big point concerns "democratization." MIT as an institution unquestionably benefits from the support that Hewlett and Mellon provide to OCW, but the real benefits are far broader. Every time that there is a discussion at Mellon of how much money we give to the most prestigious universities, I remind myself (and my colleagues) that the real benefits of many of these grants go not so much to the rich and privileged institutions that receive them as they do to all the folks "down the line" who benefit from the projects that these grants support. The data on usage that MIT-OCW has assembled demonstrate that, by and large, the greatest benefits are received by those with the least resources—in the United States and abroad. The most moving words of thanks come from the "independent scholar" in the Midwest and from faculty members and graduate students in Malaysia, India, and China. This is not a unique pattern. One of the most noteworthy aspects of JSTOR (the electronic archive of scholarly literature sponsored by the Mellon Foundation) is how important it is to the Appalachian colleges, the HBCUs [historically black colleges and universities], and resource-poor institutions in Africa, Eastern Europe, Latin America, and Asia. Similarly, the ARTstor database (the foundation's new digital archive of art images and related scholarly materials) has appealed initially to a large number of community colleges as well as to well-endowed research universities such as Stanford and Yale. By supporting digital projects of these kinds, the foundation benefits legions of users that it could never reach through traditional grant-making mechanisms.

In closing, I want to recognize the courageous leadership of Chuck Vest in conceiving and shepherding this project to this point. For OCW to have succeeded, it had to have great leadership from on high. This was not a project for the timid. But then Chuck Vest has been anything but timid in the leadership that he has brought to MIT for over almost a decade and a half.

CHAPTER 5

TECHNOLOGY, EDUCATION, AND OPPORTUNITY

ACADEMIA ONLINE: MUSINGS (SOME UNCONVENTIONAL)

❧

William G. Bowen
October 14, 2013

STAFFORD LITTLE LECTURE, PRINCETON UNIVERSITY

It is humbling to be part of a lecture series that dates from the time of President Cleveland and has included such luminaries as Albert Einstein and Gunnar Myrdal.

The topic I have chosen is "Academia Online: Musings (Some Unconventional)." So much has been said on the general subject of online learning that I run the risk of going over ground that is already familiar. To minimize that risk, I will begin by providing only the barest context. I will then discuss, in a "musing" mode with no claim of saying anything definitive, four ramifications of online learning that I regard as highly consequential: (1) "unbundling" of both faculty and institutional functions; (2) implications for the shape of the entire higher education sector; (3) impending changes in doctoral education; and (4) "equity" concerns that differ from those made famous by Myrdal but that are no less challenging. (There is a fifth topic that is very important but that I pass over because of lack of time: namely, the implications of online

Editor's note: The Stafford Little Lectures are a public lecture series at Princeton University. Other distinguished individuals who have given the Stafford Little Lecture include Daniel Kahneman, Andrew Delbanco, James Fallows, and Steven Levitt.

Author's note: I wish to thank Lawrence S. Bacow, Kevin M. Guthrie, Deanna Marcum, Michael S. McPherson, Christine Mulhern, Richard Spies, Eugene M. Tobin, Sarah E. Turner, and Derek Wu for many helpful comments on earlier drafts of this talk. I also thank Johanna Brownell for her invaluable help with the preparation of a final version.

technologies for "shared governance" and faculty roles in decision-making.) My focus will be on all of four-year higher education in the United States, *not* on Princeton. Princeton is—and will remain—an "outlier."

CONTEXT

To attempt to estimate the current extent of online learning, or to enumerate its near-limitless forms, would be foolhardy. I spare all of us that exercise.[1] Suffice it to say that not a day passes without some new initiative or some new commentary on a phenomenon that is worldwide. Driving the proliferation of online offerings are three fundamental forces, which are likely to prove lasting.

- First, dramatic improvements in Internet speed and availability, reductions in storage costs, and other technological advances have combined with changing mindsets to make possible a staggering variety of online formats that have captured the imagination of many teachers and scholars, especially those interested in reaching a wide audience.
- Second, this generation's students (the next generation's faculty members) embrace all things digital and expect to communicate in this way, whatever institution they attend.
- Third, there is a growing consensus in public discourse that current trends in both the cost of higher education and such outcomes as completion rates and time-to-degree are neither acceptable nor sustainable. There is no denying public impatience with tuition increases in higher education that have been driven in part by reductions in support (especially in state appropriations).[2] This impatience, coupled with a sense that "business as usual" will not suffice, has spurred a search for more cost-effective approaches than those we have known traditionally. Illustrative is

[1] My former colleague Kelly Lack and I attempt to provide a kind of "reader's guide" to the online learning landscape in the appendix to William G. Bowen, *Higher Education in the Digital Age* (Princeton, NJ: Princeton University Press, 2013), pp. 72–77.

[2] For an unusually explicit statement of a direct link between state funding decisions and tuition increases, see Brendan Bures, "Tuition Increase Imminent for FSU [Florida State University]; Barron Obligated to Hike Costs Against Wishes," *FSU News*, August 25, 2013.

President Obama's continuing emphasis on the seriousness of this issue; his disappointment that higher education has not, on its own, done more to address the problem; and his renewed calls for action, complete with proposals for ways of addressing the problem.[3] There is, I fear, too much complacency in much of higher education—too much of a sense that if we just "hang in there," all will be well. Higher education needs to do its part—and then some—in adjusting to new realities.

Amid all the argument over whether online learning is, in one form or another, a "good thing"—a solution to deep-seated problems or, in fact, a new problem of its own—there is general agreement that "the genie is out of the bottle." Online learning is, without question, here to stay. We can and should discuss—and with some urgency—how it can be improved, which audiences are best served by one approach or another, and what research teaches us about both learning outcomes and costs. There is, truth be told, far too little hard evidence available about what works and what cost savings, if any, can be anticipated. More rigorous research is desperately needed. Examples of flawed research abound.[4] In thinking about these issues, it is essential to compare "actuals" with "actuals" and to avoid the mistake of comparing an online offering with an

[3] See Michael D. Shear, "Obama to Offer Plans to Ease Burden of Paying for College," *New York Times*, August 21, 2013, online edition, www.nytimes.com/2013/08/21/education /obama-to-offer-plans-to-ease-burden-of-paying-for-college.html. See "FACT SHEET on the President's Plan to Make College More Affordable: A Better Bargain for the Middle Class," Office of the Press Secretary, the White House, August 22, 2013, and Kelly E. Field, "Obama's Lofty Goals on College Costs Face Long Odds," *Chronicle of Higher Education*, August 28, 2103.

[4] In September 2013, there was a report on a project at San Jose State involving a "test" of the effectiveness of a Udacity offering, and I put "test" in quotes precisely because of the problems with this "research." Particularly striking is the obvious power of selection effects (allowing students with different backgrounds and predilections to choose the teaching format that they prefer). As many of those who have commented on this project recognize, we just have to do much better than this "test" if we are to get anywhere in studying both learning outcomes for various groups of students and the costs of various kinds of "treatments." See Carl Straumsheim, "The Full Report on Udacity Experiment," *Inside Higher Ed*, September 12, 2013. See also the earlier article by the same author, "San Jose State U Posts Improved Online Course Results, but Udacity Partnership Remains on Pause," *Inside Higher Ed*, August 28, 2013. Particularly striking are the methodological problems, combined with the disappointing results for Udacity's entry-level math offering—presumably "favorable" selection effects notwithstanding. Various individuals in the California system are reported to be (properly) skeptical about the allegedly positive results cited in earlier reports.

idealized version of face-to-face teaching in some "golden age"—
such as the opportunity Henry Cabot Lodge had to study medieval
history with Henry Adams at Harvard.[5] We also know far too little
about what actually works in face-to-face environments. New online initiatives should prod us to study rigorously the effectiveness
of traditional modes of teaching as well as alternative approaches.[6]

The lack of much solid research notwithstanding, the world
moves on. We can be confident that online learning, which is in its
infancy, will improve. While there is still opportunity to affect outcomes, and to avoid unintended consequences that are undesirable, we should be giving serious thought to the broader implications of online technologies.

UNBUNDLING

Let us begin by considering the possible "unbundling" of both faculty and institutional roles in teaching. Over time, some faculty
roles could change dramatically in an online world. When I was in

---

[5] See Hunter Rawling's remarks at the installation of President Eisgruber at Princeton
University, September 22, 2013, in which he quotes Henry Cabot Lodge with respect to a
course he had taken at Harvard:

> "In all my four years, I never really studied anything, never had my mind roused to
> any exertion or to anything resembling active thought until in my senior year I stum-
> bled into the course in medieval history given by Henry Adams, who had then just
> come to Harvard.... [Adams] had the power not only of exciting interest, but he
> awakened opposition to his own views, and this is one great secret of success in
> teaching.... I worked hard in that course because it gave me pleasure. I took the
> highest marks, for which I cared, as I found, singularly little, because marks were not
> my object, and for the first time I got a glimpse of what education might be and re-
> ally learned something.... Yet it was not what I learned but the fact that I learned
> something, that I discovered that it was the keenest of pleasures to use one's mind, a
> new sensation, and one which made Mr. Adams's course in the history of the Middle
> Ages so memorable to me." Gary Wills, *Henry Adams and the Making of America*
> (Boston: Houghton Mifflin, 2005), p. 89.

My thoughts on how to improve online learning (in different contexts and for different
pedagogies), and how we should be thinking about studies of the effectiveness of learning
outcomes and potential cost savings, are in my *Higher Education in a Digital Age* (Princeton, NJ: Princeton University Press, 2013), especially on pp. 46–61.

[6] See my remarks at the inauguration of Daniel Weiss as president of Haverford, October
26, 2013.

charge of Economics 101 at Princeton in the halcyon days of yore, I was responsible for setting the syllabus of the course, crafting and giving lectures, working with others to plan the weekly sections that accompanied the lectures, leading one or two of the sections myself, responding to questions, counseling students (I recall asking one student who had great difficulty plotting points on a two-dimensional graph: "Is this really the right subject for you?"), designing and supervising the grading of the tests used to evaluate student performance, and writing recommendations. Although I certainly had help, I thought of Economics 101 as "my course." Although in some ways independent, these various components of the course were all connected and bounded by geography—all of the participants in this educational experience were together in one place, Princeton.

Now, as a result of the digitization of information and its availability nearly everywhere on ubiquitous networks, new regimes beckon in at least some parts of higher education. Who "owns" a course when

- the delivery platform comes from a MOOC [massive open online course] producer (for-profit or not);
- much of the content comes from professors/lecturers at other universities (obtained through the MOOC producer, from the institutions employing those faculty members giving the lectures, from textbook providers, or even directly from the off-campus lecturer);
- automated online quizzes and advising tools come from yet another organization;
- teaching assistance and mentoring are provided by a shifting array of TAs provided by the on-campus institution;
- and many kinds of support decisions are made by a central administration—about the amount and kind of IT and other technical and administrative support provided, the number and qualifications of the TAs assigned to the course, legal support for agreements with third-party partners and perhaps even with on-campus faculty.

Moreover, these questions become even more complicated when we contemplate situations in which one of the original participants in creating this multi-dimensional course dies, retires, or moves to another institution. Or suppose that one or another of the putative "owners" wishes to make the same course, or much of it, available to other campuses or to students with no campus affiliation—with or without compensation and with or without "credit" being offered. In prospect is a much more complicated world in which new thought will need to be given to who has (or should have) the authority to make decisions of various kinds concerning instructional methods.

Unbundling can of course occur not only at the level of the individual course but also across an institution's entire set of educational offerings—as more and more people in higher education recognize, often with fear and trembling and through clenched teeth. Unbundling at the institutional level could be highly consequential. The Internet is the classic mechanism for unbundling, and we are all familiar with how lethal technology-driven unbundling has been in many sectors (note the loss of classified ads by newspapers and the success of Amazon in bypassing bookstores). One trustee of a liberal arts college [Dan Currell] argues:

> We haven't seen unbundled education at the college level yet … [in part] because colleges have kept education and evaluation tightly bundled together. The professor teaches *and* evaluates progress; the college offers courses *and* confers a degree…. It won't necessarily stay this way. There is no reason why education and evaluation will necessarily stay bundled together, and one can already see movement in the direction of the two splitting apart.[7]

Currell is right; things need not stay as they are. It is easy to imagine, conceptually, colleges and universities unbundling a vari-

---

[7] See Dan Currell, "In Tempestuous Times, Colleges Must Decide What They're For (Essay)," *Inside Higher Ed*, June 28, 2013. Currell is a trustee of Gustavus Adolphus College and executive director with the Legal, Risk and Compliance Practice at the Corporate Executive Board. See Scott Jaschik, "Obama's Ratings for Higher Ed," *Inside Higher Ed*, August 22, 2013: "The White House also said President Obama is 'challenging' colleges to 'adopt one or more' of the practices he called 'promising' to "offer breakthroughs on cost, quality or both." Among them: competency-based learning that moves away from seat time, course redesign (including massive open online courses), the use of technology for student services, and more efforts to recognize prior learning."

ety of functions (some kinds of advising, mentoring, evaluating, and even—heaven forbid—providing entertainment in the form of big-time football and basketball!). Of course, colleges and universities have for many years outsourced support functions such as food services and facilities management. Increasingly, in recent years, activities much closer to the academic heart of the institution have also been outsourced, such as access to scholarly journals—JSTOR. More fundamentally, we are already familiar with some degree of unbundling of course offerings, especially at the introductory level, via standard transfer mechanisms. More complex forms of transfer credit or credit for competency-based learning are clearly on the horizon.[8]

THE SHAPE OF THINGS TO COME: SEEN "THROUGH A GLASS DARKLY"

Now let us contemplate the shape of things to come. The kinds of unbundling enabled by advances in technology and driven by worries about educational costs will have ramifications for the entire higher education sector that no one can foresee—hence, I think that those of us brave enough, or foolish enough, to speculate about such things need to be clear that we are viewing the future "through a glass darkly."

At one extreme there is the proposition that the coming-of-age of online learning will have truly radical effects and will mean the demise—in whole or in large part—of face-to-face teaching and the residential model. As Peter Drucker asked back in 1989, "Will tomorrow's university be a 'knowledge centre' which transmits information rather than a place that students actually attend?"[9]

It is true that *some* forms of online learning can substitute for *some* forms of face-to-face instruction in *some* settings. This has

[8] See Paul Fain, "Competency-Based Transcripts," *Inside Higher Ed*, August 9, 2013. See also Jeffrey J. Selingo, "The New Nonlinear Path through College," *Chronicle of Higher Education*, September 30, 2013, and Scott Carlson, "Competency-Based Education Goes Mainstream in Wisconsin," *Chronicle of Higher Education*, October 1, 2013.
[9] See Peter F. Drucker, *The New Realities* (London: Elsevier, 1989), p. 249.

happened already in parts of higher education, and especially for working adults in vocational fields.[10] Within the arts and sciences, colleagues and I demonstrated the cost-effectiveness of a well-designed Carnegie Mellon statistics course taught in a hybrid mode at six mainstream public universities—we retained a limited amount of face-to-face interaction, and we used a random assignment methodology to avoid selection bias.[11] But the hybrid approach that we studied is a far cry from the model envisioned by the far more sweeping assertions about the impending demise of face-to-face teaching in its entirety. Such a development is not at all likely. Indeed, I believe it to be unthinkable. Our study used one sophisticated method of teaching a beginning course in a field, statistics, extremely well suited to adaptive learning (there is, after all, one answer to the question What is a t-test?). It is far from obvious that the same pedagogy will work anything like as well in teaching subjects such as literature and international affairs. Face-to-face learning in many subjects and many settings will continue to persist for two very good reasons.

First, such teaching makes a great deal of educational sense, a priori, when we are trying to teach not only well-known concepts (the definition of a t-test) but also nuanced notions such as how to frame questions in value-laden subjects, how to distinguish evidence from opinion, how to take account of different points of view, how to formulate one's own position on complex questions, how to express oneself verbally and in writing, how to engage with others as a member of an intellectual community, and even how to approach an understanding of "life lessons." Most fundamentally, we want to engender in students the excitement associated with encountering a new idea—an experience I first had, in full measure, as a graduate student at Princeton.[12]

---

[10] See Paul Fain, "Experimental College's First Graduate," *Inside Higher Ed*, August 16, 2013, www.insidehighered.com/news/2013/08/16/new-form-competency-based-learnings -first-batch-graduates.

[11] See William G. Bowen, Matthew M. Chingos, Kelly A. Lack, and Thomas I. Nygren, "Interactive Learning Online at Public Universities: Evidence from Randomized Trials," May 22, 2012, available on the ITHAKA website at www.sr.ithaka.org.

[12] The eyes of one of my great teachers, Jacob Viner, sparkled when he demonstrated the intense pleasure of engagement with a new way of thinking. He taught me, and many oth-

A second reason for betting on the survival of good face-to-face teaching is that there will continue to be a demand for it. If application patterns are any guide (and, as a staunch believer in revealed preference, I think they are), a great many students and families will continue to pay dearly for the privilege of being part of a learning community that is about more than just acquisition of known concepts. Of course, the value proposition here includes much more than just the virtues of face-to-face teaching—it includes round-the-clock associations in settings conducive to give and take with a wonderfully diverse set of classmates. Such experiences can do wonders in the teaching of social skills as well as cognitive content, can provide invaluable opportunities to acquire leadership skills, and can lead to lifelong friendships. It would be a brave soul—and an uninformed soul, I would say—who would bet against this model perpetuating itself, even as we recognize that it will serve a small and highly privileged population which, in its demographics, is by no means a cross-section of all students.

Much more interesting than extreme models is the vast middle ground—where one can expect to find some online learning in a dizzying array of formats, in an innumerable variety of settings, and often used in conjunction with traditional forms of teaching.[13] Our system of higher education, if "system" is even the right word, is famously heterogeneous, and we are therefore blessed with literally hundreds (thousands?) of different educational models. New experiments are launched every day, and we are inundated with a surfeit of claims and counter-claims, most of them based on assertion rather than on evidence. It is my devout hope that we will indeed see "a hundred flowers bloom," and that we will avoid the stultifying effects of imitation and wrong-headed searches for a single right formula—that we will avoid forced standardization.

It would be splendid if the best of the burgeoning array of MOOCs could be harnessed to address at least some of the all-too-

ers, that learning is great fun—a lesson that has had a lifelong impact on me. But I recognize, as one of my colleagues has pointed out to me, that this kind of experience is all too rare.

[13] See, for example, the account of the growth of various kinds of online courses at Iowa State University: "Enrollment, Student Demand Fuels Growth for Online Courses at ISU," Iowa State University News Service, posted August 26, 2013, www.news.iastate.edu/news/2013/08/26/onlinecourses.

real challenges facing the large number of public colleges and universities that educate the vast majority of undergraduates in this country seeking BA degrees, as well as the army of community college students. But whether this is possible is an open question. We simply do not know. MOOCs were developed, after all, to reach vast numbers of *individual* students without reference to their institutional affiliation, if any, and without reference to existing educational infrastructures. They have demonstrated their capacity to engage large numbers of individuals all over the world (high drop-out rates notwithstanding), many of whom otherwise would have had no access to any form of higher education, and this is surely a splendid accomplishment. But engaging an individual student in a corner of India is very different from fitting within an institutional context and delivering good educational outcomes in a structured setting and in a cost-effective way. Modifying MOOCs to serve this large and highly consequential population entails overcoming very substantial technological *and* organizational challenges as we contemplate departures from the initial "one-size-fits-all" MOOC model. Right now, Ithaka S+R is carrying out a study in collaboration with the University System of Maryland to see what can be accomplished by using content and platforms created elsewhere to teach courses in a real-world institutional setting—recognizing that the hybrid courses we are testing are not really MOOCs, in that they are not "massive," not "open," and only partially "online."[14] As a former Princeton trustee, John Doar, said when leading the Nixon impeachment inquiry, "We will know more later." The jury is still out.

There are many other experiments underway. For example, the University of Texas [UT] at Austin has announced that, following almost a decade of research, two of its psychology professors will be offering what it calls "the world's first synchronous massive

[14] See "Interactive Online Learning on Campus: Testing MOOCs and Other Platforms in Hybrid Formats in the University System of Maryland," *Ithaka S+R*, November 8, 2012, www.sr.ithaka.org/research-publications/informing-innovation-higher-education-evidence -implementing-latest-online. Interim report forthcoming. This work at Maryland reminds me powerfully of the value of the enthusiasm and creativity of individual faculty members— which need to be treasured, not just tolerated, and certainly not repressed. But such creativity does need to be channeled.

online course." The course will teach up to ten thousand students who must make themselves available at 6 pm on Tuesdays and Thursdays and who will be charged a $550 registration fee. The class will be split into a number of smaller "pods" that will be monitored by former students who essentially work as online TAs. Students who finish the course will earn three transferrable credit hours. It will be exceedingly interesting to see the results of this undertaking—and to examine closely not only the educational outcomes, but also the all-in costs, which are hardly mentioned in a story about the UT initiative.[15]

Let me re-emphasize the importance of the cost blade of the online scissors. As I have said on other occasions, I am "more than bemused—actually I am dismayed"—by the lack of attention being paid, especially by faculty members, to the pressing need to control educational costs.[16] Unappealing as it may be to focus on costs (which of course can mean unwelcome changes in faculty staffing and in faculty roles), and satisfying as it may be to focus instead on the glories of teaching, in both old and new modes, it borders on the irresponsible to ignore the pressures to control costs—and the concomitant need to make the most intelligent, educationally sensitive trade-offs that can be identified. To most observers, it is crystal clear that limits on available state funding have led to reduced appropriations to higher education that, in turn, have forced up tuition and often prevented fully offsetting increases in financial aid for needy students. It is simply wrong to suggest that cost savings made possible by technology have been the driving force in reducing state support; indeed, we have seen that efforts to control

[15] See Carl Straumsheim, "UT Psychology Professors Prepare 'World's First' Synchronous Massive Online Course," *Inside Higher Ed*, August 27, 2013. The professors report that the research that led up to this offering demonstrated that their adaptive learning approach produced both better overall grades and a reduction in the achievement gap between upper, middle, and lower-income students. See Also Ry Rivard, "Georgia Tech and Udacity Roll Out Massive New Low-Cost Degree Program," *Inside Higher Ed*, May 14, 2013. Georgia Tech plans to offer a master's program for a fraction of the cost (less than $7,000 per year versus the standard program cost of $40,000 per year) to ten thousand students online.

[16] See Bowen, *Higher Education in the Digital Age*, and William G. Bowen, "The Potential for Online Learning: Promises and Pitfalls," *EDUCAUSE Review* 48, no. 5 (September–October 2013).

costs can lead to more sympathetic consideration of the need to sustain state funding.[17] Nor are reductions in state funding the only source of pressures to save money. Evidence available this fall [2013] reminds us that a number of institutions are also suffering from reduced enrollments.[18] Tuition-dependent private institutions seem especially vulnerable.

In seeking to contribute to the near-void of evidence as to what savings from the judicious use of online technologies might be achieved, Ithaka S+R, with support from the Spencer Foundation and the cooperation, once again, of the University System of Maryland, is embarking on a simulation of what educational costs might look like under a new regime in which constraints on section sizes and the need to rely on existing plant and scheduling conventions are relaxed. The intention is to study the costs of a carefully blended combination of online teaching and personalized instruction. It is entirely possible that scheduling innovations could themselves lead to improved completion rates and reduced time-to-degree without anything like commensurate increases in costs. Such new approaches could also enable colleges and universities to educate larger numbers of both traditional and non-traditional students without anything like proportionate increases in faculty and other resources, a goal recognized by policy-makers at both the federal and the state levels to be highly important in meeting the needs of our increas-

---

[17] One telling example of the direction of causation is provided by experience in the state of Maryland, where the university system reached a "compact" of sorts with the state. As the chancellor, William ("Brit") Kirwan explains (in personal correspondence, September 7, 2013): "In return for a systematic and sustained effort at cost containment, the state agreed to protect our budget, at least in relative terms and in effect 'buy down' tuition increases with general funds." Kirwan is scathing in his dismissal of the proposition that institutions should avoid seeking cost-effective reductions in educational costs. This argument, in Kirwan's words, "epitomizes why higher education is in such trouble." He goes on to say: "Few outside higher education could understand an argument that says, 'If an institution might produce better results with lower costs, then you should abandon the initiative.' " There is also abundant evidence from other states that reductions in state support have occurred in the absence of cost-saving innovations.

[18] As of May 2012, 59 percent of private bachelor's institutions and 77 percent of public master's or bachelor's institutions had failed to meet their enrollment targets. See Scott Jaschik, "Feeling the Heat: The 2013 Survey of College and University Admissions Directors," *Inside Higher Ed*, September 18, 2013, and Eric Hoover and Beckie Supiano, "In Admissions, Old Playbook Is Being Revised," *Chronicle of Higher Education*, September 16, 2013.

ingly knowledge-based economy. Online courses driven by sophisticated technology should also enable entirely new ways of studying how students learn, how to diagnose and fix common problems, and how to form new kinds of user communities. Technology should also enable us to find more cost-effective ways of discharging expensive support functions, such as advising.

To continue to muse about longer-term possibilities, I can envision a world in which more institutions adopt what I call a "portfolio" approach to curricular development. By this I mean that certain kinds of classes—and especially introductory courses in subjects in which, at least at this level, there is widespread agreement on "the right answer" to basic questions (beginning math is one example)—might be taught using online approaches plus some admixture of advising, tutoring, and mentoring; resources saved in this way might be re-deployed, at least in part, to provide the personalized instruction in seminars and in directed study that can be so rewarding. Ideally, students would be assigned, or encouraged to choose, a mix of courses that would give them a well-calibrated exposure to various modes of teaching. Only in rare cases would instruction be exclusively online.

Over time, many institutions may want to import some online instruction, particularly in introductory courses in basic subjects such as beginning math and in advanced courses in a variety of fields that small colleges, for example, could not staff properly on their own. As I have argued in *Higher Education in the Digital Age*, there is much to be said for an intelligent division of labor, with those especially well positioned to do so constructing sophisticated platforms with feedback loops, and with user campuses demonstrating at least modest capacity to customize offerings on the platform(s). We do not need a thousand versions of a basic/customizable platform; nor should we expect every campus to start from scratch in preparing its own online materials. Some wheels do not need to be re-invented.

Let me now acknowledge a pervasive problem in higher education that no one wants to talk about: the preoccupation of many in academia with what I hope will become antiquated notions of status. This is a difficult (nay, dreadful!) topic for me to discuss in this venue, at a university that is both very special to me and clearly at the top of any pecking order—but here I am, and so, as someone once said, Onward!

The more thoughtfully integrated educational structure that I envision as a successor to the increasingly homogeneous university/college system now present depends on our taking advantage of economies of scale and contemplates different roles for different players, both institutions and individuals; it values complementarities. Some institutions and some individuals are surely better positioned to be leading "producers" of sophisticated platforms and other content than are others. I also suspect that some institutions and individuals are better positioned than others (perhaps more temperamentally suited) to be extremely skillful consumers of content that originates mostly, if not entirely, elsewhere.

To be sure, different kinds of talent exist almost everywhere, and we should be careful not to exclude anyone from creative tasks for arbitrary reasons linked to wrong-headed notions of status. In fact, I suspect that market mechanisms will help achieve a sorting of people, institutions, and functions—which is certainly desirable from a system-wide perspective. At the same time, refusing to recognize the existence of institutional differences would be foolish. Some places are fortunate to have an unusually powerful combination of intellectual and financial resources—a combination that is sometimes tied to scale and even to institutional culture. If the institutions especially well positioned to make significant contributions to the development of course content and delivery mechanisms do so effectively, all of higher education will benefit. But this is certainly not to say that institutions especially well suited to be "producers" (Princeton may well be among them) should be excused from paying attention to the system-wide need to control cost increases. Ideally, they would be outstanding examples of the ability to achieve excellent educational outcomes at manageable cost.

In thinking about status issues, we need to recognize that human nature is what it is—we are not, as President Eisgruber said so eloquently in his inaugural address, "angels." Still, I think we should do our best to resist "above and below the salt" thinking. At the end of some future day, the real kudos may go to the highly creative institutional *assemblers* of intellectual content and local teaching resources. There should be a real payoff to institutions that are especially skillful in harvesting content provided by others and then adding educationally rich value of their own, including mentoring.

A closely related point is that, as Hanna Gray has suggested, major universities, and especially the multiversities that Clark Kerr made famous, should ask hard questions about the wide range of activities that many of them now undertake—in part in response to the initiatives of others. No one wants to be left behind, seemingly unable to compete for the *n*th full-paying student. The rise of "consumerism" is a reality and can easily lead to what the historian Laurence R. Veysey once called "blind imitation"—to the search by essentially all universities for a "complete" course of study and the provision of innumerable student services. In her book aptly titled *Searching for Utopia*, President Gray offers this provocative insight:

> It seems clear that universities need to confront some painful realities and become more deliberately selective in what they choose to do. Universities are overstretched in their range of programs, overbuilt in physical facilities, and overburdened by an excess of ambitions, expectations, and demands. The competition among them has led to greater homogeneity rather than constructive diversity of institutional profiles and of distinctive individual excellence. We would be better off if it were possible ... to build on each institution's comparative strengths ... Greater differentiation among institutions might encourage each to focus on its own particular mix of academic priorities.[19]

She ends her commentary by urging a rebalancing of the elements of what she calls "the stripped down university."[20]

It is by no means obvious how this country's present educational system can move in the direction which President Gray advocates,

---

[19] See Hanna Holborn Gray, *Searching for Utopia* (Berkeley: University of California Press, 2013), p. 94. After citing Veysey, President Gray gives a sobering account of recent trends (pp. 78ff).
[20] Gray, *Searching for Utopia*, p. 96.

since both current structures and assumptions about unending growth are deeply ingrained. But well-crafted incentives at the state level might make a difference in the public sector. Additional research on the costs of various programs, and their relation to student learning, might make a difference across the board.

DOCTORAL EDUCATION: IMPENDING CHANGES?

There is one super-sensitive set of activities that I feel an obligation to at least allude to, even as I recognize the pain and suffering sure to afflict anyone who even mentions this subject, never mind someone with my long ties to a prestigious university such as Princeton. I refer to the scale of doctoral education in this country, seen now in relation to ongoing trends in faculty deployment that are, in part, directly related to the combination of cost pressures and the spread of online technologies.

The current sorry state of the job market for new doctorates, trained in the traditional way, is hardly a secret.[21] There has been, without doubt, a pronounced decrease in the demand by colleges and universities for new recipients of PhDs. The intense cost pressures felt by many colleges and universities have led to both a felt need to curb faculty payrolls and an increased desire for staffing flexibility. The growth of online programs has had its own effects by reducing both the current and the prospective need for "regular" faculty trained as teacher/scholars and for individuals prepared to teach all aspects of their "own courses" in the traditional way.[22] The potential unbundling of faculty roles suggests that we may be moving toward a situation in which higher education in general needs relatively fewer "all-purpose" teacher-scholars and a larger number of individuals prepared to fill more specialized roles at various kinds of institutions.

[21] See David Mihalyfy, "Regilding the Ivory Tower," *Inside Higher Ed*, June 18, 2013.
[22] See Bowen, Chingos, Lack, and Nygren, "Interactive Learning Online at Public Universities," for very crude estimates of the potential effects of one online course on the mix of faculty needed. This crude simulation is but the tip of the proverbial iceberg, and it will be important to look closely at the results of the cost simulations the ITHAKA team is going to prepare for much more refined estimates of possible longer-term effects.

One consequence of the incipient stages of these trends evident already is the substitution of adjuncts (part-time faculty) for regular faculty. Those of us inclined to focus our attention on the most privileged institutions (such as members of this audience) may be surprised by the magnitude of what has transpired already. David Figlio and his colleagues at Northwestern have summarized data documenting the dramatic decline in the share of all faculty (excluding graduate students) in the tenure system: the fraction declined from 57 percent in 1975 to 30 percent in 2009, and it is still falling. Figlio et al. also report the results of a most interesting study at their own university that suggests that non-tenure-line faculty teaching introductory courses contributed more than regular faculty to lasting student learning.[23] These learning outcomes, based on work in introductory courses, are presumably very different from the learning that occurs through directed study and seminars, formats in which I would think regular faculty enjoy a real advantage. In any case, many institutions have concluded that adjuncts both cost less than regular faculty and provide more staffing flexibility.

Another factor to consider is the prospective reduction in the need for teaching assistants (TAs) that is likely to result from greater use of adaptive learning technologies (machine-guided learning) in many introductory courses. It is, of course, the current need for a large number of TAs that justifies (and pays for) the scale of many doctoral programs.[24]

[23] See David N. Figlio, Morton O. Schapiro, and Kevin B. Soter, "Are Tenure Track Professors Better Teachers?," NBER Working Paper 19406, National Bureau of Economic Research, Cambridge, MA, September 2013. The authors also cite a number of other studies of teaching effectiveness, measured in different ways, of various categories of faculty or teachers.

[24] My colleague Lawrence S. Bacow has emphasized repeatedly the importance of TAs in driving decisions of all kinds concerning doctoral programs. Thus he has observed: "As online learning becomes more prevalent, I think that the demand for TAs and the allocation of them across disciplines is likely to shift. Assuming that deans and provosts respond accordingly, some departments are likely to see reductions in the number of TAs they are allotted and others may see increases.... I think this has big consequences for the size of graduate programs in the affected departments. Moreover, if a department cannot support the same number of graduate students through TAships, over time the size of the department may shrink (or at least it should in my mind); of course, some may also increase. My point is that online education, depending upon how it ultimately gets implemented, could have very large consequences for the size of various graduate programs." Personal correspondence, August 12, 2013.

These developments come on top of "pre-existing conditions" in doctoral education that would be serious enough without these added stresses. Robert M. Berdahl, when he was president of the Association of American Universities (AAU), once courageously asked, "How many research universities does the nation require?" He added: "I do not know how many we should have. But it is a serious question, worthy of consideration."[25] Nor are these new concerns. In the early 1990s, Neil Rudenstine and I assembled data documenting the remarkable increase in the number and growth of doctoral programs, especially those less highly ranked, during the expansionist years between 1958 and 1972. During the subsequent "lean years," the relative share of doctorates awarded by these newer and lower-ranked programs increased dramatically.[26]

As Berdahl's failed attempt to get people to focus on this question illustrates all too clearly, it is extremely difficult to modify, never mind eliminate, programs that grew up in different times. And it is of course easy to understand why institutions that are the home of what one has to acknowledge are "middling" doctoral programs want to hold on to them. Someone once said that such programs are the "soft underbelly" of American higher education. This is, in my view, the right time to face up to the growing imbalance between supply and demand in doctoral education. We need to own up to reality. We need to recognize that, as President Hennessy of Stanford said bluntly in a discussion session following one of my Tanner Lectures in 2012, we are producing too many PhDs; we are going to have to accept the fact that in the future there will be fewer "regular" faculty positions than there are today.[27]

[25] See Robert M. Berdahl, "Reassessing the Value of Research Universities," *Chronicle of Higher Education*, July 13, 2009, online edition, www.chronicle.com/article/Reassessing -the-Value-of/47038.

[26] See William G. Bowen and Neil L. Rudenstine, *In Pursuit of the PhD* (Princeton, NJ: Princeton University Press, 1992), chapter 4. Roughly thirty years earlier, in 1960, Bernard Berelson used colorful language to describe the forces that stimulate the growth of new doctoral programs, noting: "the colonization of the underdeveloped institutions by ambitious products of the developed ones who then work to make the colony a competitor of the mother university; the need to have graduate students as research and teaching assistants, partly in order to get and hold senior staff; the vanity, pride, and legitimate aspirations of the institutions." Bernard Berelson, *Graduate Education in the United States* (New York: McGraw-Hill, 1960), p. 35.

[27] See Bowen, *Higher Education in the Digital Age*, p. 33, n. 32.

Market pressures may begin to compel changes. One might expect some prospective graduate students to shy away from doctoral programs because of evident job-market concerns—but recent data showing an unexpected boost in doctoral enrollment in the humanities offer a puzzling piece of evidence to the contrary.[28] It is true that, as one person said, "we live in a free country," and if people are informed of job prospects, they should be allowed "to pursue their dreams."[29] But such pursuits are far from cost free to the society at large.

In the public sector, in particular, both individual institutions and legislators may be more and more reluctant to support the expensive infrastructure that doctoral education requires. It is hard to know if the decision of the University of Florida to end its doctoral program in economics is any kind of harbinger.[30] Whatever the preferences of individual institutions, legislators may be reluctant to support positions at non-research universities for traditionally trained faculty—especially in settings in which it is far from obvious that research capacities are going to be required of all those engaged in an unbundled set of teaching responsibilities. The purely economic consequences of moving from one staffing model to another could be considerable; what is sometimes called "departmental research" (building into the calculation of teaching loads an assumption that all faculty must be given some time for traditional research, aimed at publication) is very expensive. As Richard Spies puts it: "Research wannabes are a luxury—or maybe an inefficiency—that we will find it hard to pay for in the future."[31]

---

[28] Data released by the Council of Graduate Schools in September 2013 are summarized by Scott Jaschik in "Humanities Doctoral Programs Show Unexpected Boost in New Students," *Inside Higher Education*, September 12, 2013.

[29] See quote attributed to Debra Stewart in *Inside Higher Ed*, September 12, 2013.

[30] See Stacey Patton, "Once Flourishing Economics PhD Program Prepares to Die," *Chronicle of Higher Education*, September 10, 2013, online edition, www.chronicle.com /article/A-Once-Flourishing-Economics/141471. It should be noted that prospects for graduates of PhD programs in economics are better than prospects for doctorate recipients in many other fields. But the costs to institutions of offering such programs are still far from negligible, as this story illustrates. The fact that this program is offered within a business school rather than within an arts and sciences program may be relevant in assessing the likelihood that other institutions will make similar decisions.

[31] Personal correspondence, September 2, 2013.

A danger, of course, is that such pressures will be excessive and will threaten support for the high-quality research, and the high-quality doctoral training, that will continue to be of critical importance. The key, as always, is to find a magical balance: to support "enough" but not "too much." But I am definitely in the camp of those who believe that we are out of balance today in the "too much" direction and need to realign our overall "system" of graduate education so that it will work more effectively in a changed (and changing) environment.

A related question of major consequence is whether renewed thought should be given to "teaching doctorates"—or at least to paying increasing attention to questions such as how to teach graduate students the skills needed to impart the kinds of education that simply cannot be provided online. I think, along with Michael McPherson, that there is a real opportunity here for academia writ large to address positively, and not just negatively, the implications of the spread of online learning.[32] Another colleague, Eugene Tobin, who has wide experience with liberal arts colleges, adds: "In an ironic way, the special human dimensions of teaching ..., including understanding how to 'flip' the classroom with more than the use of technology, may be one of every future faculty member's most needed skills."[33] Our studies at Ithaka S+R suggest that faculty are very open, even eager, to move in this direction. Whether doctoral programs will have the interest, or the capacity, to respond to such ideas is an open question—and a very important one.

---

[32] Here is the way that McPherson, president of the Spencer Foundation and a wise observer of this scene, puts it: "To have a solid academic career, at least outside the top research universities, a PhD in most fields will either need to be a really outstanding scholar/researcher or will have to be able to teach effectively in ways that computers can't easily match. We don't know for sure what those hard-to-match qualities are, but they certainly aren't going to be straightforward content delivery. This suggests to me that it may become necessary for graduate schools to take more seriously than they have the problem of preparing their students to teach well in those ways that require human qualities that we don't know how to match online. This is a very hard problem because what teaching well in college means, if we mean by good teaching more than giving high quality lectures, is not well understood." Personal correspondence, August 9, 2013.

[33] Personal correspondence, August 9, 2013.

EQUITY ISSUES

I end these musings by calling attention to what I regard as one of the most important issues to ponder as we look ahead: implications of the spread of online learning for "equity." Will the development of various forms of online learning help level the playing field or exacerbate the already large divide between educational haves and have-nots? I ask this question even as I agree with those who argue that this divide is driven largely by factors such as income inequality that are not primarily the responsibility of higher education—culprits abound![34] Still, I want to retain my focus on online learning. One of the founders of Coursera, Daphne Koller, has been eloquent in arguing that a major contribution of MOOCs is the opening of educational opportunity to students all over the world, regardless of their circumstances.[35] It would be ironic indeed if the whole gamut of online offerings were to have the perverse effect in the United States of increasing, rather than reducing, disparities in educational outcomes. This is, regrettably, entirely possible.

Let's start with Princeton. This university is making a commendable effort to see if there are ways to take advantage of technology to improve what is already an outstanding educational program. In my view, it is highly likely that the strongest liberal arts colleges, as well as the leading universities, will only get better as a result of opportunities created by advances in technology. The "haves" are not at risk. And because of generous financial aid policies, these privileged institutions will continue to offer exceptional educational opportunities not only to the well-qualified children of affluent families (who are present in large numbers in their applicant pools) but also to top students from lower-income families. But the

[34] See Catherine B. Hill, "Higher Education's Biggest Challenge Is Income Inequality," *Washington Post*, September 6, 2013.

[35] See Daphne Koller, "How Online Education Can Create a 'Global Classroom,' " CNN International, June 21, 2013, available at http://edition.cnn.com/2013/06/21/business/opinion-koller-education-petersburg-forum/index.html.

absolute number of such fortunate students from modest back-grounds will be small. Princeton will, I am confident, continue to make the direct contributions that it can to educating a diverse student body of high talent. And I hope that it will also seek ways, many of them less direct and involving its research arm and its leadership capacities, to contribute to the broader national challenge that is before us.

But what does online learning portend for less privileged educational institutions? What about the offerings available to students attending the mid-level public institutions and the community colleges that educate such a high proportion of our undergraduates? As public support for higher education diminishes, students at these institutions are increasingly the "have-nots." Will they too benefit, alongside undergraduates at the Princetons and Haverfords, from the spread of online technologies? That is certainly the hope. However, comments by some governors, feeding on the over-hyped promise of truly minimalist online offerings, suggest that inexpensive online programs, lacking in feedback loops and any real human component, could tempt states to try to meet their educational obligations "on the cheap." Such a development, if it happens, could widen substantially the existing gap between the haves and the have-nots. The less affluent, less well-prepared students are poor candidates for cookie-cutter online offerings. A widely discussed study by Columbia's Teacher's College found compelling evidence that online offerings were not equally effective with all kinds of students.[36]

Jennifer Morton, an Assistant Professor at CUNY [City University of New York], has written eloquently about the needs of her students, many of whom are first-generation college-goers and/or

[36] See Shanna Smith Jaggars and Thomas Bailey, "Effectiveness of Fully Online Courses for College Students: Response to a Department of Education Meta-Analysis," Community College Research Center, Teacher's College, Columbia University, July 2010. It should have surprised no one to learn that students from modest backgrounds with less well thought out educational aspirations were much more likely than other students to drop out of online courses. Commenting on early experience with the much-touted Udacity/San Jose State effort to use online teaching, Lillian Taiz, president of the California Faculty Association, noted that pass rates were especially low in San Jose State's remedial math course. See Carl Straumsheim, "San Jose State U, Posts Improved Online Course Results, but Udacity Partnership Remains on Pause," *Inside Higher Ed*, August 28, 2013.

recent immigrants from low-income families, for the social skills that can be helped greatly by inspired face-to-face teaching. How to make eye contact, to speak up before strangers, and to defend a position in an unfamiliar setting—these are precisely the skills that she believes her students have to be helped to acquire. Children of middle-class families often learn to navigate social relationships at home, but that is often not an option for Professor Morton's students. The danger, she suggests, is that the substitution of low-level online instruction for face-to-face teaching may simply aggravate problems that are already evident in many lecture-only settings or in any setting in which faculty do not seek to impart the kinds of social skills that are so important for success in job searches and, for that matter, in life.[37] As she recognizes, much face-to-face teaching also fails abysmally in this area—but that is hardly an argument for mindlessly substituting an educational option that is equally poorly suited to meeting real needs.

I am driven back to my advocacy of a portfolio approach to curricular development: not every course needs to have the features Professor Morton champions, and it is probably unrealistic, for financial and other reasons, to have that as our goal. Also, I recognize that the concern I have expressed about the bad qualities of some forms of online learning may lead some to advocate staying out of the online game altogether. But that is hardly an answer. What is needed is the ability, and the willingness, to develop effective online pedagogies that can then be employed, in properly limited ways, in different settings, and with different student populations. My cautionary musings are meant only to heighten our awareness of a serious danger if we approach all forms of online learning with a one-size-fits-all mentality and treat them as cure-alls, appropriate in every context.

We must believe in education as an engine of social mobility—and act on that belief. The Pledge of Allegiance refers, after all, to "one nation ... indivisible." We need to take great care that in our

---

[37] Jennifer Morton, "Unequal Classrooms: What Online Education Cannot Teach," *Chronicle of Higher Education*, August 29, 2013. My colleagues at ITHAKA believe that over time communities made possible by technology will create at least partial substitutes for the classroom discussions that many of us remember with such pleasure.

search for cost-effective ways of educating we not lose sight of the need to teach *all* students in cost-effective ways appropriate to their needs. It would be a tragedy, and nothing less than that, if new approaches to teaching widened the divide between the haves and the have-nots in our society.[38]

[38] See Elizabeth Reddem. "Higher Education in 2020," *Inside Higher Ed*, September 26, 2013, for a dire warning that government pressures to drive down the costs of degrees could lead, in an unbundled online environment, to a situation in which "the cultural divide between the elite and the rest will widen in the US and the UK."

"NEW TIMES ALWAYS, OLD TIME WE CANNOT KEEP"

~

William G. Bowen
March 18, 2013

COLBY COLLEGE BICENTENNIAL REMARKS

INTRODUCTION

This college is a long-lived, lasting embodiment of what Sir Arthur Lewis, the Nobel Prize–winning economist from St. Lucia, called "the tribute that men pay to brain." Arthur went on to put this idea into an historical perspective that antedates, probably by several millennia, the founding of Colby. "Not very long ago," he said, "men lived in caves, or under the shadow of trees. Their lives were dominated by fear—fear of the elements, of drought and flood and fire; fear of animals; and fear of other men, who wandered around in families or tribes ready to exterminate each other. The human race has pulled itself up from this by handing down from generation to generation knowledge of two sets of principles, those relating to controlling nature, which we call science, and principles relating to controlling human behaviour, which we call ethics. Human life as we know it today is based on accumulated science,

Editor's note: William D. Adams, then president of Colby College, asked Bill to be one of five speakers at Colby's bicentennial celebration. He was asked to speak about the future of residential liberal arts colleges.

Author's note: The quote in the title of my talk is attributed to the naturalist John Burroughs.

and accumulated ethical principles enshrined in laws and in the conventions of decent behaviour."[1]

> Sir Arthur then added, in addressing a university community in the struggling country of Guyana:

> The supremely important task of receiving this knowledge, adding to it, and handing it down to the next generation has always devolved on a very small body of people who specialized in using their brains. They were known as … clerks…. Here we come to the fundamental purpose of education: to produce young men and women who will join the small band of clerks stretching backwards through history and forward through generations yet unborn. Who will receive our truths, embellish them, defend them against numerous and powerful enemies, and pass them on to the next generation. If our graduates do not help to keep civilization together, to reduce the sum of human misery and to advance the cause of human brotherhood, then our university will have laboured in vain.[2]

Please note the forward-looking character of Sir Arthur's charge. The title of my talk tonight reflects that same mindset: "New Times Always, Old Time We Cannot Keep."

It has become commonplace to berate colleges and universities for their rigidities and alleged inability to adapt. Sometimes that is a fair indictment; more often, however, it is not. Just as we can be too stuck in the mud, so too can we be too eager to jump on the glitziest bandwagon in sight. These days, especially, I worry about many institutions doing A, B, and C just to be "doing something," just to avoid being "left behind," and just to avoid a risk of being downgraded by mindless national rating schemes.

At a time of rapid change in higher education—of transformational change in the view of many—it is well to have an opportunity such as this to reflect on ideas and values that are anything but transitory. A wise friend of mine said years ago that it is valuable

---

[1] Quoted in William G. Bowen, "Remarks at the Memorial Service for Sir W. Arthur Lewis," November 10, 1991, Princeton University Archives.

[2] W. Arthur Lewis, "On Hating the Sin, Not the Sinner," Chancellor's Installation Address, University of Guyana, January 1966.

for an institution to have to contend with "the heavy weight of the past." Change we must, but in contemplating change it is essential to have something to push up against.

In preparing these remarks, I have enjoyed reading a bit about the history of Colby, including the insightful rendering of its evolution provided by President Adams just over two weeks ago in his own Bicentennial Address. This is a great college today in part because it has, historically, been ahead of its time even as it has been deeply rooted in its past. Colby shed its sectarian roots early; it embraced at least an incipient version of coeducation sooner than almost all other formerly all-male colleges; it was in the forefront of the battle against slavery; it has long emphasized the obligations of the privileged to give back to society; and it has for years demonstrated the importance of being inclusive. This is an impressive record to build upon, "to push up against," if you will, as Colby contemplates what "new times" may bring.

DIGITAL TECHNOLOGIES: FRIEND OR FOE?

In thinking about our collective future in reasonably concrete terms, I want to begin by talking a bit about digital technologies and whether Colby should regard such technologies as friend or foe. Having phrased the question that way, I immediately reject the categorical thinking implied by the phrasing. In my view, all of us should avoid "either-or" thinking. It is wise, I believe, for residential liberal arts colleges such as Colby to take full advantage of digital technologies where it makes sense to do so but to sidestep the trap of emulating other places that may seek to use such technologies to replace features of present-day college life that should be retained.

Colby has, in fact, followed this simple injunction by being what one of my colleagues at ITHAKA has called a "juggernaut" when it comes to adopting and using two digital resources that I had some hand in creating: JSTOR and ARTstor. Colby has been a leader of the pack in using these digital collections of scholarly literature and art images, and, more than that, in helping to shape the future of "shared shelf" (a new ARTstor platform designed to facilitate the sharing of digital materials of all kinds).

A tougher and more controversial set of questions concerns the use of online learning models of one kind or another in classroom teaching. This is sometimes said to be the "age of MOOCs" (massive open online courses). These courses, usually offered free of charge, have attracted hundreds of thousands of registrants from all over the world. Some worthy defenders of traditional face-to-face teaching have attacked the MOOCs and other online teaching models as poor substitutes for the personalized modes of instruction for which places like Colby are famous. But, again, there is no need for "either-or" thinking.

In my view, sophisticated forms of interactive online learning (whether delivered by MOOCs or through some other approach) have real promise as a way of helping students master basic concepts in courses such as statistics. What is a *t*-test? What is a confidence interval? My colleagues at ITHAKA and I have demonstrated that in certain settings, especially at large public universities facing drastic resource constraints, machine-guided instruction can produce at least comparable learning outcomes in basic courses in which there are agreed answers to key questions—perhaps at appreciably less cost than face-to-face instruction, which in such settings is often provided by instructors of varied qualifications.[3]

Heresy of heresies, I suspect (though no one knows as yet) that such pedagogies may even be helpful in intimate, bucolic settings such as this one. We should remain open to the possibility that emerging technologies can *complement* more traditional forms of teaching and thereby allow valuable faculty time to be put to higher-value uses, such as seminar instruction and one-on-one guidance of independent work. In my experience, students benefit enormously (I know that I did) from tough-minded correction of poor writing by dedicated teachers; but instruction of this kind is enormously time-consuming and expensive. Finding ways to husband the re-

---

[3] For a short summary of this research, see Bowen, *Higher Education in the Digital Age*, and the accompanying endnotes, which contain citations to the full study.

sources to afford such tutelage is going to be a big challenge in straitened economic circumstances, as President Adams reminded us in his Baccalaureate Address; the payoff is, however, huge.

Some believe that online pedagogies can also work well in teaching discursive topics of other kinds, and there is some evidence (most of it anecdotal) that the worldwide sharing of perspectives in subjects such as introductory sociology can be highly instructive. On this question, as well as on so many others pertaining to online learning, the jury is out, and will be out for some time. And, of course, a key question has to do with trade-offs: with the availability, value, and cost of alternative teaching methods.

In thinking about the future of curricular development, I am, as I have said on other occasions, an advocate of a "portfolio" approach that can provide a carefully calibrated mix of learning styles. This mix will vary by institutional type, and liberal arts colleges should put much more weight on seminars, discussion groups, and directed study than larger institutions can hope to do. Nonetheless, even the most elite and most selective colleges and universities, which may face less pressure than other places to change, should ask if failing to participate, at least to some degree, in the evolution of online learning models is to their advantage in the long run. Their students, along with others of their generation, will expect to use digital resources—and to be trained in their use.

More generally, there is everything to be said for heeding former Harvard president Derek Bok's admonition that a determined effort should be made to help faculty teach better, in part by being sure that they are aware of, and take account of, the insights of research in fields such as cognitive science. Liberal arts colleges, in particular, should put a real premium on doing all that can be done to ensure that excellent teaching actually occurs, and is not reflected solely in the language of promotional materials, abstract pronouncements, and inspirational talks.

Next, a few words, if I may, about styles of teaching in the personalized settings that are, and should continue to be, the hallmarks of liberal arts colleges. A great teacher of mine, Jacob Viner, echoed Jeremy Bentham in decrying "nonsense on stilts," which

Professor Viner described as "a type of sophisticated nonsense, of ignorant learning, which only the [well] educated are capable of perpetuating." Viner loved to tell this story:

> A woman in a shop asked for a drinking bowl for her dog. When the clerk replied that he had no drinking bowls especially for dogs, the woman said that any drinking bowl would do. The clerk, having found one for her, suggested that he have the word "dog" painted on it. "No thanks," said the woman. "It is not necessary. My husband doesn't drink water [from a bowl], and my dog can't read." Viner's conclusion: "Learning should be kept in its place."

There is, of course, a critically important role for learning in a college such as this, assuming that it is "kept in its place." In the most selective residential institutions, the right kind of learning occurs more or less constantly, as often, or more often, out of the classroom as in it. This cliché, repeated by all presidents of residential colleges and universities, conveys real truth. Here we see clearly the limits of purely online modes of teaching. Late-night peer-to-peer exchanges, enriched by body language that sometimes tells us more than computer-generated text, offer students hard-to-replicate access to the perspectives of other smart people whom they have come to know well. And by no means all interesting questions are rooted in classroom-like inquiry. I remember well an undergraduate at Princeton extolling (and now I quote her) "the evening rap sessions that began promisingly enough with high-flown debates on free will and determinism and descended by dawn to the inevitable indictment of the frailties of the human male."

Grasping complexity—embracing it—is a critical capacity to be learned earlier in life rather than later. Liberal arts colleges have a special capacity, I think, to encourage students to learn to avoid the polarized thinking that is, sad to say, becoming the standard of our day. Einstein was right in asserting: "Everything should be made as simple as possible ... *but not more so!*" Dilemmas are real and should be acknowledged, not dismissed by sloganeering.

Online technologies will continue to improve, and we should never underestimate their potential. But I am skeptical that they will ever substitute for the skillful teacher in encouraging students to learn key habits of mind, including both how to cope with complexity and how to develop a healthy respect for evidence— combined with the ability to separate evidence from assertion. Students should be pressed to feel an incorrigible need to "find the facts." There is a wonderful little book called *The Fastest Hound Dog in the State of Maine* that illustrates this mindset. It is "thoroughly Maine," the author suggests, to "want the full facts before negotiating an opinion." He provides this exchange between two people riding on a train:

> "Is that a white horse?"
> "Seems to be from this side."[4]

Suffice it to say that I remain a strong proponent of the goals of traditional liberal arts colleges, even as I believe that the means of serving these goals must continue to evolve. These colleges should continue to act on the belief that they are there to help students learn to live a life, not simply to earn a living.

AN "OPPORTUNITY" AGENDA FOR AMERICA?

Following my theme of "new times always," I want now to turn to a distressing aspect of our prospects. I am talking about our failing efforts as a country to make anything like as much progress as is desirable in promoting opportunity.

In giving the Atwell Lecture at this year's meeting of the American Council on Education, Brit Kirwan, the exceedingly able chancellor of the University System of Maryland, bemoaned the difficulty we are having in making real the substance of the American Dream—the belief that a person's status at birth is not supposed to determine his or her status throughout life. The facts are sobering. According to Kirwan, "A child born into a family in the highest quartile of income has a roughly 85 percent chance of earning a college degree. A child born into a family in the lowest quartile of

---

[4] John Gould, *The Fastest Hound Dog in the State of Maine* (Waterville, ME: Thorndike Press, 1953), p. 92.

income has a less than 8 percent chance of earning a degree." That is a ten-fold difference! Studies at Stanford and at the University of Michigan find that education gaps between the rich and poor in this country are growing, not shrinking, and Kirwan reminds us of OECD data showing that "children of less-educated parents in the U.S. have a tougher time climbing the educational ladder than in almost any other developed country."[5] Joseph Stiglitz, a Nobel Prize–winner, has called equal opportunity "our national myth."[6]

We are in the throes of what Laura Tyson, an economist who chaired the Council of Economic Advisors under President Clinton, has termed a "vicious cycle." In a piece for the New York Times last fall, Tyson argued: "Rising income inequality is breeding more inequality in educational opportunity, which results in greater inequality in educational attainment. That, in turn, undermines the intergenerational mobility upon which Americans have always prided themselves and perpetuates income inequality from generation to generation."[7]

President Adams has steadfastly aligned Colby with the notion of equal opportunity through both his policies and his personal generosity. Small as this college is, it can serve as an example for others. What is required is, first, a continuation of thoughtful admissions policies that take into account not only what applicants have achieved but the hurdles that they have had to leap along the way. Required, too, is a continuing commitment to provide need-based aid to as many qualified students as possible. And in this connection, I should say here what I have said elsewhere: we should avoid doctrinaire statements that decry asking students to incur tolerable amounts of debt and to do reasonable amounts of work to contribute to the costs of their education. "Merit aid wars," which primarily redistribute able students from one institution to another and divert resources from more essential uses, should be avoided.

[5] William E. Kirwan, "The Completion Imperative: Harnessing Change to Meet Our Responsibilities," paper presented at the American Council on Education Ninety-fifth Annual Meeting, March 3, 2013.

[6] Joseph E. Stiglitz, "Equal Opportunity, Our National Myth," New York Times, February 16, 2013.

[7] Laura D'Andrea Tyson, "Income Inequality and Educational Opportunity," New York Times, September 21, 2012.

Moreover, all of this assumes that Colby will also resist the "consumerist" tendencies evident in parts of higher education, whereby colleges spend too much on pandering to the desires of affluent parents and their children for amenities of one kind or another. There is an institutional obligation to make the best possible use of limited funds.

Assuming (as I do) that Colby makes every reasonable effort to be inclusive and to promote opportunity, there are broader tendencies in the land that all of us should worry about and seek to correct. One is the growing stratification in higher education, with widening gaps not just between students from different socioeconomic backgrounds, but also between institutions. For reasons too complicated to go into this evening, the resources available to the wealthiest institutions have grown more rapidly than the resources available down the line. Putting at least partly to one side my economist-bred inclination to love the market, I argue in my forthcoming book on higher education in a digital age that certain forms of competition, driven by large differences in institutional affluence, can have harmful effects overall.

Let me now connect these two dots on the higher education landscape: the online learning dot and the opportunity dot. As I have continued to ponder what is likely to transpire, I confess a serious worry. The promises that online learning offers, when it is said to promote educational opportunity worldwide (as it already has), could also have the perverse effect of widening the gap in American higher education between the "haves" and "have-nots." It is highly likely that the intelligent application of the new technologies will improve education at the most privileged places— Colby among them. Is it also likely that, at esteemed liberal arts institutions like Colby (never mind at wealthy universities like Harvard), online approaches will be allowed to depersonalize instruction and deprive future generations of students of the wonderful residential experience so characteristic of these places? No way.

There will always be a coterie of families willing and able to pay the price for this kind of education, almost regardless of cost. As a believer in "revealed preference" (the notion that people reveal their beliefs through their actions), I am mightily impressed by the extraordinary number of applicants for places in the most selective (and expensive) institutions. And, as I have said, the children of affluent families are much more likely than other children to have not only the wherewithal to attend but also the requisite qualifications for admission—in part because affluent families generally invest both far more money and far more time in the educational preparation of their children than do poorer families. Because of generous financial aid, the mix of students at the most selective colleges and universities will also include some number of highly talented individuals from poorer families. But how many such students are there likely to be in this rarified subset of American higher education? The number is going to be very, very small. So, as Stiglitz has put it, the problem is not that "social mobility is impossible, but that the upwardly mobile American is becoming a statistical oddity."[8]

At the same time, recent pronouncements by the governors of some states lead me to worry that the promise of online education— and, I would say, the "over-hyped" promise of not-very-good versions of online education that lack any face-to-face component— will lead to an ever more bifurcated system of higher education. States will be sorely tempted to use relatively inexpensive online programs to serve the less affluent, less well-prepared segment of potential college-goers. If I am right in thinking that residential campuses and the other features of the more selective sector of higher education will continue to confer major advantages on those students able to attend them, it is not hard to envision the "haves" continuing to gain ground on the "have-nots."

To my way of thinking, this is a most depressing scenario. How can we prevent it from coming to pass? Or, at the very least, how can we retard the process of ever more stratification, of real bifurcation?

First, we can continue to do research that will tease out the effects of various types of online learning—and online learning comes in a great many flavors—focusing on learning outcomes for students

[8] Joseph E. Stiglitz, "Equal Opportunity, Our National Myth," *New York Times*, February 16, 2013.

from different backgrounds. A recent study by Columbia University's Teachers College found that not-so-well-prepared students at community colleges who were given online instruction with no face-to-face component dropped out at much higher rates than students who had face-to-face learning experiences—a hardly surprising finding, but certainly not reassuring.[9]

Second, we can work hard, as the City University of New York has done, to facilitate transfer flows so that able students who have done well in two-year institutions can move into appropriate four-year institutions without having to redo material or suffer unnecessarily from bureaucratic hassles.[10] It should be possible to use online technologies of various kinds to improve advising, to solve scheduling problems that at present may prevent students from finding a seat in key gateway courses, and in general to ease the flow of students through the system.

Third, as citizens, we can lend our support to political leadership that is willing to tackle the need to promote opportunity. This will require asking governments both to spend somewhat more money on education than they might otherwise and to spend money more

---

[9] In February 2013, Di Xu and Shanna Smith Jaggars of the Community College Research Center at Columbia University's Teachers College released a study of more than 40,000 students in the Washington State Community and Technical College system who had enrolled in the system in fall 2004. The researchers, who were interested in measuring what they called "adaptability to online learning," compared students' grades in online courses to those students' own grades in face-to-face courses. The study involved data from about 500,000 courses taken by study participants between fall 2004 and spring 2009. Xu and Jaggars found that students generally earned lower grades in online courses than in face-to-face courses but that some groups of students (e.g., older students and female students) "adapted" better than others (e.g., younger students and male students). See Di Xu and Shanna Smith Jaggars, "Adaptability to Online Learning: Differences across Types of Students and Academic Subject Areas," Community College Research Center (CCRC) Working Paper no. 54, CCRC, Teachers College, Columbia University, New York, February 2013, http://ccrc.tc.columbia.edu/publications/adaptability-to-online-learning.html.

[10] In June 2011 the trustees of the City University of New York (CUNY) approved a resolution creating the Pathways Initiative, which is designed to facilitate the transfer process between the system's two- and four-year colleges. Under this project, all students in the system are required to complete thirty "Common Core" credits; students who are transferring from community to senior colleges are required to take an additional six to twelve "College Option" credits. Individual colleges have substantial flexibility in determining the content of the Common Core credits, and, in the case of the senior colleges, the College Option credits. For more information on the Pathways Initiative, see www.cuny.edu/academics/initiatives/pathways.html.

effectively. It is possible, I believe, to achieve gains in productivity, and it is certainly appropriate for governors and legislators to charge colleges and universities that depend on taxpayer dollars with embracing the challenge of finding cost-effective ways to increase completion rates and reduce time-to-degree.

A concerted effort should also be made to discourage legislators and others from equating college success with how well students do in obtaining a decent-paying first job. I am certainly not against decent-paying jobs (who could be?), but it is important to adopt a longer time-horizon and look at age-graded earning profiles. Even more fundamental is the need to recognize that the value of a good education cannot be measured simply by studying earnings profiles of any kind. For many students, a good education is truly liberating and can create opportunities for service as well as money-making. It opens one's eyes to wonders of all kinds, to the benefits of a wide array of perspectives, and to one's own capabilities—and limitations.

SHOULD WE—CAN WE—TEACH VALUES?

My answers to these twin questions are "yes" and "yes"—so long as we act sensibly. Mine is most definitely not a plea for indoctrination; nor is it a plea for pontification. I remember well the comment of President Robert Hutchins when he was urged to teach his students at the University of Chicago to do this, that, or the other thing. "All attempts to teach character directly will fail," he said. "They degenerate into vague exhortations to be good which leave the bored listener with a desire to commit outrages which would otherwise have never occurred to him." Hutchins added: "Hard intellectual work is doubtless the best foundation of character, for without the intellectual virtues, the moral sense rests on habit and precept alone."[11]

---

[11] Robert Maynard Hutchins, *No Friendly Voice* (Chicago: University of Chicago Press, 1968), p. 93.

Surely it is possible, without enraging the ghost of Hutchins, to remind students that there is much to be said for generosity of spirit. It is healthy, a wise friend of mine liked to say, "to spend some time on other people's problems." Woodrow Wilson expressed a somewhat similar sentiment in his charge to the Princeton class of 1909:

> Set out to fulfill obligations, to do what you must and to exact of others what they owe you, and all your days alike will end in weariness of spirit.... There is no pleasure to be had from the fulfillment of obligations ... from doing what you know you ought to do. Nothing but what you volunteer has the essence of life, the springs of pleasure in it. These are the things you do because you want to do them, the things your spirit has chosen for its satisfaction.[12]

Let me now jump from Wilson in 1909 to our current decade and provide a second example of the kinds of questions we should pose on our campuses. I want to call your attention to a baccalaureate address that is a favorite of mine, given in 2010 by Jeff Bezos, the hugely successful CEO of Amazon. The title Bezos gave to his talk is "We Are What We Choose."[13] He began by reciting a poignant story of a trip he took with his grandparents when he was 10 years old. While riding in their Airstream trailer, this precocious 10-year-old laboriously calculated the damage to her health that his grandmother was doing by smoking. His conclusion was that, at two minutes per puff, she was taking nine years off her life. When he proudly told her of his finding, she burst into tears. His grandfather stopped the car and gently said to Jeff: "One day you'll understand that it's harder to be kind than clever."

Bezos went on to talk about the difference between gifts and choices. "Cleverness," he said, "is a gift, kindness is a choice. Gifts are easy—they're given, after all. Choices can be hard." He then challenged the graduating students to think carefully about their

[12] Woodrow Wilson, Baccalaureate Address, Princeton University, Princeton, NJ, June 13, 1909.

[13] Jeff Bezos, "We Are What We Choose," remarks delivered to the Class of 2010 at Princeton University, May 30, 2010, Princeton University Archives.

future range of choices and whether they will opt to be "clever at the expense of others, or kind." Colleges are well advised, I think, to find effective ways to help their students wrestle with just such questions—to think hard about their values. A willingness to enter such terrain, and not apologize for doing so, is one way liberal arts colleges can continue to distinguish themselves from institutions too timid to pose such questions.

As I end these remarks, I am reminded that one purpose of a bicentennial celebration is to cause all of us to think about how fortunate we are to have enjoyed the educational opportunities bequeathed to us ("given" to us) by our predecessors over two centuries and, at the same time, to recall the high purposes of Colby and the "choices" we must make—now and in the future.

TECHNOLOGY

ITS POTENTIAL IMPACT ON THE NATIONAL NEED TO IMPROVE EDUCATIONAL OUTCOMES AND CONTROL COSTS

~

Remarks by William G. Bowen
October 13, 2014

DE LANGE CONFERENCE, RICE UNIVERSITY

I begin with a framing question:

HOW ARE WE DOING IN SATISFYING THE NATION'S NEED FOR IMPROVED EDUCATIONAL OUTCOMES?

The short answer is: not very well. In my view, we need to be more sharply focused than many of us are on the inability to date of our system of higher education to meet pressing national needs for both improved educational outcomes and restraints on cost increases. (Obviously, the *quality* of the education delivered is of great importance, but I do not deal with that issue in this talk because of its great complexity.) I suspect that at least some of us fail to appreciate fully the magnitude of what is (or is not!) transpiring at the national level, and that is why I am going to devote the first part of this talk to describing in some detail four specific dimensions of what seems to me to be a very serious and interconnected

Editor's note: David W. Leebron, president of Rice University, invited Bill to participate in Rice's De Lange Conference IX: Teaching in the University of Tomorrow. Bill addresses the rapidly changing educational landscape in US higher education.

"nest" of problems. This is the context within which I hope many of the specific questions on this conference's agenda will be considered.

1. A Near-Stagnant (and Low) Overall Rate of Educational Attainment

When Matt Chingos, Mike McPherson, and I published *Crossing the Finish Line: Completing College at America's Public Universities* five years ago, we emphasized that educational attainment in the United States had been stuck on a plateau since the late 1970s. This unwelcome state of affairs followed a long period of steady increases in attainment dating back to the "high school movement" of the early 1900s that was responsible for producing the base of college-ready students that made possible this country's remarkably high level of degree completion.[1]

It would be a mistake, however, to assume that we are still on this plateau. More recently, there has been an uptick in the educational attainment of 25- to 29-year-olds, with the percentage holding BAs or higher degrees increasing from 30 percent in 2007 (it was also 30 percent in 1999) to 34 percent in 2013. Figure 1 tells the story.[2] The most recent Lumina Foundation report (2014) presents different data that show essentially the same pattern.[3]

A key question is this: can we count on continued improvement in overall measures of educational attainment? No one knows the

---

[1] See figure 1.2 and associated commentary in William G. Bowen, Matthew M. Chingos, and Michael S. McPherson, *Crossing the Finish Line: Completing College at America's Public Universities* (Princeton, NJ: Princeton University Press, 2009). Claudia Goldin and Lawrence F. Katz deserve the credit for explicating both the long record of increasing educational attainment in the United States and the subsequent plateau (see Goldin and Katz, *The Race between Education and Technology* (Cambridge, MA: Harvard University Press, 2008).

[2] I am indebted to Matthew M. Chingos of the Brookings Institution for updating figure 1.2 from *Crossing the Finish Line*.

[3] See Lumina Foundation, *A Stronger Nation through Higher Education* (2014 Report). This document reports the same recent uptick in completion rates, although it uses a different base population group (25–64), a different data source (US Census, American Community Survey), and includes both BAs and AAs in the numerator of its attainment ratio. Lumina reports that educational attainment measured in this way increased from 37.9 percent in 2008 to 39.4 percent in 2012.

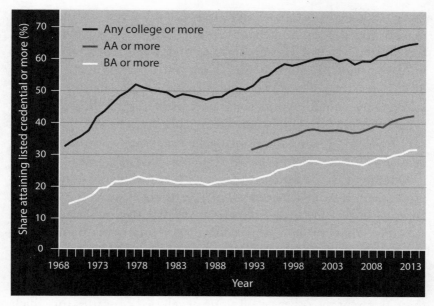

Figure 1. Educational Attainment of 25- to 29-year-olds, 1968–2013. Source: Current Population Survey.

answer. In its 2014 report, Lumina Foundation strikes an optimistic note (as did President Obama in his Northwestern talk on October 2, 2014), emphasizing that a Gallup/Lumina poll shows that "the hunger for higher education is stronger than ever." But the report is also careful to note that the changing demographics of America warn us that elements of the population with below-average attainment rates (especially Hispanics) are growing relative to the main group with above-average rates (the white population); Lumina calculates that if attainment rates were to stay the same for all racial/ethnic sub-groups, the overall attainment rate would *fall* by roughly 1 percentage point between now and 2025.[4]

Another reason for caution in extrapolating progress is that we do not know how much of the recent uptick in attainment rates is due to the 2007–8 recession.[5] As is well known, recessions induce

[4] Lumina Foundation, *A Stronger Nation through Higher Education* (Indianapolis, IN: Lumina Foundation, 2014), p. 2.

[5] Here is an important research question that, to the best of my knowledge, has not been pursued aggressively (if at all).

more students to complete high school and college, for the simple reason that the main alternative—entering the labor market—is less attractive when jobs are hard to find. Most recently, full-time undergraduate enrollment was 3 percent lower in 2012 than in 2010, presumably because of improving conditions in the labor market. We should expect some part of the uptick in attainment rates to be eroded by this enrollment dip, and one should be very cautious in predicting the slope of the prospective attainment rate curve.[6]

One thing we do know is that the absolute level of educational attainment remains unacceptably low if the United States is to compete effectively in an increasingly knowledge-driven world—a world in which other countries have been improving their attainment rates much more rapidly than we have.[7] Highly relevant, as David Autor points out in *Science*, is that the skill premium associated with cognitive achievement is much higher in the United States than in any of the other twenty-one developed countries for which data are available. This is a clear market signal that more Americans need to complete college.[8] The economic incentives are clear,

[6] US Department of Education, National Center for Education Statistics, Integrated Postsecondary Education Data System (IPEDS), "Fall Enrollment Survey" (IPEDS-EF: 90–99); IPEDS Spring 2001–Spring 2013, Enrollment component. See National Center for Education Statistics (NCES), *Digest of Education Statistics 2013* (Washington, DC: NCES, Institute of Educational Sciences, US Department of Education), tables 105.20 and 303.70.

[7] OECD, "Indicator A1: To What Level Have Adults Studied?," in *Education at a Glance 2014: OECD Indicators* (Paris: OECD, 2015), available at www.oecd.org/edu/EAG2014 -Indicator%20A1%20%28eng%29.pdf.

[8] David Autor, "Skills, Education, and the Rise of Earnings Inequality among the 'Other 99 percent,'" *Science* 344, no. 6286 (May 23, 2014): 843–51. This is an exceptionally well-crafted discussion, written in non-technical terms, of why skill premiums have changed as they have in the United States. Autor, a highly regarded economist at MIT, uses a simple supply-and-demand framework to great effect. He emphasizes: "Demand for cognitive skills has increased steadily: [The] ongoing process of machine substitution for routine human labor [benefits] educated workers who excel in abstract tasks that harness problem-solving ability, intuition, creativity, and persuasion—tasks that are at present difficult to automate but essential to perform" (p. 846). It is important to note that Autor is talking not about vocationally oriented training but about deeper, more flexible, and more transferrable skills. The supply of skills is more volatile than demand, and Autor tracks major changes on the supply side of the equation. He is careful to recognize that the power of supply and demand in the labor market does not make policy or actions by institutions irrelevant—not at all. See also David Leonhardt's article in the *New York Times*, "Is College Worth It? Clearly,

and the important question is why more Americans are not responding to them. This is an absolutely central issue that policy-makers, educational leaders, and researchers need to confront directly.

2. Long (and Increased) Time-to-Degree

A second dimension of our problem is the long time-to-degree (TTD) experienced by many of the students who do earn baccalaureates. Aggregate data from the CPS [Current Population Survey] reveal a trend of steep increases in the time it takes an average graduate to complete his or her studies that seems to have started with birth cohorts in the 1950s (who attended college in the mid-1970s) and lasted until at least the birth cohorts of around 1970 (who attended college in the late 1980s); see Figure 2.[9] The recent update of these data by Ithaka S+R colleagues suggests that the steady increase in TTD seems to have come to something of a halt among the birth cohorts of the early 1970s; subsequent increases have been very small (and are probably insignificantly different from zero). This finding is not surprising, given both the evident interest of at least some state systems in controlling increases in time-to-degree and the likely effects on students of increasing net tuition costs (see next section) associated with their staying in school for extended periods of time. In addition, the aggregate data may well conceal important differences among sub-groups that are related to the increasing stratification of American higher education (time-to-degree may well be falling at top-tier public and private institutions at the same time that it may be continuing to increase at

New Data Say," *The Upshot*, May 27, 2014. Leonhardt points out that the pay gap between college graduates and everyone else reached a record high in 2013. He goes on to quote David Autor as concluding that the data tell us that we have too few college graduates and too few people prepared for college.

[9] We are indebted to Matthew Staiger for updating the CPS data compiled for birth cohorts from 1945 through 1970 by Sarah Turner in "Going to College and Finishing College," in *College Choices: The Economics of Where to Go, and How to Pay For It*, ed. Caroline M. Hoxby (Cambridge, MA: National Bureau of Economic Research, September 2004), figure 1.6.

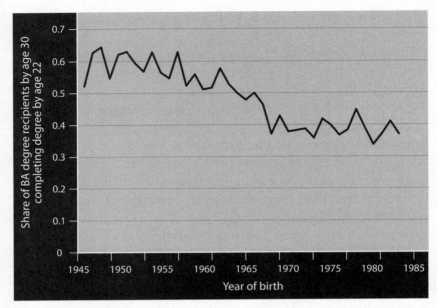

Figure 2. Time to BA by Year of Birth, Share of BA Degree Recipients Completing by Age 22

institutions that are more resource-constrained). This is another set of issues that deserves much more attention from researchers than it has received.[10]

In any case, the most important finding is that TTD has not fallen from its high levels and remains a very serious problem. A valuable window on this problem is provided by a careful comparison of evidence from two longitudinal databases (NELS-72 and NELS-88). Overall, the percentage of students completing their studies in four years fell from 58 percent for the earlier NELS cohort to 44 percent for those in the putative high school class of 1992.[11] According to the most recent CPS data available (refer back to Figure 2), under 40 percent of BA recipients complete their de-

[10] I am indebted to Sarah Turner for sharing with me (in a phone conversation) her conjectures as to what is happening. The effects of the growing stratification of American higher education (growing differences of all kinds between the "have" and "have not" institutions) deserve careful study.

[11] See John Bound, Michael F. Lovenheim, and Sarah Turner, "Increasing Time to Baccalaureate Degree in the United States," Research Report 10–698, Population Studies Center, University of Michigan, Ann Arbor, April 2010 (also published later in various places), table 1.

grees by age 22, whereas the comparable figure was about 60 percent for cohorts born in the late 1950s.

Evidence shows that increased time spent on earning a BA does not result from students' earning more credits (learning more), and increased TTD clearly raises costs for both individuals and institutions.[12] It is highly likely that the prospect of long time-to-degree deters some students from ever starting—never mind finishing—their degree programs, and thus contributes directly to low overall levels of educational attainment. Prolonged time-to-degree, then, is wasteful in and of itself, is a deterrent to raising completion rates, and is, as we will see in the next section, a contributor to increasing disparities in educational outcomes related to a child's place in the socio-economic hierarchy.

3. Pronounced Disparities in Outcomes by Socio-economic Status (SES)

A third, very troubling, "fact of life" is that in America today there are serious disparities in both completion rates and time-to-degree associated with socio-economic status—and that, once again, the problem appears to have worsened in recent years. At the turn of the twenty-first century, the odds of earning a BA were *seven to eight* times higher for a student from a family in the top income quartile in which at least one parent graduated from college than for a student with opposite characteristics—that is, from a family in the bottom income quartile with no parent having graduated from college (*68 percent versus 9 percent*).[13] While we cannot update these exact figures because more recent longitudinal data are unavailable, there are straws in the wind that are anything but encouraging. Bailey and Dynarski have shown that disparities in graduation rates by income quartile have not only persisted; they

[12] See Campaign for College Opportunity, "The Real Cost of College: Time & Credits to Degree at California Community Colleges and California State University," Campaign for College Opportunity, Los Angeles, June 2014.

[13] *Crossing the Finish Line*, figure 2.2; the data are derived from the National Educational Longitudinal Study (NELS) longitudinal database, 1988–2000.

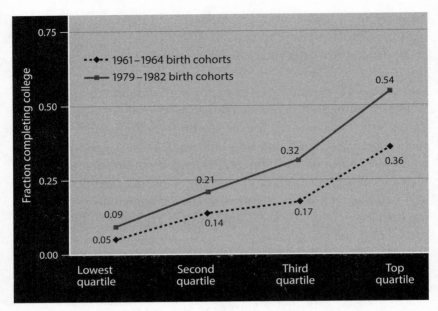

Figure 3. Percent of Students Completing College, by Income Quartile and Year of Birth. Source: Author's calculation based on data from the National Longitudinal Survey of Youth, 1979 and 1997 (US Bureau of Labor Statistics, 2010).

have widened (Figure 3).[14] This striking figure reveals two truths: (1) pronounced disparities in graduation rates by income quartile are all too evident in *both* the 1961–64 birth cohort and the 1979–83 cohort; (2) the disparities between those in the top and bottom income quintiles are appreciably greater in the more recent cohort (54 – 09 = 45 points versus 36 – 05 = 31 points).

These findings are troubling on their own terms for those of us who are concerned about inequality in America and who believe that we should be reducing disparities in educational outcomes. David Autor reminds us that, contrary to what he calls "conventional civic mythology," America has not been, and is not, anything like the "land of opportunity" that we are inclined to claim is the case. Other countries fare much better than we do when it comes to

[14] Martha J. Bailey and Susan M. Dynarski, "Gains and Gaps: Changing Inequality in U.S. College Entry and Completion," National Bureau of Education Research (NBER) Working Paper 17633, NBER, Cambridge, MA, December 2011, figure 3. (We reproduce this figure here as figure 3.)

intergenerational mobility, and these gaps appear to be widening.[15] Autor concludes that, in the United States, "lifetime relative disadvantage of children born to low- versus high-income families has increased substantially."[16] As one of our colleagues (Chancellor William E. Kirwan of the University System of Maryland) puts it: "Absent greater participation and completion rates by the poor, we will have recreated (if we have not already) the economic caste system many of our ancestors left England to escape."

A further reason for being concerned about these pronounced disparities in graduation rates by socio-economic status is that, as we have already noted, sizeable demographic changes are afoot in America. We cannot hope to reach optimistic goals in overall educational attainment, such as those enunciated by President Obama and Lumina Foundation, without making real progress—much more progress than we have made to date—in improving markedly graduation rates for students from lower-income families and certainly for the rapidly growing Hispanic population.[17] Much as we would like to do better with all groups, increasing the educational attainment rate among the relatively affluent members of the white population, which is already relatively high, will not move

[15] OECD, "Indicator A1." In its 2014 report, the OECD shows that the United States ranks second from the bottom (only Israel is lower) in the percentage-point difference since 2000 between the 25- to 34- and 55- to 64-year-old populations with tertiary education (table A1.3a.) For a lengthy discussion of the significance of this important finding, see Eduardo Porter, "Equation Is Simple: Education = Income," *New York Times*, September 11, 2014, p. B1. Porter emphasizes that America is lagging the world in reducing inequality in educational outcomes (as measured by differences in educational attainment between parents and their children). What explains this pattern—and whether it is in part inevitable—is an important research question. See the discussion in Autor, next citation.

[16] Autor, "Skills, Education, and the Rise of Earnings Inequality," pp. 848–49. Autor writes: "Contrary to conventional civic mythology, US intergenerational mobility is relatively low" (compared to other countries). "In one sense, this is not surprising, because countries with high returns to education [such as the United States] tend to have relatively low mobility for the simple reason that educational attainment is highly persistent within families. Well-off families can afford to invest heavily in the educational preparation of their children, which is a principal reason why children of higher income families do so well in the competition for places in selective colleges and universities."

[17] Regrettably, very large racial gaps in test scores persist. See Charlie Tyson, "ACT's Annual Report Shows Languishing Racial Gaps, Mediocre Scores," *Inside Higher Ed*, August 20, 2014. In 2014, "Asian-American test-takers did best, with 57 percent meeting three or more [college readiness benchmarks]. 49 percent of white test-takers met three or more standards—compared to 23 percent of Latino test-takers and 11 percent of African-American test-takers." Since 2010, these gaps have remained eerily constant.

the needle of overall educational attainment to the desired level. While elite institutions such as Rice have a definite role to play in moving us forward, the real "action" has to take place at the far larger set of mid-level educational institutions that educate both a high fraction of all students and a still higher fraction of disadvantaged students.[18]

Compounding the problem of greater disparities in graduation rates is increased disparities in time-to-degree. The Bound-Lowenheim-Turner study comparing outcomes between the NELS-72 and NELS-88 cohorts found that increases in time-to-degree were localized among those who began postsecondary education at public colleges outside the most selective universities (the non–top-fifty publics). In addition, increases in time-to-degree were most marked among low-income students. Contrary to what one might have thought, differences in college preparedness were *not* the explanation for these trends (and actually push in the opposite direction). Instead, the rich data in these longitudinal databases that allow us to link time-to-degree to individual and institutional attributes suggest that declines in resources in the less selective public sector were a major factor accounting for increased time-to-degree (mainly because of classroom crowding and limited access to gateway courses). Another factor at work was increased hours of employment among students, especially low-income students, who encountered difficulty meeting the increasing costs of college attendance; working longer hours surely impedes timely degree completion.[19]

---

[18] It is disappointing that relatively little attention is paid to the distinctive problems of this critically important sector of higher education. Without wanting to offend anyone, let me say categorically that what happens at these mid-level institutions is far more consequential nationally than what happens at the Rices (and the Michigans) of this world. Elite, highly selective institutions in both the private and the public sectors are naturally focused on improving their own already high academic standards; thus they tend to focus on how advances in technology can improve their own teaching programs. This is fine, up to a point. But it is hard to avoid asking if, at least at times, there is not too much "navel-gazing" going on and if these institutions could do more to help less advantaged places do better. This is, at its root, a problem of a national misalignment of roles and responsibilities. The institutions with the most capacity (financial resources and highly qualified faculty members) to contribute directly to meeting the needs of the less well-off institutions are not the same as the "have-not" institutions with the greatest need for new, cost-effective approaches.

[19] See Bound, Lovenheim, and Turner, "Increasing Time to Baccalaureate Degree in the United States." A wealth of data is presented in table 1 of this study, which shows, for ex-

4. Affordability?

The fourth item on my list of problems afflicting higher education is the issue of whether higher education remains "affordable." As is well known, the combination of rising institutional costs and reductions in state support has led many institutions to impose sharp increases in tuition that (setting aside the special circumstances of the wealthiest private institutions) have been offset only in part by increases in financial aid. For example, increases in Pell Grants have not kept pace with increases in tuition costs. Moreover, students just above the Pell Grant cut-off (sometimes referred to as "the near-poor") have received only modest increases in aid at most institutions, and their net costs have risen appreciably. This trend is exacerbated by what David Leonhardt calls "The Great Wage Slowdown of the 21st Century"—the fact that "the typical American family [today] makes less than the typical family did 15 years ago, a statement that hadn't previously been true since the Great Depression."[20]

One consequence of this financial squeeze is, as already noted, that many students from modest backgrounds have been driven to spend more time working while in school. Rising student debt is another, more widely publicized consequence, though the magnitude of this aspect of the problem is often exaggerated.[21] (Moreover, to speak heresy, I believe that some students borrow too little, not too much, and harm themselves by substituting long hours of

---

ample, that the percentage of students at non-top-fifty public institutions earning degrees in four years fell from 56 percent in the NELS-72 cohort to 35 percent in the NELS-88 cohort and from 41 percent all the way to 17 percent in the community college sector. In sharp contrast, the percentage of four-year finishers in the highly selective private sector *increased* from 68 to 76 percent over this interval. The empirical findings in this study on the effects of hours of employment on timely degree completion strongly support conjectures in *Crossing the Finish Line* that suggested exactly this same pattern.

[20] David Leonhardt, "The Great Wage Slowdown of the 21st Century," *The Upshot, New York Times*, October 7, 2014.

[21] See Beth Akers and Matthew M. Chingos, "Is a Student Loan Crisis on the Horizon?," Brown Center on Education Policy, Brookings Institution, Washington, DC, June 2014. See also Barry Glassner and Morton Schapiro, "Beware Higher-Ed Doomsayers," *Chronicle of Higher Education*, October 6, 2014. This generally excellent piece suffers, however, from the danger that readers will interpret the debunking of disaster scenarios as implying that "business as usual" will suffice to ward off storm clouds. I do not think that it will.

work for incurring modest amounts of debt, thereby impeding timely completion of programs.)

In addition to the direct impact of tuition increases on affordability, there is also a growing sense, justified or not (I think not), that college is "too expensive." This perception can of course lead to reluctance on the part of poor and near-poor students to earn degrees from institutions for which they are qualified.[22]

As yet another (related) dimension of the problem, mention must be made of the erosion of public support for institutions of higher education that goes beyond cutbacks in funding. Higher education has traditionally been one of our society's most trusted institutions. The trends described earlier are putting that trust at risk, not only from the perspective of politicians, legislators, and the media, but in the minds of the general public as well. There is skepticism that institutions are doing all that they can to operate more efficiently, and there are oft-stated concerns about rigidities and failures to be sufficiently forward-looking and nimble. Such criticisms are often unfair, but that does not alter the underlying loss of confidence; perceptions matter and can have long-term effects on support for research-intensive institutions, as well as on direct forms of aid to other institutions and students generally. These "ill winds" also make it harder to recruit and retain outstanding leadership. A recent issue of the *Economist* observes: "Politically, the mood has shifted.... Both Bill Clinton and Barack Obama have said that universities face a poor outlook if they cannot lower their costs, marking a shift from the tendency of centre-left politicians to favour more public spending on academia."[23] So:

[22] See two recent pieces by David Leonhardt that criticize overly dramatic complaints about affordability. Leonhardt, "Is College Worth It?" and "How Government Exaggerates College's Costs," *The Upshot, New York Times*, July 29, 2014. The first piece uses data on pay gaps to demonstrate that the return on investing in college remains very high. The second piece points out that government data on tuition increases often focus on sticker prices and ignore financial aid (though efforts are being made to fix this problem).

[23] "The Future of Universities: The Digital Degree," *Economist*, June 26, 2014, online edition, www.economist.com/news/briefing/21605899-staid-higher-education-business-about -experience-welcome-earthquake-digital.

HOW CAN WE DO BETTER? CAN TECHNOLOGY HELP?

Many voices are heard exhorting legislatures to be more generous in supporting public universities. The argument for restoring cuts in public funding is persuasive to many who believe that national priorities are askew. Improving economic conditions have, in fact, led to modest increases in appropriations in some states. It seems clear, however, that the substantial increases in public support that would be needed to make a real difference, desirable or even justifiable as they may be, are unlikely to be forthcoming in the foreseeable future, given fiscal and political constraints. Voices urging a return to the "golden age" of the 1950s represent a modern-day version of "blowing in the wind." As Hanna Gray has explained, the decade of the 1960s was an anomaly.[24] Don Quixote was right when, on his death bed, he warned against "looking for the birds of this year in the nests of yesteryear."[25]

Improving the college readiness of students would surely make a difference, is highly desirable on many counts, and is probably even essential in the longer run—but it is not going to help appreciably in the near term. Improvements in financial aid programs are certainly possible (and highly desirable), but, even if they happen, are unlikely to produce the truly substantial progress that is

[24] See Gray, *Searching for Utopia*, pp. 68–69. In this underappreciated and trenchant set of lectures, Gray called attention to the after-effects of the 1960s. She points out that this decade set expectations that continue. In her words: "Decline in federal support and public favor is seen as a precipitous falling away from what once was and still ought to be the rightful norm in the world of higher education." Gray goes on to observe: "The critical fact [is] that available resources could not continue to keep pace with the expansion of knowledge and its technologies and capital requirements or with the accelerating growth in the university's functions and programs.... [It is, she concludes,] naturally tempting to take the option of muddling through.... But that will scarcely offer long-term health.... Questions raised by current economic circumstances serve to expose and force us to confront longer-existing issues and deeper fault lines that have been building over the past decades." An exception to the tendency to downplay cost issues in the 1960s is Clark Kerr's reference, in his 1963 Godkin lectures, to "problems related to costs, identified particularly by Beardsley Ruml—faculty-student ratios, fuller utilization of the calendar, excessive numbers of courses, mechanization of instruction." See Clark Kerr, *The Uses of the University: Fifth Edition* (Cambridge, MA: Harvard University Press, 2001), p. 79.

[25] Miguel de Cervantes Saavedra, *Don Quixote of La Mancha*, edited and translated by Walter Starkie (New York: Signet Books, 1974), p. 1048.

needed—especially given the heavy use of "merit aid" by institutions. I agree with Brit Kirwan, distinguished chancellor of the University System of Maryland, when he decries the "diversion of such a high fraction of institutional aid to 'buy' high ability students already planning to go to college at the expense of capable low income students who desperately need the aid."[26] This phenomenon is related to the near-obsession with rankings based on such metrics as SAT scores and student-teacher ratios. But it is far from clear how the pernicious effects of these rankings can be arrested. Improving the quality of press reporting would also definitely help (simplistic reports that exaggerate "net costs" of college discourage students from enrolling); but, sadly, I see little basis for optimism.

Realism regarding prospects for increased governmental support, combined with the limited ability of families (or the limited *willingness* of families) to afford further tuition increases, has an obvious implication: there will be ever more emphatic calls for improvements in "productivity"—in output per unit of input. Higher education, writ large, simply has to re-engineer its processes, to alter the educational "production function" linking inputs to outputs so as to achieve more cost-effective ways of meeting students' educational needs. Put another way, it is not sufficient to seek ways of improving modestly current methods of instruction or achieving one-time savings in administrative costs (desirable as vigorous efforts of these kinds are). It is fine to postpone washing the windows this year, but what about next year, and the year after that?[27] We must approach the fundamental objective in a bold new way that will allow us to deliver improved learning outcomes in cost-effective ways—and to do so on a continuing basis.

Fortunately, advances in technology offer real opportunities to "do more with less"—if they are not over-hyped, and if the appro-

[26] Personal correspondence, August 8, 2014.

[27] This is not, of course, to disparage efforts by educational institutions to be more efficient and to cut administrative and other costs as much as they can, consistent with effective discharges of their missions (including compliance with innumerable regulations). For an example of cost-cutting actions at one university, see Douglas Belkin, "At Purdue, a Case Study in Cost Cuts," *Wall Street Journal*, August 4, 2014. However, such savings are likely to be one-time in nature. Also, as I will emphasize shortly, there is a great reluctance on the part of administrators as well as faculty to confront the need to control instructional costs.

priate technology is chosen and implemented strategically.[28] In industry after industry, well-conceived investments in technology have, in addition to disrupting processes and product lines, generated economies of scale and reduced cost per unit of output significantly. In higher education, the opportunity to spread the costs of the needed initial investments in technology and the requisite process redesign across a larger enrollment base (including, almost certainly, multiple campuses and probably multiple systems) is likely to be the key to achieving the scale needed to allow real long-term reductions in cost per student.

There are so many flavors of online learning that it is hard to focus on those approaches that have the most promise of really improving educational outcomes and controlling costs.[29] As debate continues to swirl around MOOCs and their usefulness, early indications are that their greatest value is in opening windows to knowledge for individual learners all over the world, and perhaps especially individual learners with post-secondary degrees who have the skills, self-discipline, and motivation to take full advantage of the content available on MOOCs. But what about the use of MOOCs or similar educational and content platforms to help instructors teach students pursuing degrees in a traditional institutional environment? Might those technologies be used to improve productivity at mainline institutions? To date, mainline MOOC providers have not assigned a high priority to approaches that would address these *institutional*—as distinguished from *individual*—needs. For example, an Ithaka S+R–led study of the adaptability of MOOCs to meet the needs of the University System of Maryland (USM), carried out with the full support of both Coursera and the University System of Maryland, produced mixed results, at least in

---

[28] Full disclosure: I am a convert to the potential of technology. Earlier, in my Romanes Lecture at Oxford University in 2000, "At a Slight Angle to the Universe: The University in a Digitized, Commercialized Age," I cited evidence available at that time to suggest that online offerings frequently cost more than face-to-face instruction and expressed skepticism that this would change. But there have been major advances in technology since that time, and the need for experimenting with such approaches has become all too evident. See Bowen, *Higher Education in the Digital Age*, pp. 44–46, for a discussion of the evolution of my thinking.

[29] For a good discussion of "the contours" of the online learning landscape, see Kelly Lack's appendix to *Higher Education in the Digital Age*, pp. 72ff.

part because the platform used in the study was not designed for the purpose at hand.[30]

The USM study provides examples of the potential for online teaching to both reduce costs and improve student outcomes, but it also reminds us that a substantial upfront investment is required to redesign courses to use these tools. We learned how important it is to be able to amortize such investments over large numbers of students and over time. Finally, we learned anew that, with the best will in the world, it is not easy to take systems built for individual users and adapt them to meet the needs of institutions. The appetite of MOOC providers to make heavy investments in efforts to address these institutional issues is bound to depend upon both the costs involved and the revenue streams they are able to project.[31]

What alternatives are there for campuses to improve teaching productivity through technology? The right approach cannot be for each campus to try to develop, *de novo*, the sophisticated base platform(s) required. This task is too challenging for many (most) campuses, and single campuses are unlikely to be able to realize the economies of scale that are essential if such approaches are to be sustainable.[32] In my view, the most appealing (and the most audacious) approach is the development of one or more sophisticated platforms designed specifically for use by multiple campuses. Such platforms will need to incorporate well-designed feedback loops to facilitate machine-guided learning of basic elements of subjects well suited to this approach, and they will need, too, to be designed to accommodate "hybrid" modes of instruction that in-

---

[30] See Rebecca Griffiths, Matthew Chingos, Christine Mulhern, and Richard Spies, "Interactive Online Learning on Campus: Testing MOOCs and Other Platforms in Hybrid Formats in the University System of Maryland," *Ithaka S+R*, July 10, 2014, http://sr.ithaka .org/research-publications/Interactive-Online-Learning-on-Campus.

[31] The edX initiative sponsored by Harvard and MIT intends, as does Coursera, to have the platform used to deliver its MOOCs available for other campuses to use. But so far there is little evidence of real impact at the institutional level—for many of the same reasons that made it difficult to adapt Coursera offerings to the needs of the USM.

[32] Note, however, the success achieved by Arizona State University (ASU) in expanding enrollment while controlling costs—in part through the use of relatively simple versions of online learning. More important than the technology has been the entrepreneurial spirit engendered by President Michael Crow. See Kevin Guthrie and Christine Mulhern, "In Pursuit of Excellence and Inclusion: Managing Change at Arizona State University," Ithaka S+R, January 20, 2015.

clude some face-to-face features.[33] They will also need to be flexible enough to allow some degree of customization. "Local" faculty are understandably reluctant to use courses developed entirely elsewhere.[34]

Our rigorous testing on a number of public university campuses of a Carnegie Mellon [CMU] statistics course taught in a hybrid mode (with one face-to-face meeting a week) that used an adaptive learning methodology produced encouraging results; students from all backgrounds (not just those who were especially well prepared) had learning outcomes that were equivalent to those obtained by similar students who took traditional face-to-face versions of the same course. There is every reason to believe that these are baseline results and that learning outcomes using adaptive learning approaches will improve over time. Additionally, the study reveals that there are potential cost savings to be realized.[35]

I should add that advances in technology, and the possible development of hybrid courses that will facilitate the effective teaching of some materials (especially those needed for gateway courses in basic subjects), offer promising avenues of reducing costs quite

[33] Both common sense and research tell us that, in most situations, many students, especially those with limited preparation and little experience with self-guided modes of instruction, need at least limited access to teachers who can keep them on track. See Shanna Smith Jaggars and Thomas Bailey, "Effectiveness of Fully Online Courses for College Students: Response to a Department of Education Meta-Analysis," Community College Research Center, Teachers College, Columbia University, New York, July 2010. There is an important equity aspect to this discussion. As I have argued elsewhere [see William G. Bowen, "Academia Online: Musings (Some Unconventional)," Stafford Little Lecture, Princeton University, October 14, 2013, reprinted as an appendix in the paperback edition of *Higher Education in the Digital Age* (December 2014)], there is a serious danger that legislators will be tempted to adopt cheap versions of fully online learning courses for use with "the wrong" students—students who have a special need for some face-to-face contact with instructors. Poor students, and disadvantaged students generally, would be likely to suffer from such a short-sighted approach.

[34] The controversy surrounding the use of Harvard faculty member Michael Sandel's edX course at San Jose State University illustrates this problem. See "San Jose State University Faculty Pushes Back Against edX," *Inside Higher Ed*, May 3, 2013, www.insidehighered .com/quicktakes/2013/05/03/san-jose-state-university-faculty-pushes-back-against-edx# sthash.4tPwgO7h.dpbs.

[35] See Bowen, Chingos, Lack, and Nygren, "Interactive Learning Online at Public Universities," for a full description of both the CMU course and the Ithaka S+R study of the effectiveness of this course when taught in hybrid mode (with one face-to-face session per week); the study avoided selection effects by using randomized control trials.

apart from changes in staffing configurations. Scheduling of courses and classroom space is of paramount importance, as is sophisticated advising made possible by technology. Anecdotal evidence abounds that limited ability to fit student schedules (especially, but not only, the schedules of commuter students and students with families) into constraints imposed by both existing classroom space and faculty schedules is a major factor leading to long time-to-degree and failed efforts to finish programs. The combination of hybrid course offerings (with the attendant reduction in the need for students to be in a particular place at a particular time) and scheduling technologies has the potential to ease such problems dramatically— and to save both institutions and individuals considerable amounts of money. As suggested by our earlier discussion of disparities in outcomes related to SES [socio-economic status], low-income students attending mid-level universities should be primary beneficiaries. Colleagues at Ithaka S+R are working now on simulating potential cost savings of this kind.

BARRIERS TO BE OVERCOME

To accomplish ambitious objectives that could yield both improved outcomes and cost savings on multiple campuses will obviously require large amounts of patient capital to cover start-up costs and to provide incentives for university systems to participate in such efforts. Moreover, this has to be "patient capital" since it would be foolish to expect instant results. It is an open question whether major foundations or wealthy individuals are prepared to make such investments. Localized efforts, of the kind announced regularly, are to be commended—but we have to recognize that they are unlikely to produce the needed new technological infrastructure that can be broadly shared. To be sure, my sense of our requirements may be overly ambitious or just plain wrong. But I suspect strongly that incremental approaches will prove to be inadequate to meet pressing national needs.

Financial requirements, however daunting, are by no means the only barrier that has to be overcome. A quite different set of issues involves the need to develop new protocols that can govern both the ownership and the distribution of the intellectual capital developed in the course of work on new teaching methods. It can be tempting for institutions to change as little as possible and, for example, simply assert that whatever "rights" faculty currently enjoy in owning intellectual property that they were largely responsible for creating (albeit almost always with some contribution of university resources) should apply here as well. I am skeptical, however, that such a "business-as-usual" approach is wise, and not only because needed institutional contributions of resources can be substantial (as can, in some situations, monetary payoffs to the licensing of content). A narrow vesting of "ownership" of digital content and control over its distribution may not serve larger institutional (or societal) purposes. There are important questions concerning institutional responsibility for the sustainability of technologically enhanced digital course materials to be addressed. Will a newly developed online course be available in the future, even if the person most responsible for its creation moves to another location or dies? And who will be responsible for upgrading the content and presentation of material over time?[36]

An even more formidable problem is the widespread presence of a mindset that resists confronting directly the trade-offs that must be made in considering alternative teaching methods. In particular, there is, in many settings, a deep-seated aversion to talking about costs and potential cost savings. In the 1995 edition of his Godkin Lectures, Clark Kerr offered this provocative observation: "The call for effectiveness in the use of resources will be perceived by many inside the university world as the best current definition of evil."[37]

[36] The history of JSTOR is replete with lessons applicable to online learning, and one of the most important has to do with sustainability. JSTOR would never have become the success that it is today (having just signed up its nine thousandth participating institution worldwide) had it not been able to persuade librarians and university administrators that it was sustainable, with the resources and the commitment to maintain and upgrade itself. Librarians and those responsible for library construction had to be confident that JSTOR would "be there" in the long run. See Roger C. Schonfeld, *JSTOR: A History* (Princeton, NJ: Princeton University Press, 2003).

[37] See Kerr, *The Uses of the University: Fourth Edition*, The Godkin Lectures on the Essentials of Free Government and the Duties of the Citizen (Cambridge, MA: Harvard University Press, 1995), p. 181.

If we are to make progress in addressing the national need to improve educational outcomes without commensurate increases in cost, faculty and administrators alike need to do what for many is a difficult thing: avoid treating educational quality, important as it obviously is, as the *only* crucial variable in making major decisions. There is a deeply embedded sense that talking about costs borders on the sacrilegious. But trade-offs simply have to be made.

Let us consider a sharp-edged example. If teaching method "*A*" yields results that are not "the best," not quite as good as those obtained in another way—say, the new results are 90 percent as good as those yielded by teaching method "*B*"—but if "*A*" costs two-thirds as much as "*B*," that ratio has to be taken into account in deciding which teaching method to adopt. Resources saved in one corner of the educational enterprise can be used in another or can be used to reduce the costs of attending college. It is responsible, not sacrilegious, to seek to use limited resources in the most productive way.[38]

I am not suggesting that cost considerations are generally absent from decision-making. Hardly. There is too much evidence of the pain of retrenchment to believe that. The serious generic problem is that too often cost considerations drive decisions at hard-pressed institutions *only when there is no other way to go*—when "muddling through" has hit a wall. There is also a polar tendency, at least as dangerous, seen most often in calls by legislators, regents, and trustees, for institutions to move aggressively (with or without adequate faculty consultation) to introduce cost-saving technologies. Unfortunately, far too many calls to action are made in the absence of any real concern for quality, or any appreciation that it is less well-prepared and disadvantaged students who are most likely to

---

[38] A colleague has suggested that the problem is even more serious than our "hard-edged" example suggests. He notes that there is resistance to taking account of cost savings even when it can be demonstrated that using an adaptive learning approach "does no harm" in that learning outcomes are unaffected. An eminent doctor said that exactly the same mindset exists in large parts of the healthcare system. He said that he is something of an enigma to some of his colleagues because he cares about costs of treatments as well as their results. It isn't, he said, that he is against spending money on healthcare. It is just that he wants to spend the available resources as wisely as possible. Lawrence Bacow has suggested (in personal correspondence) that it is only in education and healthcare that accepting a "trade-off" calculus would be regarded as odd or in need of justification.

be harmed by such an approach. My plea is a modest one—to occupy what Isaiah Berlin once called the "ungrateful middle ground," and to deal directly, upfront, and unapologetically with trade-offs when that can be done thoughtfully and ahead of some make-or-break crisis.

Still another development that can lead to opposition to fundamental changes in teaching methods derives from the explosive growth in the number of non-tenure-track faculty. In 1969, tenured and tenure-track faculty accounted for over three-quarters of all faculty (78.3 percent); in 2009, tenured and tenure-track faculty accounted for just over one-third of all faculty (33.5 percent). As many people have noted, the ratio simply flipped. It is a mistake, in my view, for tenured faculty to dig in their heels and resist this trend. In light of the staying power of the forces driving the huge increase in NTT [non-tenure-track] faculty—forces such as unremitting cost pressures, the "unbundling" of aspects of courses, and the availability, on the supply side, of well-qualified individuals who are satisfied with being "master teachers"—universities would be well advised to acknowledge, as some already have done, that full-time NTT faculty have been filling essential teaching roles for many years. There is a strong case for moving expeditiously to consider creating "professional teaching staff" structures. Tenure-track faculty should cooperate with such efforts and not simply bemoan reductions in their relative numbers. There is surely a place in academia, and it should be a respected place, for talented individuals who do not aspire to publish the truly distinguished work of scholarship that would make them top candidates for a tenured position at a university with an outstanding graduate program or at a wealthy college committed to inculcating scholarly skills among undergraduates.[39]

---

[39] We link the PhD-producing universities and those institutions, including elite liberal arts colleges, that focus great effort on training undergraduates to do original research, since we believe that faculty at both kinds of institutions need to be active on the research front themselves if they are to be effective in guiding others seeking to learn to do research. For documentation of data presented in this paragraph and for an extended discussion of this entire subject, see William G. Bowen and Eugene M. Tobin, *Locus of Authority: The Evolution of Faculty Roles in the Governance of Higher Education* (Princeton, NJ: Princeton University Press, 2015).

We should create conditions that will honor the "master teachers" who deserve to find a regularized, respected, decently paid way of toiling in their chosen teaching vineyards. The shifting demands of the academic marketplace writ large (related in some measure to the growth in online teaching, as well as to reluctance by some institutions to continue to subsidize teaching loads that are deemed necessary to allow faculty to produce original research) tend increasingly to favor the master teacher. Colleges and universities alike should create structures that will provide the right incentives/rewards for full-time NTT academics who prove their worth in the classroom. Of course, the need (and the opportunity) to capitalize on this set of circumstances varies greatly across the higher education landscape—these challenges are less urgent for the wealthiest privates than for the harder-pressed institutions in both the private and public sectors. But the desirability of gaining legitimacy for the concept of a fairly compensated professional teaching staff should resonate broadly and restore a needed measure of mutual respect and equity within the academy.

This entire set of staffing developments, driven in part by changes in technology that are likely to accelerate, is linked to another topic—even more sensitive—that, fortunately for me, I have no time this morning to do more than flag for attention. I refer to the need to think freshly about doctoral education in the United States, and the number (and scale) of graduate programs needed to produce holders of PhDs trained in traditional ways. Let me not be misunderstood. There will always be a need for new cadres of dedicated scholars capable of doing cutting-edge research, as well as educating their putative successors. Those of us in the academy should fight vigorously for the support needed to preserve the capacity of our universities to continue to provide leadership worldwide in developing new knowledge and educating those qualified to correct, in the future, the errors we make today. This venerable process creates the life-blood of academia, and sustaining it deserves to be our highest educational priority. But this does not mean that we can overlook (out of fear of being called "elitists") the need to economize on the resources spent nationally on doctoral education. Understandable feelings of pride and concerns for status make this a truly treacherous terrain. But, somehow, we have to marshal the courage, as well as the insight, to navigate it.

RE-THINKING "SHARED GOVERNANCE"

Finally, I want to comment, all too briefly, on an even larger subject—the crucial need to re-think aspects of "shared governance." This is a main theme of the new book that Gene Tobin and I are producing for the Princeton University Press titled *Locus of Authority: The Evolution of Faculty Roles in the Governance of Higher Education* (please forgive the blatant advertising).

Odd as it may seem to emphasize governance issues in a technological age, we believe that they are of critical importance. In the many conversations that Gene and I have had with developers of new approaches to online teaching, a common message has been that *the* biggest obstacle to experimentation with new teaching methods is *the time-consuming, costly, and frustrating process of trying to get timely (and binding) decisions made by potential testbed institutions locked into centuries-old governing structures*. It is in the twin areas of teaching methods and curricular development that decision-making mechanisms are most in need of new thinking (although these are by no means the only areas in which modifications in governing arrangements are needed).[40]

---

[40] As many commentators have observed (especially critics of the ability of higher education to adapt reasonably quickly to new demands), governance arrangements in American higher education date in many respects back to the emergence of the research university in the late nineteenth century. New thinking is clearly needed as to what governing arrangements are appropriate today. There are, however, major aspects of the conventions to which we have become accustomed that continue to serve us very well and that should be protected against onslaughts from any quarter. I have in mind especially the dominant role assigned to faculty to evaluate the qualifications of candidates for appointment and advancement. Related, of course, is the commitment of almost all colleges and universities of consequence to the freedom of faculty to speak their minds. "Academic freedom," properly understood, is absolutely essential to both scholarly pursuits and good teaching; it is also joined to responsibilities of scholars to comply with professional norms. For a cogent explanation of what academic freedom means, and does not mean, see Matthew W. Finkin and Robert C. Post, *For the Common Good: Principles of Academic Freedom* (New Haven, CT: Yale University

To be absolutely blunt, it is time for individual faculty to give up, cheerfully and not grudgingly, any claim to *sole* authority over teaching methods of every kind.[41] In the digital age, creation of new course materials is often a collaborative process involving both considerable technical support at the local level and quite often inter-organizational collaborations. Departments are traditionally the key decision-making units when it comes to curricular matters, but this vertical (silo-like) mode of decision-making is not workable when it comes to making truly big decisions affecting the development and deployment of new teaching approaches. What is needed is new ways, maybe even radically new ways, of engaging faculty and administrators in discussions of new approaches, and how to seize them, that will often be "horizontal" rather than "vertical"—that is, that will cut across departmental lines and at times across campus and even institutional boundaries. Organizational challenges are, if anything, more daunting than the technological challenges.[42]

I am NOT, let me emphasize, arguing for ignoring faculty views! Faculty expertise and faculty enthusiasm are indispensable to finding cost-effective ways of delivering excellent educational content.

Press, 2009). These legal scholars stress that academic freedom is not some God-given right but a *requirement* of universities seeking to advance knowledge. It has also been understood from early days that "rights" are joined to professional "responsibilities." Finkin and Post are very clear on this point: "A second conceptual premise [in the development of the case for academic freedom] was that faculty are professional experts in the production of knowledge—they alone can judge the competence of other faculty as scholars. Lay governing boards are competent to judge charges of habitual neglect of assigned duties, on the part of individual teachers, and concerning charges of grave moral delinquency. But in matters of opinion, and of the utterance of opinion, such boards cannot intervene." This is a claim for professional self-regulation. In short: "The traditional ideal of academic freedom [involves] twin commitments to freedom of research and to compliance with professional norms" (p. 43).

[41] In fact, there have always been limitations on faculty control of methods—for example, faculty cannot simply assume that any number of TAs is available to teach sections of courses, and access to space and facilities can also affect how course material is presented.

[42] As Clark Kerr argued years ago: "The professoriate is not well organized to consider issues of efficient use of resources. Many decisions with heavy cost consequences, including faculty teaching loads and size of classes, are made at levels far removed from direct contact with the necessity to secure resources. Departments usually operate on the basis of consensus and it is difficult to get a consensus to cut costs." Clark Kerr, *The Uses of the University*, 5th edition (Cambridge, MA: Harvard University Press, 2001), p. 180.

Absent significant faculty involvement in designing, customizing, and implementing new approaches, frustration and, yes, failure are inevitable. I wish that more high-level administrators (especially those working at the system level) and more legislators understood this essential point!

My view is that, in exchange for giving up departmentally based veto power over course development, faculty should be given an important seat at a bigger table—a table at which collaborative decision-making is needed on four aspects of online learning: (1) decisions concerning investments to be made locally in either designing online platforms that enable faculty to customize their courses or in doing the customization; (2) decisions concerning the uses at "home" of online technologies designed locally or externally; (3) decisions concerning the sharing of online technologies across institutions; and (4) decisions concerning the adoption of a "portfolio" approach to curricular development that involves a blend of courses, some mainly online, some "hybrid," and some face-to-face.[43]

In short, when it comes to teaching methods and curricular structures, we have to get away from compartmentalized decision-making. Simplistic as it may sound, I believe that "shared governance" should be viewed not so much in terms of "who owns what" but as embracing a commitment to a genuine sharing of perspectives—to the avoidance of constituency-based thinking (to the extent this can be achieved in a world of real human beings!). What is most needed on the part of all parties, including both faculty and administrators, is not just a willingness, but an eagerness to embrace good ideas generated by others. Such mutual openness to good ideas from all sources should be accompanied by recognition that nimble decision-making is required. Nimbleness implies a need for a well-understood locus of authority, with administrators expected to listen carefully to those with ideas and expertise to contribute, but then to have the confidence and courage to decide.

---

[43] For an explanation of what I mean by a "portfolio" approach to curricular construction, see Bowen, *Higher Education in the Digital Age*, p. 68.

Writing in the mid-1990s, Clark Kerr observed:

> When change comes it is rarely at the instigation of this group of [faculty] partners as a collective body. The group is more likely to accept or reject or comment, than to devise and propose. The group serves a purpose as a balance wheel—resisting some things that should be resisted, insisting on more thorough discussion of some things that should be more thoroughly discussed, delaying some developments where delay gives time to adjust more gracefully to the inevitable. All this yields a greater sense of order and stability.[44]

I do not think, however, that the most urgent need today is for "a greater sense of order and stability." It is rather for organizational machinery that can facilitate an all-encompassing set of strategic decisions that allocate human and capital resources effectively and provide a compelling set of incentives for faculty to pursue system-wide goals. Stronger central direction is political anathema to many, but it could prove necessary to strengthen educational capacities at both pre-college and college levels.[45] Informal "coalitions of the willing" are very hard to create, and even harder to sustain.

We need, now especially, courage and the will to act on the part of presidents—in short, a willingness to take some risks. It is well, once again, to heed words Clark Kerr uttered in looking back in later years on the 1960s from his vantage point as chairman of the Carnegie Commission on Higher Education and later as a prescient elder statesman. He did not pull his punches:

> I would argue for giving leadership a better chance to exert itself. Most successful new policies in higher education have come from the top. We need to reverse the denigration of leadership.... It was

---

[44] Kerr, *The Uses of the University*, p. 75.

[45] In the case of higher education, my intuition is that the best hope for making real progress lies in creating, somehow, a viable partnership between (a) one or more funders willing to make the substantial investment required, (b) an educational "system" (beyond a single campus) eager to serve as a test bed and capable of making prompt and binding decisions, and (c) an institution with real technical capacity and a willingness, as well as the ability, to design the basics of a platform that others could customize. Brokering such a tri-partite partnership would require the leadership of either a well-staffed funder or some respected third party. Faculty involvement at all levels would be essential, but faculty could not expect to have a final voice or veto in decision-making.

denigrated by students in the late 1960s and early 1970s.... Presidents were used like Kleenex. The institutions survived, but their leaders did not. Yet in a time of troubles, as then loomed and now looms again, leaders are more needed but are harder to get to serve and to keep. To the list of presidential attributes I gave in the original [1963 Godkin] lectures, I would now add the ability to withstand the frustrations from all of the checks and balances, and the criticism from all of the more active and vocal participants; that is, the possession of nerves like sewer pipes.[46]

It will be far easier to recruit and retain leaders such as Clark Kerr if academia is able, somehow, to establish an attitude of trust that is forgiving of errors (or at least of some errors) as we try out new approaches to teaching and learning.[47] We need to move ahead on the basis of what I think is a widely shared sense of mission. Most faculty, and most presidents and administrators too, would not have chosen the lives they lead if they did not believe in the lofty purposes of higher education, which clearly include progress in addressing the national needs I identified at the start of this talk. I am optimistic that, with the aid of advances in technology and fresh thinking, we can in fact do much better than we are doing now—but, realist that I am, I also know that it will not be easy. Perseverance is a virtue!

Good luck to all of us—as we seek to serve what are indeed lofty purposes.

[46] See Kerr, *The Uses of the University*, p. 137.

[47] For a current example of why recruiting and retaining able presidents is such a treacherous undertaking, see Eric Kalderman, "Why the U. of Oregon's Presidency Is Such a Difficult Job," *Chronicle of Higher Education*, August 8, 2014. The corrosive effects of big-time college sports cannot be underestimated. There are also other factors contributing to what I sense are growing pressures on presidents; this is a subject deserving of careful study in its own right.

ISSUES FACING MAJOR RESEARCH UNIVERSITIES AT A TIME OF STRESS AND OPPORTUNITY

~

William G. Bowen
April 7, 2016

RUTGERS SPEECH

I would like to begin by acknowledging some of my many debts to Rutgers. My wife and I both have Rutgers degrees, hers an earned master's degree and mine one of the "unearned" kind. Beyond that, as a close neighbor of Rutgers for many years, living right "down the road" as it were, I have watched the evolution of this great institution with intense interest.

The historical connections between Rutgers and Princeton, dating back to colonial days, are legendary. Over the years, Rutgers has made major contributions. Among her many distinguished recipients of undergraduate degrees, I must note Paul Robeson and the economist Milton Friedman—a sometime antagonist of mine! Among the PhD recipients is William "Brit" Kirwan in mathematics, a distinguished leader of public higher education, a close friend, and a current collaborator. I could go on, but the list would quickly

Editor's note: In 2016 Bill was asked to give the keynote speech at the Rutgers University academic symposium celebrating 250 years of the university's existence. The topic of his session was *What does the history of the research university tell us about its future?*

Author's note: For help in the preparation of this talk I wish to thank my colleagues Johanna Brownell and Lisa Krueger, as well as Professor Mark R. Killingsworth of Rutgers University. Also, I have borrowed liberally from two books that I have written recently with (respectively) Eugene Tobin and Michael McPherson. Of course I am solely responsible for all errors and confusions that remain.

become overwhelming. On the research front, I would mention only that streptomycin was first isolated in a Rutgers laboratory in the 1940s.

FRAMING THE DISCUSSION

Aware as we are of a truly glorious history, we should look ahead. As the title of my talk indicates, this is without question a time, for great public universities such as Rutgers, of both stress *and* opportunity. The stress, you know all too well, derives from, first of all, shrinking resources, especially when measured on a per student basis. In New Jersey, public higher education enrollment increased by 11 percent between 2009 and 2014, while educational appropriations per FTE [full-time equivalent position] fell by 23.4 percent. This is an unwelcome but inescapable historical fact of recent days. At the same time, there are also rising expectations as to the contributions that institutions like Rutgers can and should make to solving pressing national needs. These needs, which Mike McPherson and I describe in a just-published book called *Lesson Plan: An Agenda for Higher Education*, include higher completion rates for undergraduates coupled with shorter time-to-degree; a marked reduction in disparities in educational outcomes associated with socioeconomic status; and greater success in controlling increases in costs while maintaining the quality of education. The country also needs to count on leading graduate programs to continue to provide a fresh generation of intellectual leadership and ever-new additions to the stock of knowledge—as Rutgers has long done.

Moreover, all of this needs to be accomplished while stopping the pernicious erosion of trust in higher education. This well-documented season of discontent, following a long period in which higher education was highly regarded, has been fueled in part by the increasing gaps in society between the "haves" and the "have-nots"—gaps that are surely responsible in large measure for the raw anger so evident in today's political campaigns. I resist the temptation to say more on this inflammatory topic.

It is also true that many potential friends of higher education are appalled by the distortions in values and priorities that are driven, increasingly, I fear, by the overly zealous pursuit of glories on the intercollegiate playing fields of what are meant to be principled centers of learning—not purveyors of mass entertainment, and certainly not academic hideaways for both recruited athletes and complicit coaches. Rutgers appears to have had some experience with these problems—in keeping, to be sure, with many other universities. And the super-privileged places like Princeton, Harvard, and Stanford are hardly without their own challenges in this treacherous terrain. Let me not be misunderstood. I am a great sports fan, and I believe strongly in intercollegiate sports *when integrated within a sound educational program.* I am a strong proponent of the virtues of competition. After attempting to explain to my son the values of participation (whatever the outcome), I can still hear him replying: "But dad, the fun is in the winning." Fine, but the pursuit of winning should be bounded by the right set of values and not by the incentives that seem to have overtaken much of the enterprise.

These stresses notwithstanding, this is also a time of great opportunity for public universities, since they alone have the capacity to address many of these needs. The truly heavy lifting has to be done by places like Rutgers, not by their more privileged cousins. And there are steps that can be taken to make progress on many fronts. Progress will, however, require candid stock-taking of where we are, readiness to attack major issues, and a willingness to adjust some (certainly not all) modes of decision-making that date back to the nineteenth century. I remain a strong advocate of shared governance, but I believe that hallowed phrase needs to be re-thought in some ways and not misused to prevent needed changes in the way universities operate today.

Let me now discuss some specific issues before us. I focus on just five: presidential leadership; growing disparities in educational outcomes related to socio-economic status; educational costs and teaching methods involving technology; treatment of a nascent teaching corps; and principles of shared governance. I will include some historical references in this litany.

1. Presidential Leadership

In the spirit of "taking it from the top," I begin with presidential leadership. From its earliest days, American higher education, unlike higher education in much of the rest of the world, was notable for vesting much authority—and responsibility—in strong presidents. (I can explain why this occurred, historically, if you are interested.) This is, in my view, all to the good. And, having "been there," you will not be surprised to hear that I agree strongly with something Clark Kerr said more than a half-century ago: we should stop denigrating leadership, encourage risk-taking (alongside accountability), and build up rather than tear down the capacity of able leaders to, in fact, lead.

Putting in place, and retaining, able presidential leadership is no simple task. It requires, of course, both identifying the right person and persuading him or her to accept a truly demanding position—whether more or less demanding today than in days gone by is a nice question to which the answer will vary depending on institutional circumstances.

In any case, there is no substitute for the active engagement of trustee-led search committees in identifying and recruiting the right leader. The board as a whole must then be responsible for actually selecting and supporting the best candidate. This is certainly not to deny that faculty should be heavily involved. On the contrary, strong faculty involvement is today a sine qua non, as it was not in the early days. Faculty are likely to have a keen sense of what an institution needs most in a new leader; they will be able to discern whether particular candidates have the requisite sensitivities to lead an academic enterprise; and, finally, faculty can be extremely helpful in persuading the right candidate to accept a genuinely tough job. In seeking to define the faculty role in this process, we should recognize that there is no one formula that will work in all situations. Ideally, the "right" faculty will be chosen to participate actively in the search for a new leader and will accept (cheerfully) a role as trusted advisors to the board. Faculty can be, and should be, highly influential without expecting to have the final "say" in the process. In almost all situations, the best candidate will want to be sure that he or she has the support of the faculty as well as of the board. To inject a personal note, it was a trusted faculty colleague at Princeton who persuaded me, at an absurdly young age, to take on a presidency for which I was unsure I was suited. And it was faculty who propped me up at critical moments.

Outside search firms can be very helpful, but in limited ways. In particular, they can be invaluable in identifying potential candidates who might otherwise have been overlooked. But I do not think that representatives of search firms should be expected to talk effectively with leading candidates, to ascertain their interest; these firms may have agendas of their own and, in any case, are not likely to be seen by the most attractive prospects as the face of the institution. I was involved in a specific situation in which a top candidate told a search firm that he was not interested in being considered when in fact a later conversation with the chairman of the board led to a different conclusion—and to the individual's eventual election as president.

2. Disparities in Educational Outcomes, "Free Tuition," and Financial Aid Policies

This nest of issues is, to my way of thinking, enormously important—not only to higher education but also to society at large. It is more important today than ever before, in part because of the historically high premium associated with college completion. This is a knowledge-driven age. And all of us who believe strongly in social mobility should be alarmed by the fact that 60 percent of students from families in the top SES [socio-economic status] quartile earn BAs (or higher degrees) as compared with just 14 percent of students from the bottom SES quartile and 29 percent of students from families in the middle two SES quartiles.[1] Nor can this fright-

[1] See National Center for Educational Statistics (NCES), "Education Longitudinal Study of 2002" (ELS:2002), Base Year and Third Follow-up. See also Institute of Education Sciences, *Digest of Education Statistics 2014* (Washington, DC: NCES, Institute of Educational Sciences, US Department of Education), table 104.91, available at http://nces.ed.gov/programs/digest/2014menu_tables.asp.

ening disparity be explained away by referencing differences in expectations or differences in preparation. For example, it is sobering to note that low-SES students who placed in the highest math achievement quartile were far less likely to earn at least a BA than were high-SES students who also placed in the highest math quartile (41 percent versus 74 percent); moreover, 21 percent of high-SES students who placed in the lowest math proficiency quartile earned at least a BA (as compared with 5 percent of low-SES students). As one scholar opined: "Put bluntly, class trumps ability when it comes to college graduation."[2] Furthermore, the limited evidence that is available gives us no reason to believe that these disparities are diminishing. This is a terribly troubling phenomenon in search of an explanation.

More money would surely help address gaps in outcomes, but it is necessary to be careful in choosing among ways of addressing affordability issues. Sloganeering needs to be kept in its place. One recurring proposal is to make public colleges "free" for all students. There are at least three reasons for being highly skeptical about this idea. First, it would be enormously expensive—and I see no reason to believe that states would appropriate the resources required to cover essential educational costs. On the contrary, it is all too evident that pressures to reduce state support are stronger than ever. Moreover, costs associated with delivering the education will also increase, as there is evidence that "free education" lengthens time-to-degree, since the incentive to complete one's studies expeditiously is reduced. Second, such a policy would fly in the face of widely stated desires to address equity issues. The main beneficiaries of "free tuition" would be the children of reasonably affluent families who attend public universities and certainly can afford to share in the costs of educating children who, on average, benefit substantially from a college education. Do we really believe that the children of Donald Trump should be absolved from sharing in the costs of attending a fine public institution—or the children of a Bernie Sanders, for that matter? Third, there is abundant

---

[2] These are Susan Dynarski's words in commenting on the ELS:2002 study. See her column "For the Poor, the Graduation Gap Is Even Wider Than the Enrollment Gap," *New York Times, Upshot,* June 2, 2015, www.nytimes.com/2015/06/02/upshot/for-the-poor-the-graduation-gap-is-even-wider-than-the-enrollment-gap.html?_r=0.

evidence that wise targeting of limited resources on students who have demonstrated need is far more effective than "free tuition" in increasing overall completion rates and reducing disparities in outcomes.

This last point brings us directly to another sensitive but important issue: the wisdom of providing "merit aid" to students without demonstrated need. There is a disturbing trend for public universities, as well as private colleges and universities, to use merit aid to bid for students of promise, including students from relatively affluent backgrounds. Recently, 25 percent of institutional aid provided by public universities was awarded without reference to need.

There is another point that is even more powerful. The able (and courageous) chancellor of the University of Wisconsin, Rebecca Blank, from whom we have just heard, has reluctantly concluded that she has no choice but to join the party (lest she lose increasing numbers of able students to neighboring public institutions that offer generous merit aid)—even though she has agreed that this effort to redistribute able students from one place to another makes little sense from a national perspective.[3] Scarce dollars spent on merit aid could do much more good if targeted on needy students.

Implicit in what I have just said is a broader issue that is quite profound. For some time now, universities, and particularly the publics but many privates as well, have been engaged in an "arms race" on several fronts—competing to enroll top students, spending more on sports and on ancillary facilities (fancy gyms, exotic dining options, and the like). What students of game theory call the "prisoner's dilemma" applies: a single institution doesn't dare hold off on these kinds of expenditures because, if they do, rivals will gain a huge competitive advantage. So each institution is tempted

---

[3] Blank has said, "It worries me a great deal, the type of merit aid I see being offered to top students from Wisconsin.... As far as I'm concerned—I'm an economist—that's a real waste of where we should be spending our money in higher ed. But I've got to keep some of those top students in Wisconsin.... The students who are going to go to Harvard, I may not be able to keep them at Wisconsin if that's the sort of experience that they want. But I have a lot of top students who get recruited away [by] Iowa and Indiana and Illinois and Minnesota. And I'll say this, we're a better school than them. They should be coming to us and not going out of state." See Kellie Woodhouse, Playing the Aid Game," *Inside Higher Ed*, December 18, 2015, www.insidehighered.com/news/2015/12/18/university-wisconsin-ups-its -merit-aid-effort-better-compete-peers.

(driven, really) to spend scarce funds on activities that have less and less to do with real education. Most everyone becomes worse off, and the cost of education for students in general goes up. This is not a problem any one institution can solve on its own. What is required is a "non-proliferation" treaty that in turn depends on truly strong—and collaborative—leadership.

3. Educational Costs, Teaching Methods, and Technology

Important as it is to improve educational outcomes—and it is not just very important; it is essential—this must be accomplished without unduly increasing educational costs and, ideally, restraining the rate of increase in costs for institutions as well as for individuals. To be sure, the rate of increase in actual ("net") college costs is often exaggerated, and too much attention is paid to the "sticker prices" of elite private universities that enroll tiny shares of the student population. Loans incurred by typical students are also exaggerated by many. Moreover, leaders of higher education suffer from ill-founded and unsupported charges of "administrative bloat."[4] Still, there is no denying that for many students (and their families) the costs of education are a real problem. Nor is there any denying the existence in academia of a deep-seated aversion to considering ways of controlling costs, especially instructional costs. This historically rooted mindset has to change. Academia has to consider, responsibly, how to manage trade-offs and, especially, how to take advantage of new technologies to teach foundational courses in gateway fields like beginning mathematics more effectively.[5]

Nationally, one of the biggest barriers to raising completion rates, especially for students from modest circumstances, is the failure of many well-motivated students to pass gateway courses in various

[4] See William G. Bowen and Michael S. McPherson, *Lesson Plan: An Agenda for Change in American Higher Education* (Princeton, NJ: Princeton University Press, 2016), pp. 106–10.

[5] See Kerr, *The Uses of the University*, 4th edition, The Godkin Lectures on the Essentials of Free Government and the Duties of the Citizen (Cambridge, MA: Harvard University Press, 1995), p. 181.

branches of beginning mathematics.[6] As Anthony Bryk, president of the Carnegie Foundation for the Advancement of Teaching, has put it: *"developmental mathematics is where aspirations go to die."*[7]

Many efforts have been made, and more are underway, to address this critically important problem. I am, by nature, an incrementalist, and I applaud these projects. They can make a real difference—especially as they help us improve how we connect better advising, using technology, to the use of varied pedagogical approaches. To its great credit, Rutgers has been active in this area, and time precludes me from doing more than mentioning Rutgers's Center for Online and Hybrid Learning and Instructional Technologies; Rutgers also offers some fully online degrees.

But sometimes incrementalists can be ambitious and even, on occasion, advocate a "swinging for the fences" mode of attack (especially at the start of the baseball season). That is my posture. Having been skeptical for years that investing in technology has real promise in improving teaching methods at reasonable cost, I am now a convert—and an advocate of efforts that reach well beyond any single campus. I am not talking about MOOCs, useful as

---

[6] As noted in a recent report of the President's Council of Advisors on Science and Technology (PCAST), "Engage to Excel," mathematics is seen as the number-one barrier to college completion at a time when the nation needs many more mathematics majors, nonmajors with more extensive and deeper mathematics preparation, and science, technology, engineering, and mathematics (STEM) majors who are better prepared for the mathematically intensive aspects of life sciences, social sciences, engineering, information technology, business, and security. See "Transforming Post-Secondary Education in Mathematics— Report of a Meeting," University of Texas–Austin, June 20–22, 2014, https://d3n8a8pro 7vhmx.cloudfront.net/math/pages/47/attachments/original/1415904260/TPSE_Report _pages_web.pdf?1415904260.

[7] See Clyburn, "Improving on the American Dream: Mathematics Pathways to Student Success," *Change: The Magazine of Higher Learning*," September–October, 2013, p. 17, www.changemag.org/Archives/Back%20Issues/2013/September-October%202013/ameri can-dream-full.html. Of course we all recognize that pre-college education today produces too many students who are not really ready for serious college work. In the longer run, our country simply must do a better job of preparing all of our students, especially those from disadvantaged backgrounds, to have the opportunity to benefit from at least some kind of post-secondary experience. But we have two hands. Important as it is to work on pre-collegiate problems (and some of the ways of improving college teaching, such as the proposed math program, may well help at the pre-college level as well), we cannot wait for some "revolution" at the pre-college level to solve present-day problems. We must all do all that we can to help those now graduating from high school to take full advantage of post-secondary opportunities of various kinds.

they are in increasing access to knowledge to individuals (most often those with some prior training, not neophytes). But, with the best will in the world, MOOCs do not address the basic needs of mainstream public universities.

Rather, I believe that it is increasingly sophisticated forms of *adaptive learning* that have the real potential, especially when used in a hybrid mode that marries these approaches to some face-to-face contact. In essence, adaptive learning uses machine-guided methods of teaching basic concepts by means of feedback loops that provide timely hints to students and valuable data to teachers.[8] This approach makes great sense when considering how best to teach some kinds of foundational courses in fields such as mathematics and statistics to large numbers of students. Distinctions are crucial here. I am talking about subjects based on widely agreed propositions (what is a "*t*-test"?)—not the Arab-Israeli conflict! In choosing pedagogies, we have to avoid one-size-fits all thinking.

One reason for guarded optimism is that there is evidence of some success with even primitive adaptive learning approaches. The most persuasive evidence is from a rigorous study of a hybrid statistics course that used machine-guided instruction à la the Carnegie Mellon (CMU) adaptive learning approach plus one face-to-face meeting a week. This study was carried out on six public university campuses that used randomized assignment of students to either a traditional version of the course or the hybrid model in order to control for selection effects. Findings were remarkably consistent across campuses. An adaptive learning structure, with multiple feedback loops, was found to yield essentially the same

[8] The Tyton Partners report—*Learning to Adapt: A Case for Accelerating Adaptive Learning in Higher Education* (April 2013, http://tytonpartners.com/library/accelerating-adaptive-learning-in-higher-education/)—defines adaptive learning as "a more personalized, technology-enabled, and data-driven approach to learning that has the potential to deepen student engagement with learning materials, customize students' pathways through curriculums, and permit instructors to use class time in more focused and productive ways. In this fashion, adaptive learning promises to make a significant contribution to improving retention, measuring student learning, aiding the achievement of better outcomes, and improving pedagogy." They add, "If adaptive learning solutions are implemented at scale, then they have the potential—at least theoretically—to produce a higher-quality learning experience (as measured by student engagement, persistence, and outcomes) at potentially reduced cost by making high-quality instruction more scalable" (pp. 4–5).

learning outcomes with much less face-to-face staff time and less time invested in the course by students. Another key finding was that an important sub-set of students, those who were relatively less prepared academically, did as well with the adaptive learning model as did their better-prepared classmates.[9]

To be sure, adaptive learning models can be, and are being, improved significantly by organizations such as Acrobatiq (a for-profit spin-off from Carnegie Mellon). A key question right now is whether we can assemble both the institutional partners and the resources needed to test the effectiveness of an improved prototype adaptive learning platform that could scale up and yield highly cost-effective modes of teaching some kinds of basic content. This is a challenge worthy of the most forward-looking public universities, working in collaboration with both for-profit entities and their non-profit cousins (as well as with governmental agencies).

4. Rationalizing Staffing Patterns: Supporting a Teaching Corps

Another noteworthy historical fact: over the last forty years or so, there has been a dramatic shift in the mix of faculty—from tenure-track to "conditional," "adjunct," or whatever word one wants to use to describe the variety of teaching staff that comprise the non-tenure-track (NTT) faculty. In 1969, tenured and tenure-track faculty accounted for over three-quarters of all faculty; in 2009, tenured and tenure-track faculty accounted for just one-third of all faculty.[10] At the risk of aggravating (yet again!) friends in the academic world, let me suggest that this shift is the unavoidable (and irreversible) consequence of unremitting cost pressures on higher education combined with trends in doctoral output. Technological advances also play a part in this process but, to date, a minor part.

---

[9] For a full description of the study, see Bowen, Chingos, Lack, and Nygren, "Interactive Learning Online at Public Universities." www.sr.ithaka.org/publications/interactive-learning-online-at-public-universities-evidence-from-randomized-trials/.

[10] See *Locus of Authority*, pp. 152ff., for documentation of this shift and a fuller discussion of the reasons for it.

On the demand side of the equation, many institutions have felt the need to curb increases in staffing costs, and NTT faculty are of course much less expensive than tenure-track faculty: they are less well paid, they are asked to teach more hours, their performance can be assessed with less controversy than the performance of tenure-track faculty, and they can be released if need be.[11] To be sure, the country requires a heavy investment in top-level training in scholarship for the next generation of leaders of the scholarly enterprise—including, of course, those at Rutgers. In addition, a certain amount of attention to scholarship can be justified for all teaching staff as a form of professional development, but this need not be either extensive or expensive.

On the supply side, Mike McPherson and Charles Kurose of the Spencer Foundation have demonstrated that by the mid-1980s, "growth in the number of tenure-track faculty was only enough to absorb 10 to 16 percent of the PhDs produced."[12] A consequence is that the large number of aspiring faculty who cannot find tenure-track positions has provided a pool of potential teachers, many of whom prefer NTT positions to no place in academia at all.

It does no good to bemoan this shift, as a number of people insist on doing.[13] The underlying market forces are not to be denied, and people should recognize candidly that the use of NTT faculty is often justified. There are, to be sure, pronounced differences in the case for using NTT faculty in some institutions and some settings as opposed to others. The wealthiest, most selective, and most

[11] Another factor, still in its early stages, is the "unbundling" of some teaching functions as a result of technological advances. "Unbundling" reduces the need for faculty to manage all aspects of a course. See William G. Bowen, "Academia Online: Musings (Some Unconventional)," Stafford Little Lecture, Princeton University, Princeton, NJ, October 14, 2013.

[12] Michael McPherson and Charles Kurose, "Imbalance in Faculty Labor Markets," unpublished memo, September 23, 2014.

[13] See, for example, the proposal by Bernie Sanders to require institutions to retain a certain ratio of tenured to NTT faculty—an idea that ignores entirely the realities of the situation. According to Sanders, "States would have to promise that, within five years, 'not less than 75 percent of instruction at public institutions of higher education in the State is provided by tenured or tenure-track faculty.'" See Kevin Carey, "Bernie Sanders's Charming, Perfectly Awful Plan to Save Higher Education," *Chronicle of Higher Education*, July 6, 2015, http://chronicle.com/article/Bernie-Sanderss-Charming/231387.

privileged places will continue to make only limited use of this set of people, whereas the far larger number of mainstream public and private places will make more use of them. We should simply accept this situation as reality. Each institution has to do what it can afford and what is consistent with its sense of its own character and mission.

Rather than yearn for a return to an alleged "golden age" that is not achievable, it is far wiser for higher education to make the best accommodation it can to the shift in faculty mix that has transpired and find ways to make effective use of the still growing ranks of NTT faculty. There is growing evidence that NTT faculty, when properly chosen, supported, and treated, can be highly effective teachers, especially of basic, "foundational" courses.[14] Putting aside any general presumption that tenure-track faculty *must* be the best teachers (which may be justified when it comes to teaching students how to do research, but not otherwise), it is hardly surprising that in at least some situations NTT faculty have been found to be more effective than their tenured counterparts—and especially effective with disadvantaged students. After all, there are surely "master teachers," who are primarily interested in teaching.

I am persuaded that higher education should professionalize the "teaching corps" much as many universities professionalized research staff following World War II and the explosive growth of sponsored research that accompanied it. In the immediate postwar years, it became evident that the substantial numbers of highly qualified scientists needed for large-scale research projects could not possibly be accommodated within the regular teaching faculty even though they were indispensable; they required status and appropriate conditions of employment. Today there are signs that more and more universities are recognizing the need to regularize conditions of employment for a professional "teaching corps."

---

[14] Perhaps the best-known study to reach this conclusion is the one by David Figlio and his colleagues at Northwestern. David N. Figlio, Morton O. Schapiro, and Kevin B. Soter, "Are Tenure Track Professors Better Teachers?," NBER Working Paper 19406, September 2013, National Bureau of Economic Research, Cambridge, MA, www.nber.org/papers/19406, revised August 28, 2014.

Northwestern, Michigan, and the University of Maryland are among the universities that have taken the lead in this area.[15]

I will not attempt to describe in any detail the elements involved in professionalizing the teaching corps (which will, in any case, vary from institution to institution), but I do believe that they should include the following:

- A well-formulated set of titles, plus compensation and benefits commensurate with contributions. Northwestern is experimenting with the title "professor of instruction."[16]
- A clear understanding of terms of appointment and opportunities for re-appointment. I do not think that conferring tenure is necessary or appropriate, given needs to preserve staffing flexibility; there are other ways to protect the academic freedom of NTT faculty.
- A well-defined evaluation process that spells out basic protections (rights of appeal) for NTT faculty, who must enjoy the core elements of academic freedom, such as the right to express one's own views on even the most controversial issues.
- Measures to confer dignity and respect on NTT faculty, with, for example, the right to participate in faculty deliberations. The large set of NTT faculty should be regarded as within the mainstream of higher education, not as stepchildren.

5. Revisiting Shared Governance

Last on my list of challenges for higher education is the need to rethink some—but by no means all—of the principles of shared governance that have been with us since the late nineteenth century. To begin with what should *not* be changed: faculty must be

[15] Bowen and Tobin, *Locus of Authority*, pp. 157ff., contains references to evolving practice at these institutions as well as a historical discussion of the development of professional research staffs.

[16] See Colleen Flaherty, "Professors of Instruction," *Inside Higher Ed*, August 12, 2015, www.insidehighered.com/news/2015/08/12/northwestern-us-arts-and-sciences-college-updates-titles- teaching-faculty-and-offers.

relied on to vet the qualifications of their peers, and we should resist vigorously efforts by others to decide who does and who does not have the qualifications for teaching or research positions. Similarly, the core principle of academic freedom is that faculty should be expected to say and to write what they believe, without regard for the views of legislators, trustees, or fellow faculty members—provided that they follow the standards of responsible, professional utterance that have been part of the academic freedom bargain for many years. (Here again, historical context is instructive.) Tenure is the bedrock protection of this right, but it is by no means the only way to safeguard the freedom of utterance on which vigorous pursuit of truth depends—there are, for example, certainly ways of protecting the academic freedom of NTT faculty.

Faculty must be careful not to overreach, as there has been some tendency to do, especially since the late 1960s and early 1970s. History teaches us that it is a mistake to attempt to apply the principle of academic freedom to areas in which it does not belong, such as decisions as to overall staffing configurations. Administrators and trustees must be expected to make the hard financial or educational choices that inevitably affect both the size and the composition of the teaching staff. As Frederick P. Schaffer, general counsel of CUNY, has explained well: "To link to academic freedom every policy and procedure that a professional association might want for its members is to drain the concept of all meaning."[17]

Control over teaching methods is a key area in which faculty have much to contribute—indeed, their professional expertise and their enthusiasm are essential elements in the thoughtful pursuit of progress. But, on another historical note, as Gene Tobin and I argue in *Locus of Authority*: "It is time for individual faculty members to give up cheerfully, and not grudgingly, any claim to sole authority over teaching methods of all kinds."[18] In exchange, faculty should be given an important seat at a bigger table, a table at which truly collaborative thinking is needed before administrators, armed with good faculty advice, exercise their responsibility

[17] See Frederick Schaffer, "A Guide to Academic Freedom," *CUNY Bulletin*, January 2, 2012.

[18] Bowen and Tobin, *Locus of Authority*, p. 173.

for making decisions about the scale and nature of investments—judgments for which they need to be held accountable. Decisions also have to be made as to how to shape the export and import of new pedagogies across institutions as well as across fields of study. Advances in technology make it imperative to move away from historical notions that departments must drive all decisions of this kind. Moving away from a vertical, departmental "silo" approach to resolving important questions will not be easy, but it is essential. We have to organize ourselves to think more horizontally.

I know of no formulaic approach to cross-departmental decision-making that will apply in anything like all situations. It is evident, for example, that there are many complicated issues of IP [intellectual property] rights and institutional responsibility for relationships with other institutions that wish to use parts or all of platforms or content developed at university X. Some way of assuring continued access to what may seem like ephemeral content is important but very tricky. The JSTOR model may be instructive. We are in the early stages of sorting out these issues. But one thing is clear, at least to me: the right model of shared governance going forward is not "who owns what" (faculty versus administrators versus trustees) but how all parties can work together most effectively. "Shared governance" should not mean "divided governance."

As a committed empirical "bean counter," I should be expected, and should expect myself, to have rigorous answers to many questions of this kind. But, true confession, I do not. In fact, I am driven to fall back on vague notions of trust and good will. Mindsets really matter. Brian Rosenberg, the very able president of Macalester College, has it right when he says: "Organizations with a culture of suspicion make decisions to avoid the worst, while those with a culture of trust make decisions to aspire to the best."[19]

Trust, in turn, depends on a widely shared sense of educational mission and a commitment to advancing the important humanistic goals for which higher education has stood for generations. The cynicism of today notwithstanding, I believe that the great majority

---

[19] Personal correspondence, July 2, 2014.

of faculty and administrators continue to believe strongly in what they do—which is why they came to the party in the first place. Otherwise, they would have chosen a different life path. What those of us in academia do really matters, as a reasonable dose of introspection should remind those of us who have benefitted so much from attending great institutions such as this one. We should be unabashedly proud of having chosen what is indeed a noble calling.

CHAPTER 6

PROFILES IN LEADERSHIP

TOO SOON TO BE TIRED

~

William G. Bowen
June 23, 2016

LEON HIGGINBOTHAM TALK, PHILADELPHIA
BAR ASSOCIATION

Speaking as I am here at the Philadelphia Bar Association, I cannot help but let you know that I have a modest claim to be one of you. At the height of the campus turmoil of the early 1970s, a leader of the radical students at Princeton came to my office to debate the meaning of a campus statement on the limits of dissent. He complained that I was reading the statement "as if it were the Talmud." He then exclaimed: "Mr. Bowen, you have a very good *little* mind; you would have been a great lawyer!"

It is a genuine pleasure to be here today to join in celebrating the legacy of Leon Higginbotham, who was indeed a great lawyer. I had the privilege of serving with Leon on the Board of Regents of the Smithsonian. More than that, along with countless others, including many in this room, I watched with admiration as he stood up for rights that should be common property but that too often have fallen prey to what Glenn Loury has called our "unlovely racial history."[1]

It is unnecessary to recite Judge Higginbotham's history and accomplishments, especially before this audience. That would be

Editor's note: Bill was invited by the Philadelphia Bar Association (PBA) to give the Higginbotham Lecture at the PBA's quarterly meeting. The lecture series is named for A. Leon Higginbotham, a prominent African American civil rights advocate and federal appeals court judge.

[1] See Glenn C. Loury, introduction to the paperback edition of *The Shape of the River* (Princeton, NJ): Princeton University Press, 1999).

"carrying coals to Newcastle." But I cannot refrain from mentioning a coincidence. One of my great friends in life is Derek Bok, distinguished former president of Harvard and co-author of *The Shape of the River*. It was Derek's father, Judge Curtis Bok, who gave Leon his first opportunity to clerk after he graduated from Yale Law School with a distinguished record; apparently no one else in Philadelphia legal circles at the time was interested in even giving this remarkable black man an interview. Times change— fortunately.

But they have not changed fast enough or moved us far enough in the right direction. Hence the title of my talk today: "Too Soon to Be Tired."

When LBJ gave his last major speech, in the early 1970s shortly before he died and against the strong advice of his doctors (he was very ill), he gave it at a symposium on civil rights. In this much under-appreciated speech, LBJ said: "To be black, I believe, to one who is black ..., is to be proud, is to be worthy, is to be honorable. But to be black in a white society, is not to stand on level and equal ground. While the races may stand side by side, whites stand on history's mountain and blacks stand *in history's hollow*."[2] A great phrase.

To be sure, much progress has been made since Judge Higginbotham first met Curtis Bok and since LBJ gave that speech. The situation today is indistinguishable from the situation then. LBJ could not have imagined that our president today would be Barack Obama—a black American who, in my opinion, dominates others on the political stage with his intelligence, eloquence, common sense, and courage.

But we should not be deceived; racial prejudice remains a potent force, and I am persuaded that many of the attacks on the president reflect a deep, if unacknowledged, racism. And this deep undercurrent of lack of respect is reflected in present-day political realities.

[2] See Lyndon B. Johnson, "Remarks," in *Equal Opportunity in the United States: A Symposium on Civil Rights; Co-sponsored by the Lyndon Baines Johnson Library and the University of Texas at Austin*, ed. Robert C. Rooney, pp. 161–75 (Austin: Lyndon B. Johnson School of Public Affairs, 1973).

Stereotypes based on atypical instances of success only mislead. An example: At Princeton, I recruited to the faculty a Nobel Prize–winning economist from St. Lucia in the West Indies—Sir Arthur Lewis. A white woman from England asked if she could have the honor of serving as Sir Arthur's secretary. Fine. At the time of the Johnson-Goldwater election, Arthur and his secretary fell to discussing politics. She said that she was going to vote for Goldwater. Arthur, in his direct manner, asked: "Why are you going to do a thing like that?" She responded, "Because of the race question." Undaunted, Arthur asked: "What about the race question?" She said, "Well, Johnson will force me to sell my house to a Negro." Arthur replied: "That's not a practical policy; there aren't enough Negroes; imagine what the housing velocity of sales to Negroes would have to be!" Arthur, who was telling me this story, went on to say, with a grin, "And, I have to report that my aunt, in Harlem, is going to vote for Goldwater for the same reason." To the secretary, Arthur was not black; he was "Sir Arthur." Both the secretary and the aunt misunderstood the character and depth of the race problem in America.

In preparing this talk, I originally contemplated driving home my point about present-day realities by presenting a brief scorecard. But I then decided that that would be superfluous before this audience.

You are all too familiar, for example, with the statistics showing the vast disparity in incarceration rates by race. The Pew Research Center here in Philadelphia tells us that, in 2010, "black men were more than six times as likely as white men to be incarcerated."[3] Six times! Gaps in mortality rates and in health generally are also dispiriting. In the field I know best, education and labor force behavior, figures are less dramatic but—especially from a long-term perspective—no less alarming. Among all Americans 25 and older, 38 percent of whites have attained a BA or higher degree; the corresponding figure for blacks is 27 percent—just three-quarters of

[3] See George Gao, "Chart of the Week: The Black–White Gap in Incarceration Rates," *Fact-Tank*, Pew Research Center, July 18, 2014, www.pewresearch.org/fact-tank/2014/07/18 /chart-of-the-week-the-black-white-gap-in-incarceration-rates/.

the white rate. On average, weekly earnings for full-time black workers are also three-quarters those of whites. (A parenthetical note: These widely cited gaps in earnings and income are not nearly as pronounced as gaps in wealth—an indicator much harder to measure but very important. It is wealth, and especially liquid assets, that permit a parent simply to write a check when circumstances threaten to derail the college plans of an offspring.) Finally, as is well known, the black unemployment rate is twice the white rate—and unemployment rates fail to capture differences in labor force participation (the fact that some unemployed become so discouraged by their limited job prospects that they simply stop looking for work and thus are no longer counted as unemployed).

Of course these problems interact, and we will continue to debate to what extent crime and incarceration are the products of inequality and despair. A former colleague of mine, Marion J. Levy Jr., was the author of a pamphlet titled *The Ten Laws of the Disillusionment of the True Liberal*.[4] One of these laws went something like this: "That segment of the community with which one has the greatest sympathy as a liberal inevitably turns out to be one of the most narrow-minded and bigoted." A colleague, Stanley Kelley, paraphrased this observation as follows: "Last guys don't finish nice."

But simply wanting things to be better will not do the trick. Another of Levy's Laws was this: "Always pray that your opposition be wicked. In wickedness there is a strong strain toward rationality. Therefore there is always the possibility of out-thinking them." He provides the corollary that "good intentions randomize behavior."

Education can help close gaps in opportunities—and then in outcomes. "Opportunities" and "outcomes" are not, I hasten to add, the same. My wife, Mary Ellen, and I were present when, in her installation address as vice chancellor of the University of Cape Town, Mamphela Ramphele (mother of Steven Biko's son) told her audience, including many South African black students who may have thought that finally they had it made: "Everyone deserves opportunity; no one deserves success. Success has to be earned."

---

[4] See Marion J. Levy Jr., *The Ten Laws of the Disillusionment of the True Liberal* (Princeton, NJ: M. J. Levy, 1981).

Too much is made, I'm sure, of where students go to college. But it does matter. There is abundant evidence that most students who are fortunate enough to go to highly selective schools do, in fact, benefit greatly, whether outcomes are measured in terms of life-time incomes or in other ways, such as prestigious opportunities for public service. We do well, I think, to reject categorically one of the most pernicious myths that continues to circulate. It is called "the mismatch hypothesis," and it holds that affirmative action often harms the intended beneficiaries by enticing poorly prepared minority students to attend schools that are too demanding for them, schools where they will be intimidated, out-gunned, and doomed to fail. Better, the argument goes, that they attend easier schools and not try to rise above their station.

This is an empirical proposition, and tons of data show that the mismatch hypothesis is, in fact, baloney. As Derek Bok and I first demonstrated in *The Shape of the River*, black students who enroll at schools where the average test score is higher than their own do far, far better than black students with comparable credentials who attend less selective schools. Apparently the combination of pressure to excel and strong educational environments pays off. Of course we should give admissions deans some of the credit for this impressive result: they are not admitting black students (or any students, for that matter) whom they do not believe can handle the challenges a school provides. Just recently a talented Israeli sociol-ogist, Sigal Alon, published a book containing extensive findings from Israel as well as the United States that document once again that there is *no* support for the mismatch hypothesis.[5] The failure of this proposition to die a peaceful death, in spite of innumerable blows to its vital organs, is a sad commentary on the lack of re-spect in America today for evidence.

A friend of mine, Charles Exley, legendary chairman of the NCR Company and a staunch conservative who describes himself as "to the right of Attila the Hun," agrees with what I have just said. Chuck much prefers leaving the judgment about matters of admission to

[5] See Sigal Alon, *Race, Class, and Affirmative Action* (New York: Russell Sage Founda-tion, November 2015).

presidents like me than to having them subject to efforts to impose more and more "objective" tests of who deserves a place in a class. He worries about the pernicious effects of bigger and bigger rule books. "You will make mistakes," Exley said to me, "but I can study outcomes and if you make too many mistakes, I can fire you!" He is right to join accountability to discretion. Those of us in higher education should want to be held to account.

Judge Higginbotham understood exactly what I have been saying, and I remember well the open letter he wrote to Justice Clarence Thomas bemoaning the fact that Thomas never acknowledged the advantage he received by having been admitted to Yale Law School.[6] Sadly, not all of our ducks are swans.

But those of us gathered here today (including the ducks among us) will, I would hope, press on. We know that the work so boldly advanced by Judge Higginbotham in his day is far from over. It is, as I hope we can agree, much too soon to be tired.

[6] See A. Leon Higginbotham Jr. "An Open Letter to Justice Clarence Thomas from a Federal Judicial Colleague," *University of Pennsylvania Law Review*, November 29, 1991, pp. 1005–28.

REMARKS AT MEMORIAL SERVICE FOR TONY MARUCA

~

William G. Bowen
September 14, 2007

Sally, members of the family, friends: All of us here today are fortunate people. We were privileged to know Tony Maruca, as we are privileged to be part of this memorial service.

It was my great good fortune to get to know Tony professionally through, first, the good offices of two of our great mutual friends, Ricardo Mestres and Bob Goheen, two giants with whom Tony worked from 1962 until 1972, when I became president. Tony and I were then the closest of colleagues from 1972 until 1988, when both of us left the university. At the time that Tony decided to retire, having suffered with me through thick and thin all those years, I remember him saying: "I have carried my spear long enough!"

What a spear it was—a sturdy, powerful, and exceedingly effective instrument used always in the service of Princeton. But somehow the image of the spear is not right. We think of spears as having sharp points and inflicting pain on those who attack us or simply are in the way. Tony was never one to inflict pain, and he went to inordinate lengths to protect people from pain and to cushion any fall that could not be prevented. What a gentle man he was.

Editor's note: Bill delivered these remarks at the funeral service for his dear friend and colleague Anthony J. Maruca. A Princeton graduate, Maruca was a member of the Princeton University administration for thirty years, including as a senior administrator during the sixteen years when Bill was president.

And how much he accomplished, on an astonishing variety of fronts. Tony's title during his last years at Princeton was "vice president for administration." That title sounds innocuous enough, but it encompassed responsibility for personnel (a function that became far more important under Tony's leadership than it ever had been before), athletics (and I could go on and on about what discharging that duty entailed, including serving as midwife to the creation of the Patriot League), public safety (during, we should recall, some of the more tumultuous days in Princeton's modern history), the University Health Services (itself awash in controversies over such topics as sex education and counseling), purchasing, and who knows how many other necessary but unglamorous activities. Never once did he even question whether he should do this, that, or the other thing that we wanted him to do, never mind fail to do whatever was asked of him in an exemplary fashion.

He was superb at what he did—and he never felt left out of the major decisions being made all around him about academic directions and university priorities—for the simple reason that the rest of us had the good sense not to leave him out. He could, and did, contribute to decisions of every kind: examples include an increased emphasis on minority recruitment, the building up of student aid, the move to coeducation, the genuine opening up of the chapel and the university to people of different faiths, the strengthening of the life sciences, creation of the residential colleges, and the general positioning of Princeton to play a leading role in scholarship and teaching worldwide. He was involved in decision-making and execution all across the board—again, for the simple reason that his colleagues on the academic side of the house as well as those involved in administration knew that he was a wise man, that he had extraordinary judgment, and that he would never put a personal agenda ahead of a university agenda.

This discussion of activities and accomplishments, important as it is, fails, however, to recognize Tony's greatest strength and his most important contribution to Princeton. He had an uncompromising commitment to the values of the university that was combined with an extraordinary generosity of spirit and an irrepressible desire to help other people. He was one of the least self-centered people I have ever known. What mattered to Tony was not who got credit for A, B, or C (he never sought credit for himself) but that the university run well and that people were able to take real satisfaction from being part of a great institution. As someone once said of Sam Hughes, legendary Washington civil servant, "He achieved without fanfare results beyond the reach of those who seek the limelight."

Tony was an ombudsman without the title, and I was struck on so many occasions by the range of staff, faculty, and students who went to him for advice, or just to confide their troubles, confident (rightly confident) that he would do everything he could to help them. He was everyone's friend without ever condescending, playing favorites, or compromising the integrity of the university. He knew where to draw lines, and that was one reason, I think, why he was so universally respected. From his post in Nassau Hall, Tony was the glue that often held people together at the same time that he held the institution together. In the words of one of his long-time colleagues, the dean of the Graduate School, Ted Ziolkowski, "He was just such a decent man."

In talking with friends about this service, and what points I should emphasize, I learned that, as Marcia Snowden put it, everyone seemed to have a "special kindness story" about Tony: a young administrator getting a bottle of wine from him when her confidence needed a boost, a colleague in Nassau Hall being given one of the pictures that she had admired on the wall of Tony's office, a faculty member who received financial help at a crucial time, a young minority student who was encouraged when he needed encouragement, and a young man from Tennessee (here today), a classmate's grandson who wanted a pen pal. Mary Ellen has reminded me of how extraordinarily kind and helpful Tony was to Ann Rogerson, the widow of football coach Ron Rogerson, not only after his sudden death but also in all the years since.

In reflecting on these and other stories, I am struck again by Tony's common touch. He cared about everyone, and he treated everyone the same, whatever their status or station. At Christmas time he used to take me to the party at the powerhouse, so that I could thank the people who did so much for Princeton with so little recognition. He also had a wonderful appreciation of the genuinely funny moments in life. One morning during a time when we were dealing with unusually weighty (and aggravating) matters, he came into my office very early, doubled over from laughing. He had just overheard two gardeners in front of Nassau Hall talking (in Italian) about the beat-up car I drove to work (I think it was still the Dodge Dart with a hole in the floor behind the front seat). Never imagining that Tony understood what they were saying, one asked the other: "Why do you suppose the president drives such a pile of junk?" The second gardener replied: "Maybe they don't pay him any better than they pay us." On another occasion, I recall Tony's comment on the "position description and analysis form" that the inimitable Fred Fox '39 had been compelled (by Tony) to prepare. It included 161 separate functions including "Soothed Yale professor whose bulldog was stolen by our undergraduates. Petted his dog." Tony's observation: "the position and the incumbent defy classification—which is as it should be." He understood the limits of bureaucratic rules, and he always insisted on treating each person as an individual.

Nor did Tony's appetite for being helpful end when he left Nassau Hall. He worked for a time at the Rockefeller Family Office in New York, and one Sunday night at my New York office, I was struggling with the need to get a mass of detail sorted out so that a group for which I was responsible could conclude the sale of Rockefeller Center to Mitsubishi Estates. Tony obligingly responded to my call for assistance, trooped over to my office, helped stuff envelopes, and managed somehow to calm down a secretary who was on the edge of hysteria. Some years later, after he returned from Martha's Vineyard, he agreed to work with Paul LeClerc at the New York Public Library on some of that great organization's multiple organizational challenges—and Paul has never stopped singing Tony's praises. Closer to home, Tony was helpful, I know, to Peter Dougherty when Peter took over as director of the Princeton University Press. And then there was a situation that required the most sensitive kind of counseling and tutelage. There was no doubt in my mind who should be called upon. In thinking about Tony's core commitment to helping people, I am reminded of a great phrase of Harold Helm: "It's healthy to spend some time with other people's problems."

Another of Tony's most remarkable qualities, evident I hope in all that I and others are saying, was his unshakable loyalty: to the values he believed in, to the institutions he served, to the people around him, and of course to Sally and his family. Maruca family ties, their love for one another, and their mutual dedication were—are—beyond description. In Tony's last days, I saw first-hand how strong and courageous he was, and how remarkable Sally was—a duo that surely deserved each other.

Having mentioned Harold Helm, I want now, in closing, to say a word about Manning Brown and how similar I think Tony and Manning were in many ways. As most of you know, Manning was Princeton's "top trustee" (as a student once put it) during incredibly trying and contentious days. Tony and Manning were both characterized by an inner strength, unselfishness, and what I can only call a "thoughtful steadiness." Nothing flashy, just always ready to do the right thing, and for the right reasons. Just always ready just to get the job done. At one commencement I referred to a poem by Jack Gilbert entitled "The Abnormal Is Not Courage" that speaks to me about both of these stalwarts. The poet reminds us that courage is not "the bounty of impulse," but rather

> ... The beauty
> That is of many days. Steady and
>   Clear.
> It is the normal excellence of long
> Accomplishment.

So it was with Tony: "Steady and clear ... the normal excellence of long accomplishment."

IN PRAISE OF PRESIDENT
CHUCK VEST

~

William G. Bowen
October 4, 2004

MIT OPENCOURSEWARE CELEBRATION

President Vest has stood squarely for the unqualified pursuit of both excellence and opportunity. As I look at the group of people assembled in this room, I realize that I risk saying the obvious if I dwell on the standing that MIT enjoys today. The leadership that this faculty provide in many fields of knowledge is so well known that no amplification is required. All I would add is that recruiting and retaining a great faculty is the work of many days; it requires both a discerning eye for promise and a talent for building the collegiality that alone is worth more than almost anything else— save, perhaps, state-of-the-art laboratories! I am reminded of what I was once told by a Nobel laureate in physics at Princeton who was being wooed by a university prepared to double his salary: "I am not going," he said, to reassure me. He then added: "Excellence can't be bought, but it has to be paid for." Which is of course why President Vest has worked so tirelessly to raise the money needed to justify retaining on this faculty some of the world's finest academics.

Editor's note: Charles "Chuck" Vest was a long-time friend and colleague of Bill's and served on ITHAKA's board of trustees. He was a founding trustee and began his tenure when the certificate of incorporation was filed in 2002. He remained on the ITHAKA board until his death in December 2013. Vest was president of MIT from 1990 to 2004. From 2007 until his passing, he was the president of the National Academy of Engineering. When Vest wanted to launch OCW, he worked with Bill to secure start-up funding from the Mellon Foundation (and the Hewlett Foundation).

If possible, I admire President Vest's determined pursuit of opportunity even more than his success in building the excellence for which MIT is known. Let me cite three instances. First, it was President Vest who led the resistance to the ill-advised effort of the Justice Department to alter established financial aid polices and practices designed to concentrate financial aid funds on students who really need them. He characterized the Justice Department's decision to bring a suit under the Sherman Antitrust Act as "bizarre," and he and MIT then fought a long battle in the courts to defend a principle that was important to all of higher education. As a participant in this process (as a witness for MIT), I can speak about President Vest's leadership on the basis of personal experience. Eventually, MIT won at least a moral victory in the appeal court and, in the process, sent a strong signal about its beliefs to all who would listen. Higher education is not about exploiting a monopoly position to maximize profits (if that were the goal, why not just auction off places in the entering class to those who will pay the top price?); it is about husbanding scarce resources to serve societal goals in the most effective way possible.

Second, I would mention President Vest's candor in addressing the issue of the treatment of women faculty members at MIT. It is hard to imagine many university presidents acknowledging deep-rooted problems so openly. Throughout much of higher education —by no means only at MIT—the effective inclusion of women academics as full participants in the educational enterprise remains very much a work in progress. Needed is not only a strong commitment to "do the right thing" but also more research that will help us understand better when, and where, and why impediments to the advancement of women continue to take a toll.

My third example is President Vest's dogged and highly principled defense of programs designed to extend educational opportunity in America to more members of racial minorities. Most of you in this room are familiar with both the outcomes of the University of Michigan cases heard by the Supreme Court in 2003 and the protracted battle over summer enrichment programs sponsored by MIT that was fought out more or less concurrently. In the course of these contentious debates, Chuck and I had many personal conversations, and I never failed to feel better afterward. This was in part because he helped me understand the nuances of some complicated situations. But there was more to it than that. Like so many of you, I drew strength from his strength. I suspect that there are more than a few here today who heard Chuck's eloquent speech at the Martin Luther King Day event at MIT. Let me say simply that the prospects for blending opportunity with excellence in American higher education—and in America—have been enhanced greatly by Chuck's personal leadership. For him, these are far more than abstract issues. At bottom, they are about our values, our aspirations, and our common humanity.

In preparing to give this talk, I reread Chuck's 2004 report entitled "Moving On"—something he himself is about to do. In its tonalities as well as its substance, this report reminded me in so many ways of a talk given by an economist of distinction, Sir Arthur Lewis, when he was being installed as the chancellor of the University of Guyana at a time (1967) of great racial turmoil in that country. Arthur took his audience back in time as he spoke about the role of universities:

> Universities did not begin with science; we are the guardians and transmitters not merely of science, but of all human knowledge. Let me put this into historical perspective. Not very long ago men lived in caves, or under the shadow of trees. Their lives were dominated by fear—fear of the elements, of drought and flood and fire; fear of other animals; and fear of other men, who wandered around in families or tribes ready to exterminate each other. The human race has pulled itself up from this [condition] by handing down from generation to generation knowledge of two sets of principles, those relating to controlling nature, which we call science, and principles relating to controlling human behaviour, which we call ethics. Human life as we know it today is based on accumulated science, and accumulated ethical principles enshrined in laws and in the conventions of decent behaviour.
>
> The supremely important task of receiving this knowledge, adding to it, and handing it down to the next generation has always devolved on a very small body of people who specialized in using

their brains. They were known as clerks.... Here we come to the fundamental purpose of education: to produce young men and women who will join the small band of clerks stretching backwards through history and forward through generations yet unborn. Who will receive our truths, embellish them, defend them against numerous and powerful enemies, and pass them on to the next generation. If our graduates do not help to keep civilization together, to reduce the sum of human misery and to advance the cause of human brotherhood, then our university will have laboured in vain.

Do those themes sound familiar to those who have known Chuck at MIT? I suspect that they do. He and Arthur Lewis also have in common an understanding of the need for passion (and courage), coupled with a recognition that passion has to be channeled appropriately. Arthur's Guyana talk concludes with these words:

What distinguishes the civilized man from the barbarian is not that he lacks passion, but that his passion is mingled with compassion. He hates the sin, but not the sinner. He can therefore reach out to exploiter and exploited alike, with understanding and therefore some chance of reconciliation. The great leaders of our day, the Hammarskjolds and Bunches and arbitrators of our innumerable disputes, are those who are welcomed on both sides not because they lack passion—for if they lacked passion they would not care to take on such tasks—but rather because their passion, mingled with compassion, makes them dispassionate.

Please join me in saluting this far-sighted, principled, courageous, passionate, yet dispassionate, man who has provided such great leadership for OCW, MIT, and the world beyond this campus.

REMARKS AT THE ANDREW W. MELLON FOUNDATION DINNER IN HONOR OF HANNA HOLBORN GRAY

~

William G. Bowen
March 20, 2003

In considering what I might say about Hanna's stewardship of the foundation, and how much our close working partnership, our friendship, has meant to me personally, I first of all turned away several suggestions by one-time colleagues. The first idea I rejected was that a small group, led by Chuck Exley, might provide a musical tribute in the form of a rendition of a specially composed ballad that a former senior advisor of the foundation found on the Internet. It is titled "Hanna Blue," and I will say no more about it than that—though I will report that it has Chicago roots, not Yale roots. I will provide a different Yale reference at the end of these remarks. The second idea I rejected was also proposed by a former senior advisor (and you may begin to understand why the adjective "former" keeps being used to identify these creative souls). This individual suggested that we encourage Hanna to regale us with an account of her encounter with Deidre in the Chicago airport. Now

Editor's note: Gray was a dear friend of Bill's and worked closely with him as a trustee of the Andrew W. Mellon Foundation for twenty-four years, six of which she served as chair, until her retirement in 2003. Gray was the first woman to serve as president of Yale University, where she was acting president in 1977–78, and the first woman president of the University of Chicago, where she served from 1978 to 1993. Bill delivered these remarks upon her retirement from the Mellon Foundation's board.

this is very much an insider's story, which perhaps at some other occasion those of you interested in it can persuade Hanna to tell you. It does speak eloquently both to the wide range of her admirers and to her legendary story-telling ability—but somehow this doesn't seem like the time or place for it.

My intention is to be more prosaic, since I have a serious purpose in mind: to try, however inadequately, to sum up what Hanna has meant to the foundation and to all of us. At the conclusion of this year's annual report I intend to tell those who follow the foundation's affairs that a major change in board leadership is to take effect in March 2003. I will go on to say that words and descriptive phrases, however carefully chosen, are bound to fail to capture the spirit, as well as the substance, of Hanna's dedicated and truly inspired, inspiring leadership of the board. How to characterize it? I would describe her leadership as

- always thoroughly informed (homework done meticulously);
- thoughtfully independent (with an emphasis on both words);
- ready to ask the probing question (as we all know so well), but ready as well to make and support difficult decisions;
- creative and forward-looking as well as traditional in the best sense of the word;
- always aware of the difference between responsibility for overseeing an organization and for managing one; and, finally
- ever mindful of both the foundation's core mission and the attitudes, assumptions, and habits of mind that help us maintain a somewhat distinctive style of grantmaking.

In this latter regard, I want to recall the quite extraordinary tribute to Paul Mellon that Hanna wrote shortly after his death. In this tribute Hanna credits Paul with, among other things, establishing a style of philanthropy that sets clear directions, establishes priorities, and identifies "trends and opportunities where [the foundation] might make a distinctive contribution." This approach involves, in her words, "understanding the long-term goals to be sought, and then relying on the ablest people and institutions to carry out the programs in their own best way." She then added: "This kind of philanthropy *sets high expectations and assumes, in the collaboration between foundation and grantee, a high level of trust.*" I would observe that it was not Paul alone that established and maintained this line of thought.

An obvious question is what explains our chairman's prodigious capacity to lead the Mellon Board as she has done so ably. There are, I'm sure, many elements at play, and I will suggest only three.

First, *Hanna is exceedingly knowledgeable*—about not just this foundation, not just foundations in general, but the wide range of institutions with which we work. She has an intimate familiarity with the humanities, with the worlds of teaching and scholarship —in the United States and abroad, at every level from undergraduate college to university to center of advanced study—and with closely related fields such as the arts and music. Yes, we have here, in our midst, a polymath, a real child of the Renaissance.

Second, *Hanna cares so much*. The words "commitment" and "dedication," which we sometimes use loosely, have real meaning when it comes to Hanna and the Mellon Foundation. No one, not even someone with her breadth of knowledge and longstanding interest in the fields central to the work of the foundation, could have made the contribution she has made absent a strong desire and determination to do so. I have in mind her willingness to sit on as many runways as necessary, to read as many docket items as we could produce, to think hard about the detail as well as the large picture before her, and then to preside over us with evident zest.

Third, she "*practices what she preaches*." Or, more accurately, she "lives by her learning"—a lovely phrase suggested to me by James Shulman. James went on to suggest that one of the greatest fears for those who care about the humanities is that their subjects will become playthings for the curious—baubles taken out for amusement when idle hands can afford to indulge themselves in philosophy or literature or art or … history. In sharp contrast, Hanna's profound engagement with her academic field is revealed not just in the ways she teaches and writes, but in the way that she *lives*: presiding over a board meeting, attending a reception, or participating in a lively conversation—always ready to challenge a weak proposition and test and promote a strong one. Her humor, her style, and her ability to persuade are not "mere" rhetoric. Her technique embodies the lessons learned from the legendary figures from whom she has inherited more than texts—lessons that she has understood and integrated into her life.

Consider, for example, her citation of Machiavelli discussing Alexander the Great (from her famous, oft-quoted 1963 article "The Pursuit of Eloquence"):

> Countless times situations arise in which an army will come to grief if the captain does not know how or does not undertake to speak to it. For such speech takes away fear, fires souls, increases determination, uncovers snares, promises rewards, points out dangers and the way to escape them, reproves, entreats, threatens, fills again with hope, praises, condemns, and does all those things by which human passions are allayed or incited.

What better description can there be of Hanna's ability to wield her language to fit the situation—to guide us. The key point, which Hanna's article makes clear, is that such dazzling rhetorical flair is not *just* that—not "mere" rhetoric—but a powerful means of living life and communicating values in a world populated by all who need to learn. And learn we have.

There is one other aspect of Hanna's leadership of the board that I want to highlight, and I will do so by borrowing parts of the final paragraph of her essay "The History of Giants," to which Neil has already referred. But I will take the liberty of modifying her language so that it applies to the role she has played among us, here at the foundation, rather than to the somewhat different role of president of a great university ... another role that she understands all too well. In concluding this essay, she suggests that the role of leadership relates to "service" and "enabling." It entails (and now I quote) "enabling people to meet their own highest standards in an environment at once supportive and demanding, enabling institutions to reach, over the long term, toward their goals. Such enabling, at its best, will rest on a foundation of collegial respect, disciplined restraint, constancy of purpose, and old-fashioned courage, on a willingness to pursue what may be unpopular at the moment and speak out against the merely popular, and on faithfulness to the ... calling itself. Such enabling leadership does not presume to rule but is not afraid to lead, to take decisive positions, and to accept accountability."

She ends her essay on giants by allowing Sir Winston Churchill to provide a coda, which I would not be so bold as to suggest applies to our Hanna (or to any of the rest of us, heaven forbid). But you can judge. In his memoirs, Churchill wrote: "I did not suffer from any desire to be relieved of my responsibilities. All I wanted was compliance with my wishes after reasonable discussion."

Finally, I want to add a personal word of gratitude for all that I have learned from our friend, and for all that she has given to me. Thank you, Hanna, for so much wit, wisdom, and friendship—for always being there for me, and for always being you.

ANDREW J. GOODPASTER

80TH BIRTHDAY CELEBRATION

~

William G. Bowen
April 7, 1995

It is a great privilege, nothing less than that, to participate in this tribute to Andy Goodpaster. My role is to discuss Andy's contributions outside the military. While I shall try my best to fulfill this assignment (happy obligation that it is), it will not be easy: first, because Andy has been such a resolute soldier that it is hard to think of him in any other way, and, second, because I am familiar with only a small part of Andy's other life and know, for instance, far less than others gathered here about his contributions to the Atlantic Council. My remarks, then, will be both highly selective, focusing perhaps inordinately on Princeton associations (which I know best), and only partly compartmentalized, since one of my themes will be how perceptively this consummate military man has understood a civil society.

I first met Andy Goodpaster in the early 1960s—under extraordinarily auspicious circumstances. Princeton University received a gift of unprecedented magnitude ($35 million then, which is equivalent to over $150 million today) to strengthen and expand its graduate program in the Woodrow Wilson School of Public and

Editor's note: Andrew J. Goodpaster was an army general who served as supreme allied commander, Europe (SACEUR), for NATO and commander in chief of the US European Command (CINCEUR) from May 5, 1969, until his retirement on December 17, 1974. Goodpaster was a Princeton graduate, and Bill cultivated and maintained a good relationship with him from his time as provost and then president of the university until Goodpaster's death in 2005.

International Affairs. The gift was anonymous at the time, but a subsequent announcement indicated that it had been made by Charles and Marie Robertson, two extremely private people who just didn't like a lot of attention or fanfare. They wanted only to do a good thing, for their country and for the world, by expanding dramatically opportunities for individuals of high talent to be educated for public service, with particular emphasis on international affairs. I always thought it ironic that the skeptics among us were convinced that the money had come, somehow, from the CIA.

Through some set of associations that were never entirely clear to me (though they were obviously inspired, if not designed, by some great Tiger in the sky), Andy Goodpaster turned out to have been an absolutely key figure, along with Bob Goheen and John Gardner, in orchestrating this drama. A few years later I was asked to be the director of a rapidly expanding Graduate Program, and that is how I first came to know Andy, who was then (and is now) a highly influential member of the board of the Robertson Foundation—the entity established by Princeton's trustees and the donors to oversee the progress of the program made possible by this extraordinarily generous gift. I tell you this bit of local history not only because it explains why I happen to be at the podium tonight, but also because it is embedded in a larger story that tells us so much about Andy Goodpaster. Let me try to explain.

The story has its beginning shortly after the end of World War II, when our honoree, then a 32-year-old member of the War Department General Staff, chose to pursue graduate study at Princeton, first in engineering. Even then, he had what I can only call a precocious sense of the role of higher education—and especially of the kind of education that he (and others) would need to be of maximum usefulness in a world of high technology and increasing interdependence that was, in many respects, still in its infancy. In a letter written to a professor before he began his graduate study, Lt. Colonel Goodpaster articulated "the need, on the part of Army officers at least, for the broad basis of education which civilian schools might give. Such schooling should pay off in widened horizons, better perspective, and increased objectivity. The need for such improvement is all too apparent." He added: "There is a need for understanding of the forum in which [policies and strategies] are determined, and for an awareness of the fundamental elements of history, philosophy, and social forces which orient national policies." We see in this early letter a conception of education for service that Andy has always maintained—and that we need to reemphasize today. Breadth of vision and a non-parochial view of the world are two of Andy's notable characteristics.

The ability to "get it done" also ranks high on that list of attributes, along with obvious intelligence. The record shows that Andy earned three advanced degrees, including a master's in engineering and a master's and PhD in international politics, all in the space of three years. You do not want to know the average time-to-degree for doctoral candidates—then or now. Andy's doctoral dissertation is a 377-page analysis, "National Technology and International Politics." You will not be surprised to hear that he made a lasting impression on his teachers. His primary faculty advisor was the late Professor Harold Sprout, who told one of my colleagues that, as a student in seminars, Andy had one quite unusual habit: "Rather than just take notes, he *listened*; and then prepared his own response." Here we have another of Andy's enduring characteristics: never to assume either that he already knew it all or that what he still needed to learn could be learned by rote. Listening to other people, considering their ideas, and then preparing one's own position—these have always been Andy's rules of intellectual engagement.

Andy is such a quiet, unassuming person that I cannot imagine he would ever consider enumerating the major institutions that he has influenced profoundly. That is a task that the rest of us have to perform for him. Others here tonight can explain better than I can his lasting influence on the military, NATO, West Point, the Atlantic Council, and the White House itself. But I hope Andy will allow me to add the Woodrow Wilson School of Public and International Affairs to the list. Its very existence, in its present form, owes so much to him. I can attest, from personal experience, that his educational philosophy played a major role in shaping the development of its program and, in turn, the preparation received by a stream of graduate students that will be, I trust, never-ending.

Those who studied, taught, and administered at Princeton were the beneficiaries not just of Andy's intellectual grasp of the complexities of the modern world and their implications for education. They were also the beneficiaries of his *personal* example—as were, I'm sure, innumerable fellow officers, members of other organizations, cadets at West Point, and more than a few presidents of the United States. You couldn't be around Andy without recognizing, and being influenced by, his steadiness, loyalty, courage, and integrity. Henry Adams made the oft-quoted observation that a teacher never knows where his influence ends, and Andy is one of the world's great teachers, outside the structure of any normal classroom. Those of us who worked with him on the board of the Robertson Foundation appreciated his faithfulness in holding the program of the Woodrow Wilson School to its original intentions, but never foolishly, and never without taking into account changes of every kind that were occurring worldwide. Steadiness and loyalty were certainly in evidence when, for example, the excitement generated by Great Society initiatives might have tempted others to downplay the long-term importance of international affairs.

I can illustrate Andy's courage and integrity, and their impact, by recalling one event that is stamped indelibly on my memory. At the time of Vietnam, Andy wrestled personally, as well as professionally, with the agonies felt by so many others, including students and faculty on campuses that were undergoing enormous stress and fractiousness. Emotions were running so high, and feelings were often expressed with such stridency, that anyone who looked at all "military" generally elected to stay at a good distance from college campuses. Well, Andy certainly looked "military"—he was, after all, deputy commander in Vietnam for a short period—but he was incapable, by personality and character, of staying out of contentious debates in situations that would have been too trying for almost anyone else. So Andy accepted an invitation to come to the Woodrow Wilson School and engage in a discussion of Vietnam with a large number of irate students who were no doubt overjoyed at the prospect of confronting a "dumb general."

Andy's presence, and especially his evident respect for those who were staunchly opposed to the war, combined with his ability to present another point of view in a calm and considered way, led to one of the most genuinely educational events I have ever observed. Andy's critics may not have been persuaded that he was right on all counts (truth be told, many of us were not persuaded); but no one there that evening left without a new appreciation for the complexities of the issues, or for the need to listen respectfully to divergent points of view. It was a lesson in citizenship, taught brilliantly. That same lesson, taught over and over, in every imaginable setting, all around the world, is surely one of Andy's greatest contributions.

I once wrote an honorary degree citation for another public servant (Sam Hughes) who had achieved, I suggested, "results beyond the grasp of those who seek the limelight." How true of Andy. A search of news clippings reveals that editors were regularly at a loss to know how to write about a man who was a public figure, in high positions, and yet was so opposed to anything that might smack of self-promotion that he almost never granted interviews. Andy has proven hard to honor. But the Class of 1939 at Princeton managed to make him an honorary classmate, and the inimitable secretary of that class, Fred Fox '39 (who collected donations for the rebuilding of the Princeton gym from soldiers who were with him on a landing craft about to reach the beaches of Normandy) decided that the appropriate way to recognize Andy's election to membership in the class was by giving him a box of K-rations.

Subsequently, Princeton awarded Andy the highest distinction that can be conferred on an alumnus of the Graduate School when it presented him with the Madison Medal on Alumni Day in 1976. It was singularly appropriate, I think, that the other principal honoree on that occasion was George Kennan. Later, after his distinguished service at West Point, Andy was awarded an honorary doctor of laws degree by the trustees. The official citation refers to Andy's "constancy in commitment" and to his "persistence in maintaining reasoned discourse." But I like even more a reference in an earlier draft to one of Andy's statements that comes close, I believe, to summing up his own life: "Integrity ... takes a thousand forms."

So thank you, Andy—for your steadfastness, leadership, integrity, and devotion, given without quarter to your country over a lifetime.

A GENTLE GIANT

A GATHERING IN HONOR OF
NICHOLAS KATZENBACH

～

Remarks by William G. Bowen
June 21, 2012

It is my privilege to welcome you today. I do so on behalf of Lydia, her family, and Princeton University. Thank you for coming to this "gathering" (Lydia's word) in honor of Nicholas Katzenbach.

As one of our mutual friends said immediately after learning of Nick's death: "He was a national treasure!" So he was, but I want to talk about Nick more "locally"—as a Princeton trustee and personal friend.

At the risk of violating Nick's intense dislike of any reference to "credentials" (more on this in a moment), I should note that Nick was a key member of the Princeton board of trustees during almost all of my time in the president's office (fourteen of the sixteen years), and I knew him very, very well. He was truly one of a kind: A GENTLE GIANT—in physical presence, to be sure, but even more in character and humanity. He was as kind and compassionate as he was brilliant.

Nick was so multi-dimensional, so understated yet so deep that, simple as he was in many ways, he is hard to capture. But this can

Editor's note: Nicholas deB. Katzenbach was US Attorney General under President Lyndon B. Johnson. A Princeton graduate, Katzenbach served on Princeton's board of trustees from 1971 to 1975 and from 1977 to 1987, where he and Bowen worked closely together and became friends. In 1963, Katzenbach was responsible for delivering President John F. Kennedy's orders to integrate the University of Alabama and allow two African American students to attend. He drafted what became the 1964 Civil Rights Act.

be said emphatically and without qualification: he was a man of unassailable integrity, of precise judgment, and of impeccable values.

A few vignettes:

An attorney of matchless ability, Nick represented me (and Princeton) in countless legal disputes, always pro bono. He hated pretense, had no use for it, and certainly no need of it. I remember one case in which a pompous lawyer for the other side, resplendent in three-piece suit, introduced himself by recounting his legal pedigree at inordinate length. Nick then rose, in a rumpled suit, and said simply, "My name is Katzenbach, and I represent Mr. Bowen."

As a trustee, Nick chaired the board's Committee on the Curriculum, which oversaw all academic initiatives and the faculty appointment process—at a time when the university was building much of its present-day strength in fields such as the life sciences. He also worked actively on every imaginable issue, including investments in South Africa (and some unimaginable issues!). At one testy moment when we were debating, yet again, ROTC, another trustee, apparently annoyed by Nick's insistence on taking account of the implications of whatever we decided, challenged Nick by asking pointedly: "Don't you believe in principles?" To which Nick responded, "Of course I do, but I also believe in consequences." His steadfast belief in *both* principles and consequences informed all that he did, at Princeton and beyond.

Nick had exceptionally good relationships with trustees of every size and shape. They had great respect for his moral compass and admiration for his incisiveness, combined always with good humor. I will never forget one meeting when, as chairman of the Curriculum Committee, he concluded his report without having presented one set of recommendations. I turned to him and said, "Mr. Katzenbach, I think you have another item to present." He looked down at his papers and, with that wonderful smile of his and perfect timing, said: "Yes, I stand corrected ... for the first time!"

Tom Wright, who served as secretary of the board, had this to say about Nick: "He, more than any other single trustee over thirty years, would lift a discussion to a higher level of discourse. His combination of intellectual acuity and subtlety, of moral steadiness, and of ironic warmth and humor, made his presence transforming."

Another of our close colleagues, Neil Rudenstine, said: "I try to think about him at dinners, where his mind was always in play and his wit always on alert. An easy conversation with Nick could be relaxed and informal, but there was always that element of probing.... There was also the sense of deep untapped resources— untapped until the moment required them. So this was a very large man with a wonderful mixture of gravitas, deftness, and lightness of touch."

Nick and I were much more than colleagues on the board. We were, I am privileged to say, close friends for half a century. After one dinner at Lowrie House, I happened upon our daughter, Karen, then a junior in high school, talking earnestly with Nick. She was inviting him to speak to her class about a Supreme Court case. I protested vigorously (as Karen recalls to this day!), saying that it was inappropriate for her to take advantage of a guest in our house to plead her case. Nick cut me off: "This is between Karen and me," he said. And of course he spoke to her class. Karen explained to me just a few weeks ago that she had asked him to come to her class not, in her words, "because of his CV" (which was something of a mystery to her at that time) but simply because "he was kind and approachable."

One of our family's favorite possessions is a famous Richard Avedon photograph of Nick, John Doar, and James Meredith (signed by all three), celebrating the integration of the University of Mississippi twenty-five years later. It hangs in my study—as it always will.

A final story about dinners. Nick and Lydia were in the habit of joining Mary Ellen and me for an early New Year's Eve dinner at the Homestead restaurant on the edge of Trenton. We did this every year for nearly twenty years, and we always ate at the one table in the kitchen. It was over that table that we heard stories about matters great and small, including Nick's legendary encounters with Governor Wallace—in the school-house door in Alabama and in the White House. Many, but by no means all, of those stories made their way into his splendid Norton book, in which he detailed his Washington years working alongside two antagonistic personalities, Bobby Kennedy and LBJ. That book bears the apt title "Some of It Was Fun," which he told me was the contribution of daughter Mimi.

Committed as he was to large causes in the public arena, Nick was nonetheless most strongly committed to Lydia, his wife of more than sixty-five years. Nick was simply devoted to Lydia. As those of us who visited him at Stonebridge in his last days can testify, just mentioning her name always brought a smile to his face. The dedication of the Norton book on his Washington years reads simply: "For Lydia, of course."

Being in Nick's presence was stimulating, instructive, and, yes, inspiring. One could not help but reflect on how much he did for the lives of people of every kind, in all parts of this country and all over the world. But it was more than that. Being with Nick was *fun*, pure and simple. We are assembled here today, then, to express not just our gratitude for a long life, lived to the full, but our *pleasure* in having known this remarkable man. In language often associated with Eleanor Roosevelt, he was always inclined to light a candle, never to curse the darkness. Miss him, we do—and we will. But we can never be in darkness for long if we remember his truly luminous spirit.

WILLIAM J. BAUMOL 90TH BIRTHDAY CELEBRATION

~

Remarks by William G. Bowen
April 24, 2012

NEW YORK UNIVERSITY

By an odd coincidence, it was almost exactly twenty years ago that I was privileged to say a few words at a celebration of Will Baumol's contributions to Princeton. In the intervening decades, my appreciation for this wonderful friend has grown—I want to say "exponentially," but I worry that Will might object to a loose use of language.

I will end with a toast, to both Will *and* Hilda, since it is the "joint products" of these two irrepressible New Yorkers that have enriched us all. I am hard pressed to think of another couple that, as it were, "complete each other" so perfectly.

Hard as it is to believe, it was more than half a century ago, in the fall of 1955, that I found myself as a terrified graduate student in Professor Baumol's graduate theory course. We used a text by J. R. Hicks (*Value and Capital*) that defied comprehension, and we covered, if my memory serves me, all of thirty-five pages in an entire semester. I learned so much: that clear thinking has to precede clear writing, though the former certainly does not guarantee

Editor's note: William J. Baumol was an economist and Bill's PhD advisor at Princeton. There they began what would become a sixty-plus-year friendship. They collaborated together a number of times, most notably on *Performing Arts, the Economic Dilemma: A Study of Problems Common to Theater, Opera, Music, and Dance*, which introduced the phenomenon known as Baumol's cost disease.

the latter, and that while it might take me quite a while to understand something (longer than it took some of my classmates), if I persevered I could figure most things out. I gained a quiet confidence that has been a gift of incredible value.

I continued to learn from Will and Hilda as we worked together on a study of the economics of the performing arts that yielded a proposition about "the cost disease" that has had an incredibly long shelf life; it has now led to Will's most recent book, to be published soon by the Yale University Press. How's that for staying power! Over the years, I found that if I was puzzled about anything, all I had to do was ask Will and he would set me straight. But it was Hilda, not Will, who taught me to navigate the New York subways. She has always been there when I needed her—my quintessential "Jewish mother."

Of all the other principles of economics I learned from Will, I will recall tonight only one: *revealed preference*. If you want to know what will happen to the quantity of peas purchased if the price were to rise, you don't ask countless people hypothetical questions. You let the price go up and see what happens. People will reveal their preferences through their actions. This is a principle of life, not just of economics. We "reveal our preferences" by being here tonight with two of the most remarkable people any of us will ever know.

Will's "reach" and gift for language are evident in the prologue to his great book *Welfare Economics and the Theory of the State*, in which, before demolishing pillars of classical economics, he quotes the boatswain in *The Tempest*, who, when reminded to take care in the storm, for his boat is carrying the king, remarks that there is "none [in this boat] that I more love than myself." Our friend's amazing versatility is revealed in the art that resides today in my home and my offices—including a memorable painting, *Death of the Pope*.

It is not, however, these manifold fruits of high intelligence, cultural sophistication, and endless productivity that I would highlight. Rather, it is personal gifts bestowed unstintingly on everyone. What Will and Hilda have revealed most clearly through their lives is that it is possible to think rigorously without abandoning the capacity to *feel* as well as to think—to be cheerful forces for good in a troubled world. Head and heart go together, they have taught us. So I raise a glass to Will and Hilda: for their wise heads and loving hearts—for their inspiration and, most of all, for their friendship.

APPENDIX
A SELECTED LIST OF PUBLICATIONS

~

BOOKS

1. *Lesson Plan: An Agenda for Change in American Higher Education.* Princeton, NJ: Princeton University Press, 2016.
2. *Locus of Authority: The Evolution of Faculty Roles in the Governance of Higher Education.* Written with Eugene M. Tobin. Princeton, NJ: Princeton University Press, 2015.
3. *Higher Education in the Digital Age.* Princeton, NJ: Princeton University Press, 2013.
4. *Lessons Learned: Reflections of a University President.* Princeton, NJ: Princeton University Press, 2010.
5. *Crossing the Finish Line: Completing College at America's Public Universities.* Written with Matthew M. Chingos and Michael S. McPherson. Princeton, NJ: Princeton University Press, 2009.
6. *The Board Book.* New York: W. W. Norton, 2008.
7. *Equity and Excellence in American Higher Education.* Written with Martin A. Kurzweil and Eugene M. Tobin). Charlottesville: University of Virginia Press, 2005.
8. *Reclaiming the Game: College Sports and Educational Values.* Written with Sarah Levin. Princeton, NJ: Princeton University Press, 2003.
9. *The Game of Life: College Sports and Educational Values.* Written with James L. Shulman. Princeton, NJ: Princeton University Press, 2001.
10. *The Shape of the River: Long-Term Consequences of Considering Race in College and University Admissions.* Written with Derek Bok. Princeton, NJ: Princeton University Press, 1998.
11. *Universities and Their Leadership.* Edited with Harold T. Shapiro. Princeton, NJ: Princeton University Press, 1998.
12. *The Charitable Nonprofits: An Analysis of Institutional Dynamics and Characteristics.* Written with Thomas I. Nygren, Sarah E. Turner, and Elizabeth A. Duffy. San Francisco: Jossey-Bass, 1994.
13. *Inside the Boardroom.* New York: John Wiley & Sons, 1994.
14. *In Pursuit of the PhD.* Written with Neil L. Rudenstine. Princeton, NJ: Princeton University Press, 1992.
15. *University Libraries and Scholarly Communication.* Written with Anthony M. Cummings, Marcia L. Witte, Laura O. Lazarus, and Richard H. Ekman. A study for the Andrew Mellon Foundation. Washington, DC: Association of Research Libraries, November 1992.

16. *Prospects for Faculty in the Arts and Sciences: A Study of Factors Affecting Demand and Supply, 1987 to 2012.* Written with Julie Ann Sosa. Princeton, NJ: Princeton University Press, 1989.

BOOKLETS

1. *Barriers to Adoption of Online Learning Systems in U.S. Higher Education.* Written with Lawrence S. Bacow, Kevin M. Guthrie, Kelly A. Lack, and Matthew P. Long. New York: ITHAKA, 2012.
2. *Interactive Learning Online at Public Universities: Evidence from Randomized Trials.* Written with Matthew M. Chingos, Kelly A. Lack and Thomas I. Nygren. New York: ITHAKA, 2012.
3. Introduction to *Unlocking the Gates*, by Taylor Walsh. Princeton, NJ: Princeton University Press, 2011.
4. *At a Slight Angle to the Universe: The University in a Digitized, Commercialized Age.* The Romanes Lecture for 2000, delivered before the University of Oxford. Princeton, NJ: Princeton University Press, 2001.

SELECTED ARTICLES:

1. "The Painful Lessons of Sweet Briar and Cooper Union." Written with Lawrence S. Bacow. *Chronicle of Higher Education*, September 24, 2015.
2. "Commentary: Scott Walker's Test of Academic Freedom." Written with Eugene M. Tobin. *Chicago Tribune*, June 22, 2015.
3. "Demanding Universities to Divest Is Often Bad Policy." *Washington Post*, March 27, 2015.
4. "The Potential for Online Learning: Promises and Pitfalls." *EDUCAUSE Review* 48, no. 5 (September–October 2013).
5. "Online Learning in Higher Education." *Education Next* 13, no. 2 (Spring 2013).
6. "Trustees and Directors Matter." *Forum Futures 2009* (EDUCAUSE, Cambridge, MA), October 2009.
7. "Race-Sensitive Admissions: Back to Basics." Written with Neil L. Rudenstine. *Chronicle of Higher Education*, February 7, 2003.
8. "Winning and Giving." Written with Sarah E. Turner and Lauren A. Meserve. *Social Science Quarterly*, Winter 2001.
9. "Get In, Get Ahead: Here's Why." Written with Derek Bok. *Trusteeship*, November–December 1998.
10. "No Vacation from the Bottom Line." *Trusteeship*, January–February 1995.
11. "Do Boards Matter?" *Princeton Alumni Weekly*, February 22, 1995.
12. "When a Business Leader Joins a Nonprofit Board." *Harvard Business Review*, September–October 1994.
13. "Income-Contingent College Loans." Written with Alan B. Krueger. *Journal of Economic Perspectives* 7, no. 3 (Summer 1993).
14. "The NTEE Classification System: Tests of Reliability/Validity in the Field of Higher Education." Written with Thomas I. Nygren and Sarah E. Turner. *Voluntas* [Manchester University Press, Manchester, UK], Spring 1993.

15. "Student Aid: Price Discount or Educational Investment." Written with David W. Breneman. *Brookings Review*, Winter 1993.
16. "The B.A.–Ph.D. Nexus." Written with Sarah E. Turner and Marcia L. Witte. *Journal of Higher Education* [Ohio State University Press, Columbus], 63, no. 1 (January–February 1992).
17. "Measuring Time to the Doctorate: A Reinterpretation of the Evidence." Written with Graham Lord and Julie Ann Sosa. *Proceedings of the National Academy of Science* 88 (February 1991).
18. "Colleges Must Have the Flexibility to Designate Financial Aid for Members of Minority Groups." Written with Neil L. Rudenstine. *Chronicle of Higher Education*, January 9, 1991.
19. "The Flight from the Arts and Sciences: Trends in Degrees Conferred." Written with Sarah E. Turner. *Science* [American Association for the Advancement of Science, Washington, DC] 250, October 1990.
20. "Prospects for Faculty in the Arts and Sciences." Written with Julia Ann Sosa. *Princeton Alumni Weekly*, April 4, 1990.
21. "Thinking about Tuition." *AGB Reports* 29, no. 2 (March–April 1987).
22. "Thinking about Tuition: What People Are Saying About College Prices and College Costs," *Princeton Alumni Weekly*, May 21, 1986.
23. "Market Prospects for PhDs in the United States," *Population and Development Review* 7, no. 3 (September 1981).

CHAPTERS IN BOOKS AND CONTRIBUTIONS TO CONFERENCE PROCEEDINGS

1. "Information Technology and Independent Scholarship: The Efficiencies of Collaboration." From an address delivered at the Centennial Meeting of the Association of American Universities, Washington, DC, April 17, 2000.
2. "Scholastic Aptitude Test Scores, Race and Academic Performance in Selective Colleges and Universities." Written with Fredrick E. Vars. In *The Black-White Test Score Gap*, ed. Christopher Jencks and Meredith Phillips. Washington, DC: Brookings Institution Press, 1998.
3. "Inside the Boardroom: A Reprise." From an address at the National Conference of the American Society of Corporate Secretaries, June 30, 1995. In *Nonprofit Governance: The Executives Guide*. New York: American Society of Corporate Secretaries and the American Bar Association, Section of Business Law, 1997.
4. "No Limits." From an address delivered at a Cornell University symposium in honor of Frank Rhodes, May 21, 1995. In *The American University*, ed. Ronald G. Ehrenberg. Ithaca, NY: Cornell University Press, 1997.
5. "How Libraries Can Help to Pay Their Way in the Future." From an address delivered at the Summit of World Library Leaders, New York Public Library, April 27, 1996. *Logos* 7, no. 3 (1996).
6. "Inside the Boardroom: A Reprise." From an address delivered at the meeting of the American Philosophical Society, November 10, 1994. *Proceedings of the American Philosophical Society* 139, no. 4 (December 1995).

7. "Comments on '"The Functions and Resources of the American University of the Twenty-first Century' by Harold T. Shapiro." *Minerva* 30, no. 2 (Summer 1992).

8. "Productivity: A Journalist's Perspective." In *Dimensions of Productivity Research: Proceedings of the Conference on Productivity Research*, ed. John D. Hogan and Anna M. Craig, vol. 1. Houston, TX: American Productivity Center, April 1981.

AFTERWORD
WILLIAM G. BOWEN

I first met Bill some forty-five years ago. He had been elected president of Princeton to take office the following academic year and was taking time to visit various institutions and people to expand his acquaintance with them and with current developments in higher education. The itinerary brought him at some point to Chicago, where he invited me to a lunch at which we had a vigorous and enjoyable discussion about all kinds of issues, starting with coeducation. I did not realize that this was in fact an interview until, out of the blue, Bill asked whether I might consider an administrative position at Princeton. I declined with thanks, and he said, "Oh, what a shame. We need some *older* people in my administration." I had recently turned 41, until that moment unaware of having crossed my geriatric threshold. Bill's youth, on the other hand, amazed me. Yet I was always to think of him over our long acquaintance as actually older than myself, not for reasons of chronology, obviously, but because of his wisdom and his commanding habit of authority.

At this first meeting, Bill and I quickly found common ground in our thinking about universities, about their missions and the essential conditions for their necessary autonomies, about the then state of higher education and its challenges, about the opportunities as well as the problems ahead. That essential agreement continued throughout the course of an association in which we often acted as co-conspirators in meetings like those of the Association of American Universities [AAU] presidents and also of boards and committees on which we both sat. I have an especially vivid memory of taking on the vice president of the United States, who had demanded a special meeting of the Smithsonian Board of Regents in order to impose his own close friend and candidate as the next secretary of the institution. It was splendid to watch Bill, exuding an air of menacing politesse, eviscerate the vice president, and it was very satisfying to be allowed the spot of cleanup batter for the final inning. Bill and I were to repeat this partnership in other contexts, taking a perhaps unseemly pleasure in acting as provocateurs.

I do not have to tell this gathering of Bill's gift for friendship, how generous and steadfast his encouragement and his concern, how forthcoming and effective his assistance in the most varied of circumstances, how deep his impulse to help, to bend every effort to improve the lot of those—and they were many—about whose welfare he cared. I am infinitely grateful to recall the reach of his unwavering kindness and support over so many years. In Bill I found a special colleague as well as friend. From the outset, he treated me as an equal at a time when women were not, if I may put it delicately, entirely welcome in the councils of the Ivy League. Bill had always taken coeducation entirely for granted as a natural condition of existence, as it had been in his own educational experience. He was incredibly helpful, always without condescension, when I had for a brief period to join the Ivy presidents at their usually boring meetings that dealt almost entirely with athletics. After I had been turned away at the door of the University Club of New York—the club had automatically given membership to a new president of the University of Chicago, but without checking her gender, and a very large doorman said he had never seen a member who looked like me and barred the way—Bill was outraged, I think even more than I was. He initiated a boycott of the club and leaned on the AAU presidents to join him. This was no doubt a real nuisance for many of them, an inconvenience prolonged after the club held a vote to admit women that was defeated by members who wanted to continue a still more important tradition, that of swimming naked in the club's pool.

Unlike some of his peers, Bill never succumbed to academic snobbery. Ivy could not wind itself around him, nor did the ambition and competitive search for prestige that constitute so prominent and unworthy a priority in the world of higher education today. Bill judged institutions by their quality. He took a great interest in public higher education. He certainly did not assume that any scholar or academic program existing outside the so-called elite universities would necessarily be less than the best. He himself lived the life of meritocracy, and he believed in it deeply.

Bill's sheer intelligence struck one immediately on contact. He relied on rigorous research and the meticulous analysis of evidence to arrive at his ideas and proposals, considering theory of no real merit unless tested and applied in practice. His was a practical outlook driven by the hope of making a difference, creating some value, as a contribution to improving the state of things, especially in all that concerned higher education and its social benefits. At his core, Bill was a teacher with a large breadth of interests and an abiding intellectual curiosity, an educator whether in his professorial or presidential or philanthropic role. He was a teacher who taught about higher education in a number of books and in countless lectures and annual reports, a teacher who while serving the foundation went on teaching in his work with its staff and grantees and in his mentorship of the talented young researchers whom he brought to the foundation, a teacher who took enormous pride in the success of those he mentored and to whom he gave the fullest credit of co-authorship in the work they jointly pursued. He was, indeed, a teacher by example for all of us.

Bill never left behind his Mid-Western roots. He loved and remained passionate about Denison University, devoted to the liberal education and enduring friendships he had found there. His Midwestern heritage sometimes showed up in his vocabulary, for example, in his speaking of being "aggravated," a usage you are less likely to find in the effete East. Quite a few things aggravated him. He was aggravated by stupidity, a trait to which he gave a very wide and inclusive definition, and he was aggravated by hypocrisy and pomposity, by windbags and charlatans, by most politicians, by simplistic views of the world, and by those who clung to unyielding absolutist positions of black and white on the vital questions it posed. He was aggravated most of all by the failures of principle, decency, courage, and fair-mindedness that occurred all too often when clarity and strength of purpose should have prevailed.

Bill was by nature a moderate. He was neither a puritan nor a utopian; he could see, even if he regretted, the imperfections of human existence, the ambiguities and complexities of its conditions. Some battles he deliberately avoided as not worth fighting, whether deeming them unwinnable or as demanding an investment and expenditure of a president's inherently limited capital that needed to be saved for matters that could be foreseeably managed. Bill insisted on the highest standards. He professed an economist's faith in the over-riding power of reason and an academic's faith in the power of education despite the irrationality and willful ignorance that seemed so frequently to dominate. He believed that the forces of education and civil persuasion could be effective, understanding that this would likely occur only gradually, but by first setting out goals that could be embraced in common and by nurturing a shared respect for the process that followed. These in turn could illuminate a path directed to putting in place at least a framework for identifying possible solutions and establishing at least a relative peace. He looked always to creating and managing a process that could shape an adequate consensus and accept constructive compromise not as an unfortunate concession or selling out, but as a step toward reaffirming basic goals while listening to and accommodating views and ambitions that had been in conflict or had posed seemingly irreparable divisiveness. Bill was a master of negotiation and of finding the ground on which such steps could be identified without sacrificing the things that mattered most. His sense of direction in these matters, of where he was headed and why, never faltered. At the same time, he was an excellent listener who often modified or subtly shifted some position after thoughtful discussion. Bill might appear to have made up his mind and staked out a position, sometimes intimidatingly so, and of course he usually got his way. But in the meantime he listened and pondered and took in what he had heard. Similarly, Bill shared his draft manuscripts and thoughts and took seriously the reactions and critiques these provoked. He did not always agree. But he thought about each comment as an invitation to rethink and perhaps revise his original thinking on specific points and conclusions.

Bill possessed what I might call a kind of impatient patience. When seized of an idea or project or cause or one of his sudden enthusiasms, he became single-mindedly persistent, never letting go of trying to find ways to make the seemingly impossible or relentlessly difficult happen, and taking on every intractable detail until he had finally wrestled it to the ground. In his zeal, Bill sometimes got out ahead of the troops, ready to commit to a proposal that excited him before the rest of us—and here I am speaking of the Mellon board—had had sufficient time or information to share in its consideration, totally ready to act right away. Being Bill, however, he usually came to agree on the need and utility for slowing down at least very slightly. When challenged, he would remind himself of his own firmly held convictions about the responsibilities and benefits of effective boards, a subject he wrote about more than once. After swift consultation, he would then apply his customary prudence and intensity of focus to building his new venture step by deliberate step, following his own favorite call to action, "We press on!" And so he did.

Bill brought to the foundation an interesting mix of risk-taking and caution. Within the foundation he strengthened a culture that sought to work in collaboration with and to find an enabling partnership with its grantees as opposed to enacting a role of lordly patronage dispensing alms from on high to carry out its own predetermined ideas and its own predicted outcomes. Bill understood that not every genuine experiment would or even should necessarily work—in either case, successful or not, there would be something significant to learn. He respected, if somewhat unwillingly, the stately pace of change and development, despite all urgent prodding, that marks the worlds of higher education, as also of the arts and the humanities and their institutions more generally. At the same time, Bill made sure that the foundation continued to fuse these points of departure with the regular and rigorous review of its activities. He oversaw the introduction of new initiatives that emphasized what the foundation could do, within its central purposes, that spoke both to its own comparative strengths and to the best possibilities and most compelling needs of its constituencies. And he was in addition a very creative and imaginative creator or co-creator of programs that have had an enduring effect on the practices of scholarship and the experience of higher education itself. I can, for example, no longer imagine a world without JSTOR.

As there was sometimes a tension between Bill's desire to get things done no later than yesterday and his belief in the worth of consultation and his knowledge that things take time, so there was between his staying the course in a meeting and his hatred of meetings that veered off course or went on longer than he thought necessary. He was always practically on his feet and out the door when ready for a meeting to be over and poised to rush on to his next meeting or, what mattered more, to his computer and his research, paying as little attention as possible to the usual social chitchat among those who lingered at meeting's end. If at a luncheon meeting, he would be lunging out before dessert was served (I once saw David Rockefeller almost in tears after Bill's abrupt departure left him bereft of the sorbet to which he had happily looked forward.) Bill's work was all-consuming, although of course he did not let it get in the way of his many other responsibilities, including his many board roles in both the corporate and not-for-profit worlds. He was a leader in every one and somehow got about twice as much done and decided or moved along on any given day as anyone I have known. But his central preoccupation always rested with the work on his computer. It drew him like a giant magnet.

Bill rather assumed that everyone was, or should be, as productively workaholic as himself. He also wanted to be sure that you knew he was not slacking off. Each year, before leaving with Mary Ellen for their winter visit to St. Croix, he would call to reassure me that he would be working hard, for this would be no vacation, except for an hour a day on the tennis court, and that he would begin drafting his annual report as soon as they had boarded the plane.

Bill never, of course, asked people to work harder than he did, but what a standard he posed. On 62nd Street, lights burned late. I thought the foundation board should have set up something like a bank's examining committee, a group that arrives unannounced, makes everybody put down whatever they are doing, and then looks at whatever it chooses to examine. Our trustee examining committee might have dropped in on the foundation, say around 9:00 pm, on almost any week night. It would presumably have found many of you who are present this evening working feverishly away while receiving an insistent flow of messages and visits from Bill all evening long, asking you to revise for the fourteenth time a board docket due tomorrow that you thought you had already perfected, or describing in detail the latest statistics he had uncovered on the unrecognized scandals of collegiate athletics.

Bill loved what he did and concentrated on his work with fierce devotion, caring little for the usual worldly rounds and social expectations of those in his position. He was always happier at his desk or patrolling the hallways of the foundation. There was absolutely nothing pretentious in his way of life. Or, indeed, in his self-presentation. As the day wore on, Bill's nice suits began to look as though tailored by Goodwill Industries. His shirt hems seemed reluctant to make contact with his waistband. So far as I could tell, he owned two neckties for regular wear and perhaps a third for special occasions. These were lovable characteristics, but I fear that my speaking of them would have caused Bill terrible aggravation.

So I will press on to say that, just as Bill disdained the competition for prestige, so, too, he made appearance entirely secondary to substance. That substance had to do with the values and purposes of intellectual integrity, with institutional clarity, with a principled sense of mission and of adherence to its imperatives, with an uncompromising fidelity to his ideal of humane service within the collegial community of those he worked with and cared for. I am forever grateful to have been among its many beneficiaries at Mellon and elsewhere, and I am thankful for this opportunity to recall and to affirm Bill's exceptional leadership, and the spirit that informed it, as well as to express admiration and affection for a man of singular character and accomplishment whose life was one of such consequence for us all.

Hanna Holborn Gray
March 9, 2017

INDEX

Page numbers for entries occurring in figures are followed by an *f*.